HAMLET
THE 1-HOUR GUIDEBOOK

AN ILLUSTRATED GUIDE FOR MASTERING SHAKESPEARE'S GREATEST PLAY

David Grey & Gigi Bach, editors

A Division of Barnes & Noble Publishing

Text and illustrations copyright © 2005 Bermond Press

All rights reserved. No part of this book, including illustrations, may be reproduced or transmitted in any form or by any means, electronic or mechanical, including photocopying, recording, or by any information storage and retrieval system, without prior permission in writing from the Publisher.

This edition published by Spark Educational Publishing in agreement with Bermond Press.

SPARKNOTES is a registered trademark of SparkNotes LLC.

Spark Educational Publishing
A Division of Barnes & Noble Publishing
120 Fifth Avenue
New York, NY 10011

Printed in the United States of America

10 9 8 7 6 5 4 3 2 1

ISBN 1-4114-0446-7
Library of Congress Catalog-in-Publication Data available on request.

Cover and book design by Dreamedia, Inc.

LIMIT OF LIABILITY / DISCLAIMER OF WARRANTY: THE PUBLISHER AND AUTHOR HAVE USED THEIR BEST EFFORTS IN PREPARING THIS BOOK. THE PUBLISHER AND AUTHOR MAKE NO REPRESENTATIONS OR WARRANTIES WITH RESPECT TO THE ACCURACY OR COMPLETENESS OF THE CONTENTS OF THIS BOOK AND SPECIFICALLY DISCLAIM ANY IMPLIED WARRANTIES OF MERCHANTABILITY OR FITNESS FOR A PARTICULAR PURPOSE. THERE ARE NO WARRANTIES WHICH EXTEND BEYOND THE DESCRIPTIONS CONTAINED IN THIS PARAGRAPH. NO WARRANTY MAY BE CREATED OR EXTENDED BY SALES REPRESENTATIVES OR WRITTEN SALES MATERIALS. THE ACCURACY AND COMPLETENESS OF THE INFORMATION PROVIDED HEREIN AND THE OPINIONS STATED HEREIN ARE NOT GUARANTEED OR WARRANTED TO PRODUCE ANY PARTICULAR RESULTS, AND THE ADVICE AND STRATEGIES CONTAINED HEREIN MAY NOT BE SUITABLE FOR EVERY INDIVIDUAL. NEITHER THE PUBLISHER NOR AUTHOR SHALL BE LIABLE FOR ANY LOSS OF PROFIT OR ANY OTHER COMMERCIAL DAMAGES, INCLUDING BUT NOT LIMITED TO SPECIAL, INCIDENTAL, CONSEQUENTIAL, OR OTHER DAMAGES.

NEW & UPCOMING TITLES

IN THE 1-HOUR GUIDEBOOK SERIES

Hamlet
Romeo & Juliet
Macbeth
Julius Caesar
A Midsummer Night's Dream
Othello

CONTENTS

Foreword ix

Character
    Hamlet's Family 12
    Hamlet's Girlfriend's Family 24
    Hamlet's Friends 34
    The Minor Characters 42

Power Bases 54

Plot
    Main Plot 70
    The Subplots 84
    The Finale 100

Scene By Scene 112

Appendices
    Appendix A: Dramatic Maps 157
    Appendix B: Background 181

ACKNOWLEDGEMENTS

The editors would like to extend our warmest gratitude to the following people who supported us with their encouragement, feedback, proofreading and inspiration: Barbara, David and Beverly, Lisa, Brian, Professor Louis A. Montrose and Professor Harold Bloom.

FOREWORD

This book emerged from our desire to provide the unfamiliar reader with the most comprehensive, clear picture of *Hamlet* in the least amount of time. In addition, our awe of Shakespeare's masterpiece nurtured a passion to present the information in a way that complemented the greatness of his work. Why shouldn't the beauty of a Shakespeare primer at least attempt to mirror the beauty of the subject? Briefly stated, why does a literary guidebook have to look ugly? The obvious answer is that it doesn't, especially when illustration collaborating with text is the best way to accomplish our desire for clarity and quick assimilation. Neither text nor graphics is exclusive to the brain. We think in pictures; we think in words. The cognitive interaction between the two is the quickest path to understanding.

When developing a picture of our audience, therefore, we held these characteristics foremost: frightening lack of time, need for clarity, desire for beauty.

Certain innovations arose in attempting to satisfy this model—visual distillations, plot timelines, dramatic maps, quick reviews of the characters, scene by scene illustrations and more. By the same criteria, certain traditional elements were eliminated—you won't, for example, find lengthy commentary in this book. Most of the commentary we have found in other study guides to Shakespeare was either overly obvious or arguably incorrect. To take up valuable time with our own commentary would be counter to our purpose, which we felt demanded concrete summary rather than questionable surmise.

As far as our specific decisions regarding *Hamlet*, we tried to eliminate speculation whenever possible, treating it as a pitfall, rather than an intrinsic necessity. There is also a movement among some scholars to exalt Hamlet at the expense of the other characters. As understanable as this temptation is, we feel this does a disservice to the playwright's intent. While Claudius is no Iago, for example, his pragmatic, Machiavellian opportunism makes him the perfect antagonist to the speculative, principled prince. Concerning Hamlet's relationship with Ophelia, we took the stance that he did in fact love her, as she herself believed, but found Ophelia's loyalty to her father insurmountable at a time when his own energies were strained beyond recovery. Other defensible readings exist.

Our scene by scene summaries give equal, single-page weight to each scene division, except in the case of 2.2, which by sheer volume needed to be split into two parts, and 4.2-3, which we felt could best be dealt with in combination. We ask your indulgence.

Congratulations on your adventure into Shakespeare's inimitable masterwork.

David Grey & Gigi Bach, editors

Let him who would move the world
first move himself.
Socrates

Hamlet's *family*

Hamlet's family is the hub around which the play turns: the concerned Gertrude, the pragmatic Claudius, the wronged Old Hamlet and the deeply analytical prince himself. These characters form a central core of human issues that touch on the lines between loyalty and betrayal, examination and action, veracity and falsehood, life and death. In the middle of that core is Hamlet—or more specifically Hamlet's mind—who must make sense of these issues and navigate the truth within a sea of uncertainty.

...TO DIE, TO SLEEP.

To sleep, perchance to dream. Ay, there's the rub;
For in that sleep of death what dreams may come,
When we have shuffled off this mortal coil,
Must give us pause.

3.1.65-69

THIS IS HAMLET

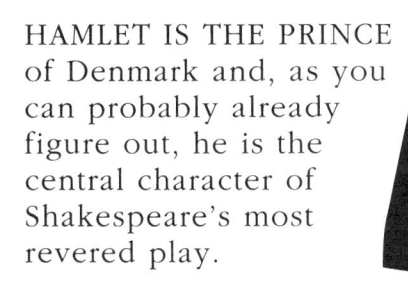

HAMLET IS THE PRINCE of Denmark and, as you can probably already figure out, he is the central character of Shakespeare's most revered play.

As we shall see, the questions Hamlet struggles with during the course of the play are of fundamental importance. In one sense, Hamlet's *mind* is the play's true central character.

TO BE, OR NOT TO BE...

Hamlet is placed in circumstances of great ethical and emotional strain by events occurring very early in the play. His famous soliloquies examine these issues in wonderful detail, exposing us to the process of human thought.

STUDENT
Hamlet is a student at the University of Wittenberg, Luther's university and the birthplace of Protestantism. This is an anachronism, however, as the university would not have existed in Hamlet's time.

IDENTITIES
Hamlet is a son whose father has just been murdered; a prince whose claim to the throne has been interrupted; a student who is unable to return to school; a friend who is about to be betrayed by his ex-schoolmates; and a suitor whose relationship will decay beyond repair. Shakespeare is setting him up to confront an epistemological crisis—is there an underlying, objective truth?

GOOD HAMLET,
*cast thy nightly colour off,
And let thine eye look like a friend on Denmark.
Do not for ever with thy vailéd lids
Seek for thy noble father in the dust.
Thou know'st 'tis common—all that lives must die,
Passing through nature to eternity.*

1.2.68-73

QUESTION
Hamlet comes from the royal family of Denmark. What is his title? (ANSWER ON PAGE 18)

HAMLET HAS A MOTHER

HER NAME IS GERTRUDE. She is the queen of Denmark, having been so through two regimes. She is concerned for Hamlet's well-being and genuinely loves him.

As we shall see, despite Hamlet's reciprocal love for his mother, his relationship with her becomes psychologically problematic because she has married Hamlet's uncle quickly after the death of Hamlet's father, the king.

THE LADY
PROTESTS TOO MUCH

The extent to which Gertrude is culpable in the king's death is left unclear and may even seem to change as the play progresses. This is because the degree to which Hamlet blames his mother vacillates throughout the play—climaxing at its midpoint. From then on, their relationship begins to mend and nearly heals by the play's end.

FAITHFUL
One of the translations of Gertrude's name is "very faithful" (from the Old German: gerdraut). The question of Gertrude's faithfulness will plague Hamlet for the bulk of the play. Like many large issues in Shakespearean tragedy, it is left unresolved.

I AM THY FATHER'S SPIRIT,

Doomed for a certain term to walk the night,
And for the day confined to fast in fires,
Till the foul crimes done in my days of nature
Are burnt and purged away.

1.5.9-13

ANSWER
Hamlet is the prince of Denmark.

QUESTION
What is the chief reason Hamlet is upset at his mother, Queen Gertrude? (ANSWER ON PAGE 20)

HAMLET HAD A FATHER

HIS NAME WAS OLD HAMLET (which is just like saying Hamlet, Sr.). He was the king of Denmark and a good general when he was alive. We see him in the play only as a ghost who appears briefly and then vanishes.

The ghost tells Hamlet that he was murdered by his brother, Hamlet's uncle. While the king was asleep, his brother poured poison into his ear and then told everyone that the king had been bitten by a snake.

MURDER
MOST FOUL

Shakespeare goes out of his way to ensure that the identity of the ghost is unclear—is he Hamlet's dead father? An angel? Demon? Hallucination? The lack of resolution is a deliberate device for maintaining tension and interest.

PURGATORY
In Catholic theology, purgatory is the place of redeemable sinners—a liminal, unresolved space. Some in Shakespeare's time believed purgatory was a land from which the dead could return, under strict circumstances, to give warnings to the living. Luther believed purgatory was a theological distortion. Shakespeare's England was divided and vexed by such doctrinal differences.

VENGEANCE
The ghost of Old Hamlet directs Hamlet to avenge his "foul and most unnatural murder." He calls his murderous brother "that adulterate beast." But, the ghost warns Hamlet to "taint not thy mind," asking him to leave Gertrude's punishment to heaven (God). Regicide—a favorite topic of Shakespeare's—was an important subject to Elizabethan audiences.

CHARACTERS | Hamlet's Family | 19

...OUR SOMETIMES SISTER,

now our queen,
Th'imperial jointress of this warlike state,
Have we, as 'twere with a defeated joy,
With one auspicious and one dropping eye,
With mirth in funeral and dirge in marriage,
In equal scale weighing delight and dole,
Taken to wife.

1.2.8-14

ANSWER
Hamlet is most upset at his mother, Queen Gertrude, for marrying his uncle, Claudius.

QUESTION
What does the ghost of Old Hamlet ask Hamlet to do? (ANSWER ON PAGE 23)

THIS IS HAMLET's PROBLEM

THIS IS CLAUDIUS, HAMLET's uncle. He has recently become king and married Hamlet's mother, upon the death of Old Hamlet. Hamlet believes Claudius is the murderer of his father. Hamlet's inner struggle with and resolution of this belief is the central problem of the play.

As Hamlet is the chief protagonist, Claudius is the chief antagonist. The two plot against one another, and often square off in a battle of words.

SUCCESSION
Hamlet's succession to the throne has been interrupted by his uncle. It was not uncommon for the Danish council to vote for the next head of state. The play, however, focuses more on the prince's vengeance of his father's murder than on his claim to the throne.

MORE
THAN KIN

Claudius asks Hamlet to think of him as a father, even naming him first successor to the throne. Hamlet will have none of it. In his opening line, Hamlet riddles, "A little more than kin, and less than kind," meaning, in essence, "You're married to my mother, so you are more than just kin, but you're not my natural father, nor are you loving" (quibbling over *kind*, meaning both *lineage* and *good-hearted*). In return for Hamlet's coldness, Claudius asks Hamlet not to return to school—undoubtedly to keep him under his watchful eye.

CHARACTERS | Hamlet's Family | 21

A SUMMARY of HAMLET's FAMILY

mother

Gertrude
QUEEN OF DENMARK

Hamlet's mother. Her name in the Old German means "very faithful." Widow of Hamlet's father, she quickly marries Claudius, Hamlet's uncle and the new king. Hamlet suspects his uncle of foul play and the marriage greatly upsets him. Some directors choose to have her wear a locket containing a portrait of Claudius (which Hamlet refers to midway through the play). The extent of her guilt is kept intentionally unclear.

locket of Claudius

uncle

Claudius
KING OF DENMARK

Hamlet's uncle, brother to Old Hamlet. He is the play's chief antagonist, as he murders Hamlet's father and marries Gertrude, Hamlet's mother. By the play's opening, this has already occurred, and Claudius is the new king, presumably by vote of the council—thereby interrupting Hamlet's claim to the throne. Claudius murdered Old Hamlet by pouring poison into his ear. Hamlet will force him to drink his own poison at play's end.

cup of poison

dead father

Hamlet
PRINCE OF DENMARK

His father is murdered by his uncle, who then marries his mother. His claim to the throne is interrupted. He is prevented from returning to school and is betrayed for profit by his friends. It's said the unexamined life is not worth living. If so, then Hamlet's life is supremely worthy. His need to second-guess his actions—to deeply examine both his motives and his humanity—makes him one of the most heralded figures in all of literature.

cross of Denmark

Old Hamlet
EX-KING OF DENMARK

Hamlet's dead father. In Hamlet's estimation, he was a well-respected king, a loving husband and a good general when he was alive. His ghost directs Hamlet to avenge his murder. He tells Hamlet that he was murdered while sleeping and therefore was unable to make amends for his sins before dying. He is confined to purgatory, doomed temporarily to "fast in fires" by day and walk the world by night as a spirit.

royal crown

ANSWER The ghost of Old Hamlet wishes Hamlet to avenge his "foul and most unnatural murder" while leaving Gertrude to God.

CHARACTERS | Hamlet's Family | 23

Hamlet's girlfriend's family

The second most significant family in the play is that of Hamlet's girlfriend, Ophelia. She is trapped between the forces of her father and her one-time suitor, leading her to madness and death. Ophelia's father, Polonius, acts as chief court advisor—it is his death that provides Claudius the chance to regain the initiative against Hamlet. The quest of Ophelia's blood-thirsty brother, Laertes, to avenge Polonius' murder is skillfully shaped by Claudius to become the instrument of Hamlet's demise.

AND I, OF LADIES

most deject and wretched,
That sucked the beauty of his music vows,
Now see that noble and most sovereign reason
Like sweet bells jangled out of tune and harsh;
That unmatched form and feature of blown youth
Blasted with ecstasy. O woe is me
T'have seen what I have seen, see what I see.

3.1.156-162

QUESTION
What is the name of Hamlet's mother and what does her name mean? (ANSWER ON PAGE 28)

THIS IS HAMLET's GIRLFRIEND

HER NAME IS OPHELIA. She is both a loving girlfriend and an obedient daughter. Unfortunately for her, these roles will clash.

Ophelia's father tells her that Hamlet's words of love are hollow—just a young man's attempt to seduce her. Moreover, he forbids her to see Hamlet, except to help him to spy on the prince. This upsets Hamlet greatly, and in effect kills the play's only loving possibility.

GET THEE
TO A NUNNERY

Ophelia then becomes a bittersweet casualty of her father's cynical views and her boyfriend's cryptic, desperate displays of affection. By the time Hamlet suggests she escape to a convent, their love has been irreparably damaged. Hamlet's accidental murder of her father, triggers Ophelia's complete psychological unraveling.

MADNESS
Hamlet feigns madness, but Ophelia's insanity is real. After the death of her domineering father, she sings and talks incoherently. At one point, she passes out flowers to the others—flowers that hold special significance, such as fennel (identified with infidelity) to Queen Gertrude. Ophelia drowns as she is stringing garlands in the branches over the brook.

THIS ABOVE ALL—
to thine own self be true,
And it must follow, as the night the day,
Thou canst not then be false to any man.
Farewell—my blessing season this in thee.

1.3.78-81

ANSWER
Getrude is the name of Hamlet's mother, the queen. In the Old German it means, "very faithful."

QUESTION
How does Hamlet's girlfriend, Ophelia, die? (ANSWER ON PAGE 30)

THIS IS OPHELIA's FATHER

HIS NAME IS POLONIUS. He is a member of the council of Denmark, acting as chief advisor to King Claudius. He is also overprotective of his daughter, Ophelia: he tells her early on that Hamlet's intentions toward her are not honorable and he forbids her to speak with the prince.

Thus begins Hamlet and Polonius' antagonistic relationship in the play. Hamlet counts him a "tedious old fool."

DEAD
FOR A DUCAT

Polonius loves to spy. He sends his servant to spy on Laertes, his son. He spies on Hamlet from behind a tapestry on two occasions. The second time costs him his life—Hamlet believes he is King Claudius, so he skewers him, rug and all, with his sword.

VERBOSE
Polonius often frustrates those around him by using verbose speech to express a minor point. He always loses the verbal challenge with Hamlet, as he is no match for the prince's wit.

FATHERS
Polonius is the classic overprotective father of Shakespearean theater: cynical, dogmatic, over-bearing and fearful—unable to connect with his daughter or see past the destructive energies that lie dormant in his social values. If such a father's grip is turned aside or overruled, then a comedy ensues, ending in multiple weddings. If the father's fears are unabated, then death follows close behind.

CHARACTERS | Ophelia's Family | 29

HOW CAME HE DEAD?

I'll not be juggled with.
To hell, allegiance! Vows to the blackest devil!
Conscience and grace to the profoundest pit!
I dare damnation. To this point I stand;
That both the worlds I give to negligence,
Let come what comes; only I'll be revenged
Most throughly for my father.

4.5.130-136

ANSWER
Ophelia, daughter of Polonius and sister of Laertes, drowns hanging flower garlands in the branches over the brook. She is insane at the time.

QUESTION
Hamlet "accidentally" kills Polonius, although he actually intended to kill someone else. Who did he think was behind the tapestry? (ANSWER ON PAGE 33)

OPHELIA HAS A BROTHER

HIS NAME IS LAERTES (pronounced, Lay-air-tease), the son of Polonius. He is away at school in France for the bulk of the play, after receiving the king's blessing in Act One.

When Laertes returns, he finds his father murdered at the hand of Hamlet and his sister insane. He is then bent on revenge and will stop at nothing to accomplish his aim. King Claudius shrewdly fans the fires of Laertes's vengeance. The two conspire to kill the prince: Claudius with poison drink, Laertes with a poison sword tip.

TO CUT
HIS THROAT I' TH' CHURCH

Laertes is easily persuaded by the king. In the final scene, he wounds Hamlet with the fatal sword tip, and then is wounded by it in return. Hamlet then stabs Claudius and forces him to drink his own poison. At their deaths, Hamlet and Laertes absolve each other of their crimes.

CONTRAST
Laertes' actions are a headstrong contrast to Hamlet's strategic hesitations. An obvious counterpoint to Hamlet's question: "What dreams may come?" stands Laertes' unconcerned "Let come what comes." Laertes represents quick action on behalf of personal revenge (much as Fortinbras will represent quick action on behalf of political gain.)

ACTION
Like Hamlet, Laertes has a murdered father. Unlike Hamlet, however, Laertes acts immediately to take revenge. But to what end? Laertes, not possessing Hamlet's cognition, goes full speed ahead in the wrong direction. In the end, he begs the prince's forgiveness and blames Claudius for his provocation.

CHARACTERS | Ophelia's Family | 31

A SUMMARY of OPHELIA'S FAMILY

Hamlet's girlfriend

Ophelia
MAIDEN

Trapped between her love for Hamlet and her obedience to her father, Polonius, Ophelia is truly the undeserving tragic figure of the play. She is enlisted to help Polonius spy on Hamlet, which greatly upsets the prince. After the man she loves murders her father, Ophelia undergoes a mental breakdown. She sings and talks incoherently, oblivious to the social decorum of the court. While hanging garlands, she falls into the brook and drowns.

symbolic flower

her father   *her brother*

Polonius
COUNCIL MEMBER

Acting as the chief advisor to King Claudius, Polonius is the long-winded father of Ophelia and Laertes. Believing Hamlet's intentions dishonorable, he forbids Ophelia to see him. Later relenting his decision, and convinced Hamlet's madness (which is actually feigned) is caused by the prince's love for Ophelia, Polonius begins to spy on him. While spying from behind a tapestry, he is killed by Hamlet, who mistakes him for King Claudius.

spying eye

Laertes
STUDENT

Son of Polonius and brother to Ophelia, Laertes is away at school in France for the bulk of the play. He returns to find his father murdered and his sister mad. Quick to act and easily persuaded, Laertes conspires with Claudius to kill Hamlet at a fencing match by poisoning the tip of his unprotected sword. Hamlet is scratched and then uses the same sword to scratch Laertes. Dying, Laertes repents and the two exchange pardons.

poison sword

ANSWER Hamlet believes King Claudius is standing behind the tapestry when he murders Polonius.

CHARACTERS | Ophelia's Family | 33

Hamlet's *friends*

The title for this section is a partial misnomer, for Rosencrantz and Guildenstern quickly become Hamlet's ex-friends. The two childhood companions of the prince are commissioned by the king and queen to discover the origin of Hamlet's madness. Hamlet uncovers their deception with ease—their loyalty to Claudius necessitates him keeping them at arms distance. In contrast, Horatio is profoundly loyal to the prince. Hamlet's friend from university, Horatio is privy to the secret of the prince's feigned madness. He is the only major character on hand to eulogize Hamlet, whose dying breath commissions Horatio to tell his story.

AND LET ME SPEAK

*to th' yet unknowing world
How these things came about. So shall you hear
Of carnal, bloody, and unnatural acts,
Of accidental judgements, casual slaughters,
Of deaths put on by cunning and forced cause;
And, in this upshot, purposes mistook
Fallen on the inventors' heads. All this can I
Truly deliver.*

5.2.332-339

QUESTION
Which word best describes Ophelia's brother, Laertes—headstrong or thoughtful? (ANSWER ON PAGE 38)

THIS IS HAMLET's BEST FRIEND

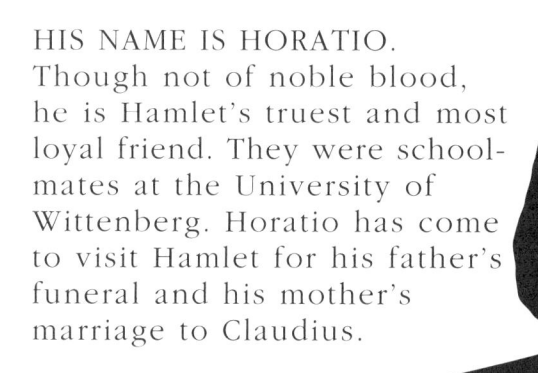

HIS NAME IS HORATIO. Though not of noble blood, he is Hamlet's truest and most loyal friend. They were schoolmates at the University of Wittenberg. Horatio has come to visit Hamlet for his father's funeral and his mother's marriage to Claudius.

Though Rosencrantz and Guildenstern betray the prince for the king's favor, Horatio remains loyal. He is the only character (besides Gertrude near the end) who knows, as well as understands, Hamlet is feigning madness. He is present for much of the prince's wordplay with others.

TELL
MY STORY

The name Horatio shares the same Latin root as *orate*, to speak publicly. So it comes as no surprise when, with his dying breaths, Hamlet tasks his most loyal friend with the telling of his story to future generations. Thus, Horatio takes the play full circle to the beginning—when the curtain drops we can almost imagine it reopening as Horatio begins it anew.

LOYAL
Horatio is, if nothing else, the most loyal to Hamlet of all those in the play. Even Ophelia must divide her loyalties between Hamlet and her father. Claudius and Gertrude may realize this, as they request Rosencrantz and Guildenstern, rather than Horatio, to spy on the prince. In the final scene Horatio struggles to follow Hamlet into death by drinking the poisonous cup—though Hamlet stops him and gives him the more worthy commission of storyteller.

POOR
Horatio is not from the royal court, nor is he wealthy; he is merely a scholar and friend of Hamlet's.

R: HE DOES CONFESS
*he feels himself distracted,
But from what cause he will by no means speak.*

*G: Nor do we find him forward to be sounded,
But with a crafty madness keeps aloof
When we would bring him on to some confession
Of his true state.*

3.1.5-10

ANSWER
Laertes is best described as headstrong, playing counter to Hamet's thoughtful deliberation.

QUESTION
What task does Hamlet give Horatio at the end of the play? (ANSWER ON PAGE 41)

THESE ARE HAMLET's
EX-FRIENDS

ROSENCRANTZ AND Guildenstern, old friends of Hamlet, have been asked by the king and queen to come to Elsinore and ascertain the reasons for his madness.

They are happy to accommodate the royal request, presumably to win favor. Hamlet sees through their ruse at once (he is never easily fooled) and chides the now ex-friends for their betrayal of his trust.

THE HEART
OF MY MYSTERY

Later, Claudius has the pair escort the prince to England on the pretense of a diplomatic mission. The ex-friends carry a letter for Hamlet's execution. While they sleep, Hamlet slyly switches the letter with one asking for the *bearers* of the letter to be executed. Thus, Rosencrantz and Guildenstern come to an untimely end.

ROSE-STAR
The Danish names *Rosencrantz* and *Guildenstern* mean "rose crown" and "golden star." These inseparable fair-weather friends of Hamlet may have been named after two cousins of the famed astronomer Tycho Brahe, who each visited England in 1592—Frederick Rosenkrantz and Knut Gyldenstierne.

A QUICK REVIEW of

Hamlet

- Prince of Denmark
- Student in Germany
- Son of Gertrude and Old Hamlet
- Nephew and stepson of Claudius
- Angry
- Deeply analytical
- Feigns madness
- Accidentally murders Polonius and Laertes
- Brings about the deaths of Rosencrantz and Guildenstern
- Horatio's friend
- Ophelia's boyfriend
- Killed by Laertes' poisoned sword tip

Old Hamlet's Ghost

- Was King of Denmark
- Was married to Gertrude
- Now trapped in purgatory
- Murdered by his brother, Claudius
- Sad and angry
- Calls for vengeance
- Mysterious
- Was a good king and general
- Protective of Gertrude

Polonius

- Councilman of Denmark; Chief advisor to Claudius
- Father of Ophelia, Laertes
- Cynical and suspicious
- Loves to spy
- Verbose
- Killed while spying from behind a tapestry
- His death a catalyst for Hamlet's death

Ophelia

- Hamlet's girlfriend
- Daughter of Polonius
- Sister of Laertes
- Loving
- Innocent; naive
- Confused
- Used by father to spy on Hamlet
- Goes insane and drowns in brook

THE MAJOR CHARACTERS

Gertrude
- Queen of Denmark
- Wife of Claudius
- Widow of Old Hamlet
- Mother of Hamlet
- Caring
- Deeply concerned
- Extent of culpability left unresolved
- Drinks from poison cup Claudius intended for Hamlet

Claudius
- New King of Denmark
- New husband of Gertrude
- Uncle and stepfather of Hamlet
- Poisoned his brother, Old Hamlet
- Gregarious
- Clever, scheming
- Persuades Laertes to murder Hamlet
- Accidentally poisons Gertrude
- Stabbed and poisoned by Hamlet

Laertes
- Brother of Ophelia
- Son of Polonius
- Headstrong; vengeful
- Kills Hamlet with poison sword in fencing match
- Scratched by Hamlet with his own poison sword and dies

Horatio
- University student in Germany
- Best friend of Hamlet
- Loyal confidant
- Asked by Hamlet to tell his story to future generations

Rosencrantz & Guildenstern
- Paid spies of Claudius
- Transparent to Hamlet
- Killed in clever letter-switching ruse by Hamlet
- Ex-friends of Hamlet

ANSWER Horatio is given the task of telling Hamlet's story to future generations.

CHARACTERS | The Major Characters | 41

the Minor *characters*

The minor characters help dimensionalize the play of Hamlet. *The Norwegians—led by the aggressive, opportunistic Prince Fortinbras—along with the ambassadors, are the necessary political element beyond the claustrophobic borders of Denmark. The pirates are a plot convenience to interrupt Hamlet's fateful journey to England. The servants lend support to some delightful comic moments. The soldiers establish a side of Hamlet worthy of loyalty and the players assist the prince in exposing the king's guilt. Finally, the grave crew— pragmatic and irreverent—simultaneously humanize and universalize death.*

LET FOUR CAPTAINS

Bear Hamlet like a soldier to the stage;
For he was likely, had he been put on,
To have proved most royally; and for his passage,
The soldiers' music and the rites of war
Speak loudly for him.

5.2.348-353

The Norwegians mirror the main plot: Prince Fortinbras' father, the king, was killed and Norway, Fortinbras' uncle, succeeded to the throne. In contrast to the main plot, Prince Fortinbras' penchant for action runs counter to Hamlet's rational deliberations. In the end, Prince Fortinbras' opportunism and eagerness to act allow him to be in the right place at the right time, as Hamlet names him ruler of Denmark.

QUESTION
Rosencrantz and Guildenstern are asked to escort Hamlet to what country? (ANSWER ON PAGE 46)

THE NORWEGIANS

PRINCE FORTINBRAS—Hamlet's Rival
He is a prince of Norway, a rival to Denmark. Fortin-bras literally means "strength in arms." It is appropriate: he is an aggressive military leader and a man of action. Hamlet admires Fortinbras for his impulse to act, although he questions the thoughtfulness of his campaigns. Like Hamlet, Prince Fortinbras' uncle took over after his father died. With his dying breaths, Hamlet names Prince Fortinbras the ruler of Denmark.
Aggressive • Man of action

KING FORTINBRAS—Old Hamlet's Rival
Prince Fortinbras' father. He is dead and we never see him in the play, but he is referred to enough that it is a good idea to know who he was. In the past, he challenged Old Hamlet to a one-on-one combat to the death. Whoever lost was to forfeit a great deal of his land. Contracts were drawn up, they fought and Old Hamlet won, killing King Fortinbras. Prince Fortinbras is now angry because his father gambled away his inheritance.
Bested by Old Hamlet • Lost his son's inheritance

NORWAY—Claudius' Counterpart
Named only by the title of the country he rules, Norway is Prince Fortinbras' uncle and the king of Norway. Like King Fortinbras, he also never appears in the play, but he is discussed second-hand by Claudius and the ambassadors. When Claudius' ambassadors tell Norway his nephew, Prince Fortinbras, is building an army against Denmark, Norway diffuses the situation and keeps the peace.
Uncle king • Past his prime • Peacemaker

MOST FAIR RETURN
of greetings and desires.
Upon our first, he sent out to suppress
His nephew's levies, which to him appeared
To be a preparation 'gainst the Polack;
But, better looked into, he truly found
It was against your highness...
2.2.60-65

ANSWER
Hamlet, Rosencrantz and Guildenstern are sailing under the pretense of diplomacy to England.
QUESTION
Young Fortinbras is prince of what country? (ANSWER ON PAGE 48)

THE AMBASSADORS

VOLTEMAND AND CORNELIUS
Denmark's peacemakers

Early in the play, when King Claudius hears Prince Fortinbras is raising an army against Denmark, he immediately communicates his concerns to Norway by sending his two ambassadors, Voltemand and Cornelius. These two ambassadors reappear a little later to tell Claudius that Norway has diffused the situation and that his petitions for peace have been heard.

THE ENGLISH AMBASSADOR
"Where is our thanks?"

At the end of the play, Hamlet, Claudius, Gertrude and Laertes lay dead on the stage. The English ambassador enters and asks, rhetorically, who will thank England for carrying out Claudius' request for execution (actually, Hamlet switched the names, but that's of no matter here). Horatio says no one is left, the monarchy is in ruins—thus, Shakespeare uses the English ambassador to focus our attention on the state of chaos in which Denmark is left at the end.

THE PIRATES

SAILORS 1 AND 2
Hamlet's way back to Denmark

Hamlet is sailing to England with Rosencrantz and Guildenstern on the pretense of a diplomatic mission when the ship is suddenly attacked by pirates. In the fighting, Hamlet boards the pirate ship and they return him safely home, hoping to win favor with the king of Denmark.

CHARACTERS | The Minor Characters | 47

THE KING, SIR,
*hath laid, sir, that in a dozen passes
Between you and [Laertes] he shall not exceed you three hits.
He hath laid on twelve for nine; and it would come to
Immediate trial if your lordship would vouchsafe the
answer.*
5.2.128-132

ANSWER
Prince Fortinbras is the Prince of Norway.

QUESTION
To whom are Claudius' two ambassadors, Voltemand and Cornelius, dispatched? (ANSWER ON PAGE 50)

THE SERVANTS

REYNALDO
Polonius' servant and spy
Polonius sends his servant, Reynaldo, to spy on Laertes, who is away at school in France. Polonius' verbose, circuitous advice borders on the comical as he cautions Reynaldo to uncover the extent of Laertes' wild behavior without interfering with the young man's necessary sowing of his wild oats. Reynaldo is not seen again in the play.
Spy • Comic straight man to Polonius

OSRIC
King Claudius' messenger
Claudius, having conspired with Laertes to kill Hamlet in the deadly fencing contest, uses Osric to deliver the challenge to the prince. We enjoy some comic relief as Hamlet and Horatio engage in wordplay at the courtier's expense, poking fun at his affected mannerisms, speech and overblown sense of self-importance. Osric maintains his composure and does not stoop to defend himself from their insults.
Courtier • Self-important and affected

THE SOLDIERS

BARNARDO, FRANCISCO AND MARCELLUS
The first to see the ghost of Old Hamlet
The first scene of the play has the king's guard, along with Horatio, on watch at the castle walls. They see the ghost of Old Hamlet and report his appearance to the prince. The next night, Hamlet sees the ghost for himself. He swears the soldiers to secrecy. They agree out of loyalty to the prince.
Loyal guard • Frightened by the ghost

GIVE ME LEAVE.

*Here lies the water—good.
Here stands the man—good. If the man go to this water
and drown himself, it is, will he nill he, he goes. Mark you
that. But if the water come to him and drown him, he
drowns not himself. Argal, he that is not guilty of his own
death shortens not his own life.*

5.1.14-19

ANSWER
Voltemand and Cornelius are dispatched to Norway, uncle of Prince Fortinbras
and brother to the late King Fortinbras.

QUESTION
Who is Reynaldo sent to spy on and who sends him? (ANSWER ON PAGE 53)

THE GRAVE CREW

THE GRAVE DIGGERS
Clowns for wordplay
The final act of the play opens with two grave diggers who joke in Shakespearean fashion about death. Hamlet joins them, in high spirits, having just returned on the pirate ship. They engage in low-comic wordplay about the universal experience of death. Little does Hamlet know, the crew are digging Ophelia's grave.
Low station • Pragmatic • Irreverent

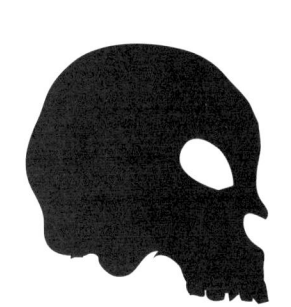

YORICK
The silent jester
Hamlet notices a skull the grave digger has tossed aside and, after finding out it was his father's court jester (a childhood friend), Hamlet ruminates on the shared fate of kings and jesters—the grave. Jesters in Shakespearean drama were reserved as truth-tellers, allowed to speak the truth because of their inconsequence. Yorick maintains this position in his silence: all will eventually die.
Childhood friend • Father's court jester • Silent witness

THE PLAYERS

THE ACTING COMPANY
The play-within-the-play
Hamlet is exuberant at the sight of the players as he has enjoyed their performances in the past. Hailing their arrival, he gets an idea—he will have them perform a play that mirrors the murder of his father by his uncle. He will watch Claudius' reaction and therefore test his guilt.
Touring actors • Well-known and well-liked by Hamlet

A QUICK REVIEW of

The Norwegians

Prince Fortinbras
- Prince of Norway
- Son of the late King Fortinbras who lost his son's inheritance
- Name means, "Strength in Arms"
- Man of action
- Given Denmark by Hamlet at end of play
- Nephew of Old Norway

King Fortinbras
- King of Norway in Old Hamlet's time
- Challenged Old Hamlet to a solitary combat: was killed and lost his son's (Prince Fortinbras) inheritance
- Only referred to in the play; never seen
- Brother of Old Norway

Norway (Old Norway)
- Current king of Norway
- Keeps the peace between Prince Fortinbras (his nephew) and Denmark
- Brother of the late King Fortinbras

The Ambassadors

Voltemand and Cornelius
- King Claudius' ambassadors
- Sent to Norway to restrain Prince Fortinbras's aggression
- Return successful

The English Ambassador
- After all have died, he arrives to ask, "Who will reward us for executing Rosencrantz and Guildenstern?"

The Pirates

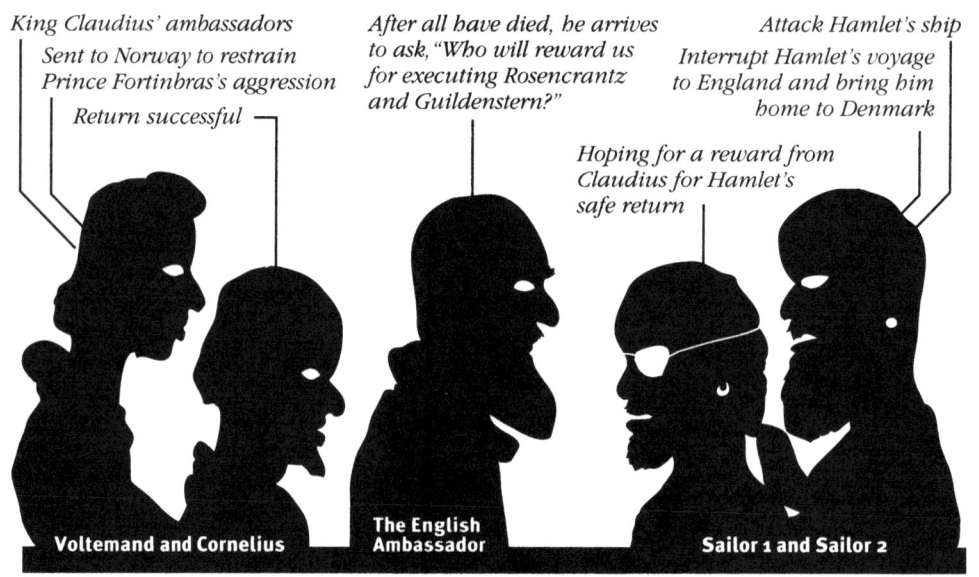

Sailor 1 and Sailor 2
- Attack Hamlet's ship
- Interrupt Hamlet's voyage to England and bring him home to Denmark
- Hoping for a reward from Claudius for Hamlet's safe return

THE MINOR CHARACTERS

The Servants

Reynaldo
- Servant of Polonius
- Dispatched by Polonius to spy on Laertes
- Has to listen to Polonius' long-winded direction

Osric
- Courtier dispatched by Claudius to present the challenge
- Affected manners and speech

The Soldiers

Francisco / Barnardo / Marcellus
- King Claudius' guard
- First to see the ghost of Old Hamlet; they, with Horatio, tell Hamlet about the ghost
- Sworn to secrecy by Hamlet

The Grave Crew

Clown 1 and Clown 2
- Digging Ophelia's grave
- Low-comic wordplay with Hamlet about death

Yorick
- Skull of Old Hamlet's jester, Hamlet's childhood friend
- Silent witness of the universal fate of both kings and jesters—death

The Players

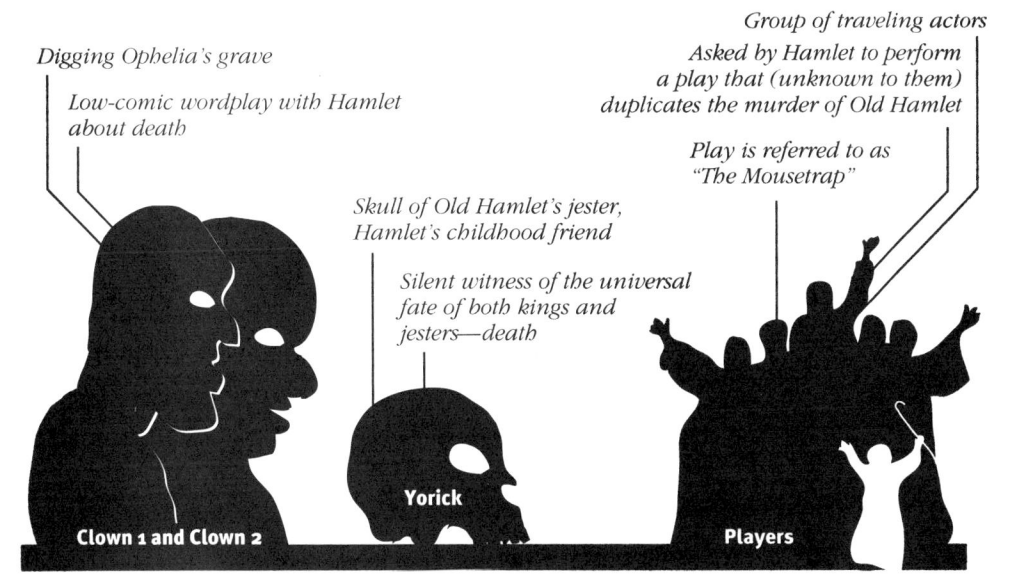

Players
- Group of traveling actors
- Asked by Hamlet to perform a play that (unknown to them) duplicates the murder of Old Hamlet
- Play is referred to as "The Mousetrap"

ANSWER Reynaldo is sent by Polonius to spy on Laertes.

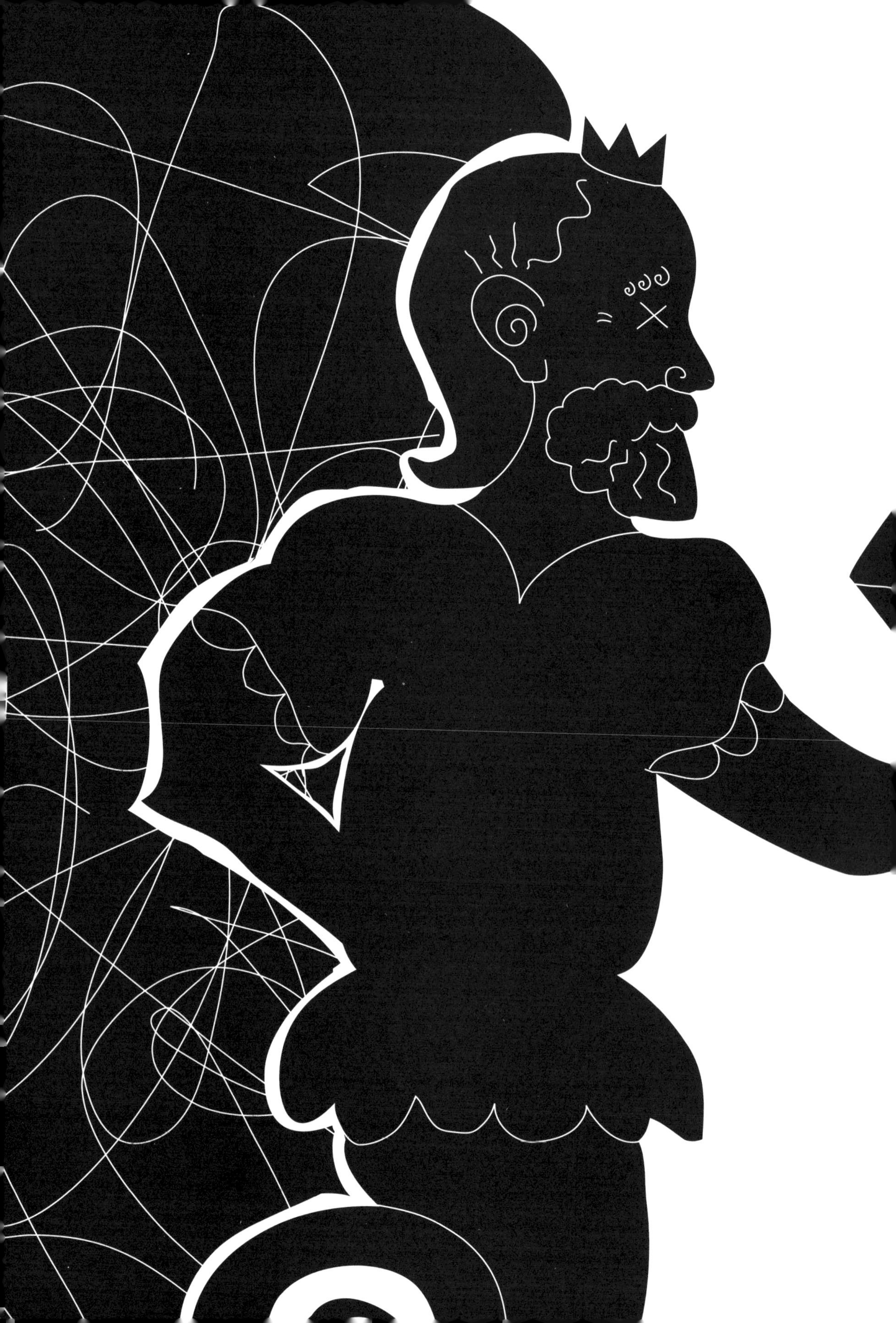

Power *bases*

The power bases in Hamlet are not difficult to recognize. Knowing them will increase your understanding of how the characters motivate each other's actions. In this chapter, we will examine the power bases as they polarize around Hamlet—the central protagonist—and Claudius—the central antagonist. We will draw special attention to Laertes' independence of Polonius; Gertrude's ambivalence (which causes her to straddle both power bases); Polonius' minor power base; and, finally, Old Hamlet's indirect control of the prince.

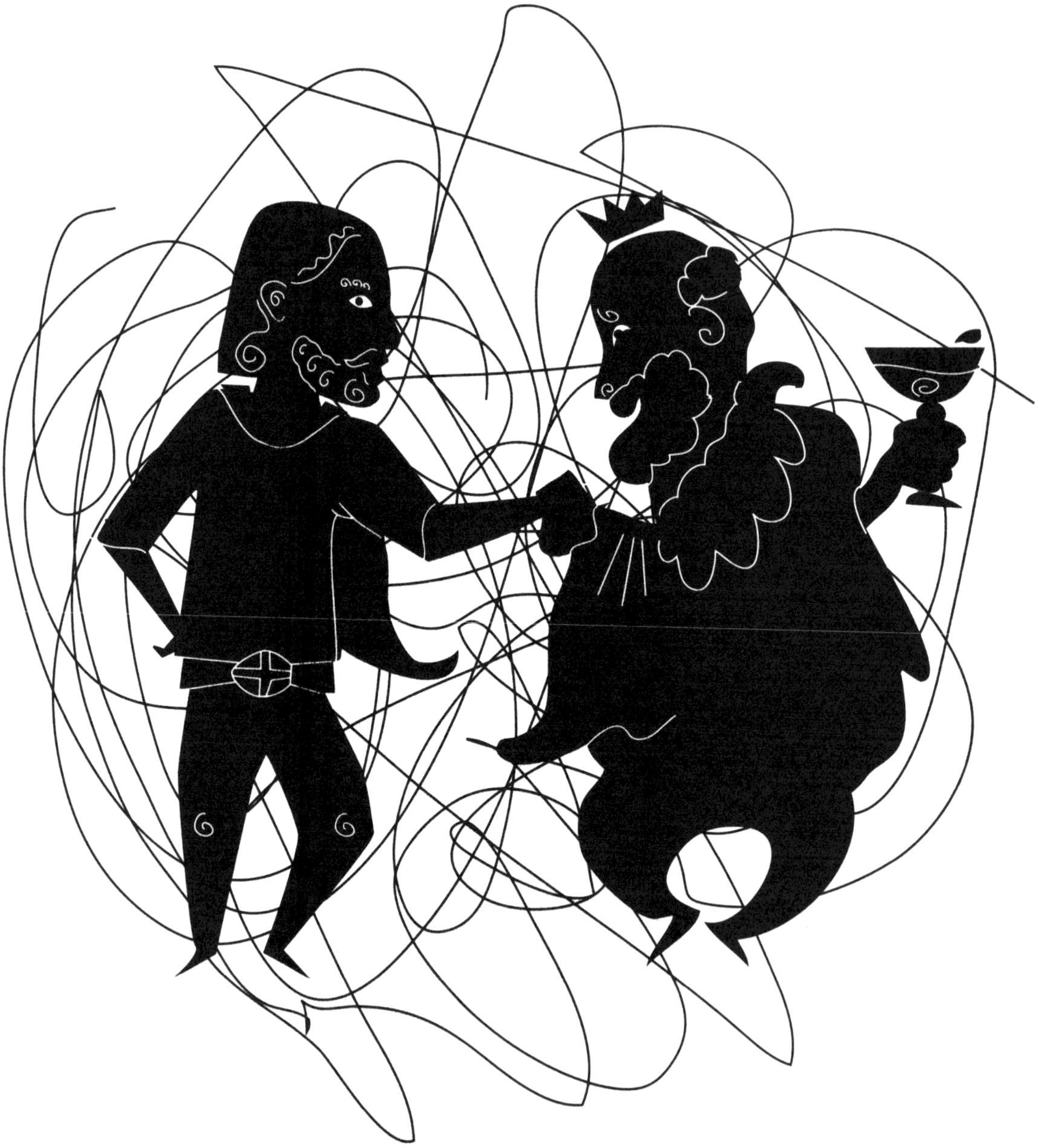

Hamlet and Claudius are caught in a classic power struggle.

ONE WAY OF LOOKING at the play is in terms of the protagonist, Hamlet, versus the antagonist, King Claudius. As the play opens, Hamlet's father has died under suspicious circumstances, Hamlet's mother has married Hamlet's uncle (which violates church doctrine), Hamlet's succession to the throne has been interrupted and he is soon asked not to return to university. During the course of action, Hamlet discovers that his uncle—and possibly his mother—is guilty of his father's murder. Hamlet wishes to avenge these wrongs, setting up all the elements of a classic power struggle:

Hamlet vs. **King Claudius**

Protagonist   *Antagonist*

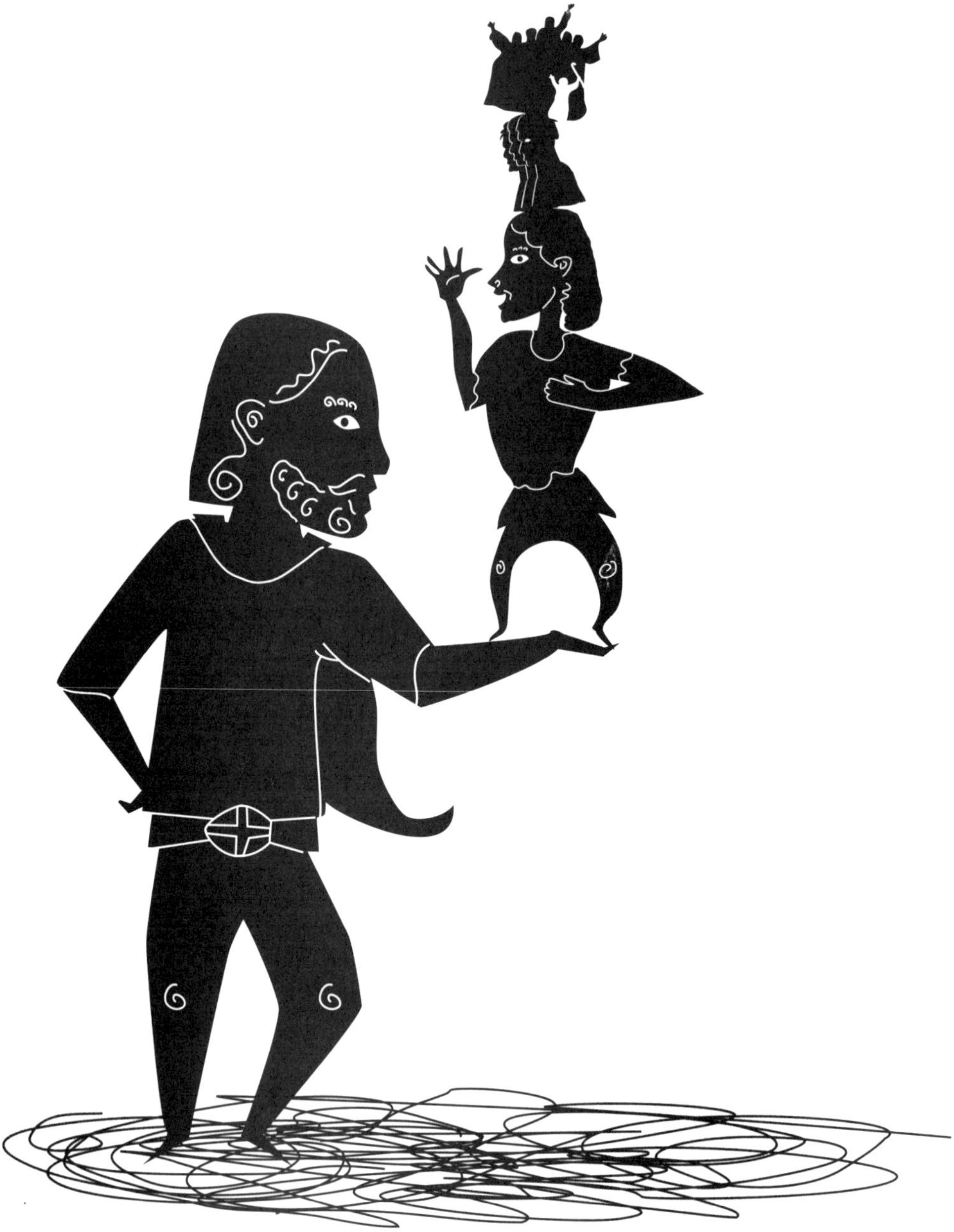

Hamlet has a fairly simple power base.

THROUGHOUT THE PLAY, the two major characters of Hamlet and Claudius direct or control the actions of characters within their respective power bases. Hamlet's power base consists of the soldiers, Horatio and the Players. It is relatively simple.

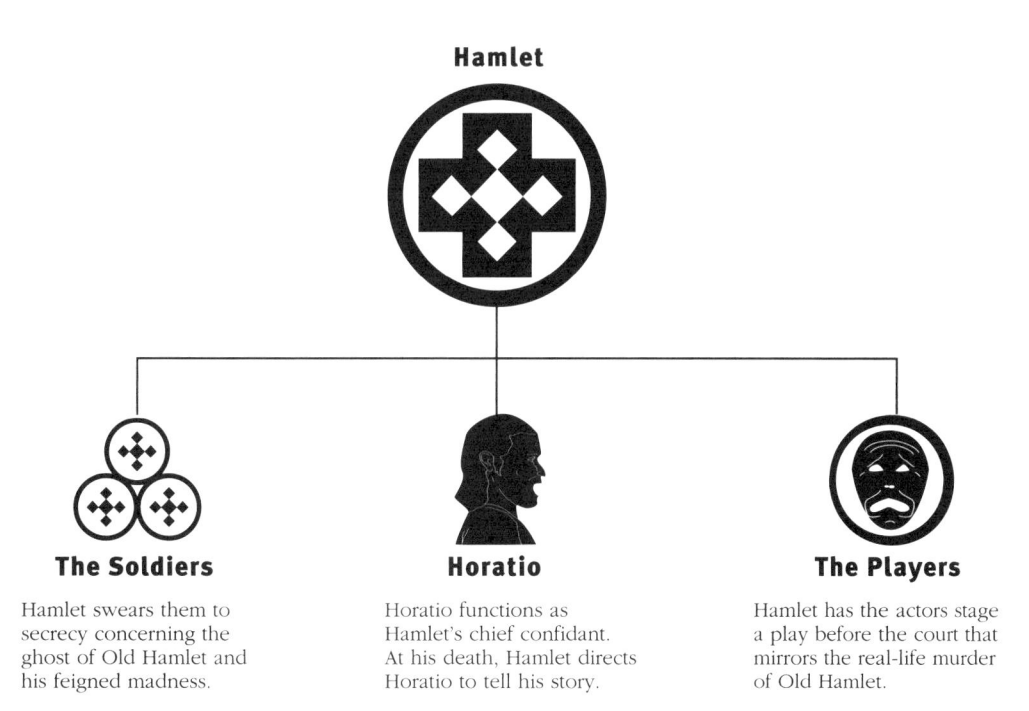

Hamlet

The Soldiers
Hamlet swears them to secrecy concerning the ghost of Old Hamlet and his feigned madness.

Horatio
Horatio functions as Hamlet's chief confidant. At his death, Hamlet directs Horatio to tell his story.

The Players
Hamlet has the actors stage a play before the court that mirrors the real-life murder of Old Hamlet.

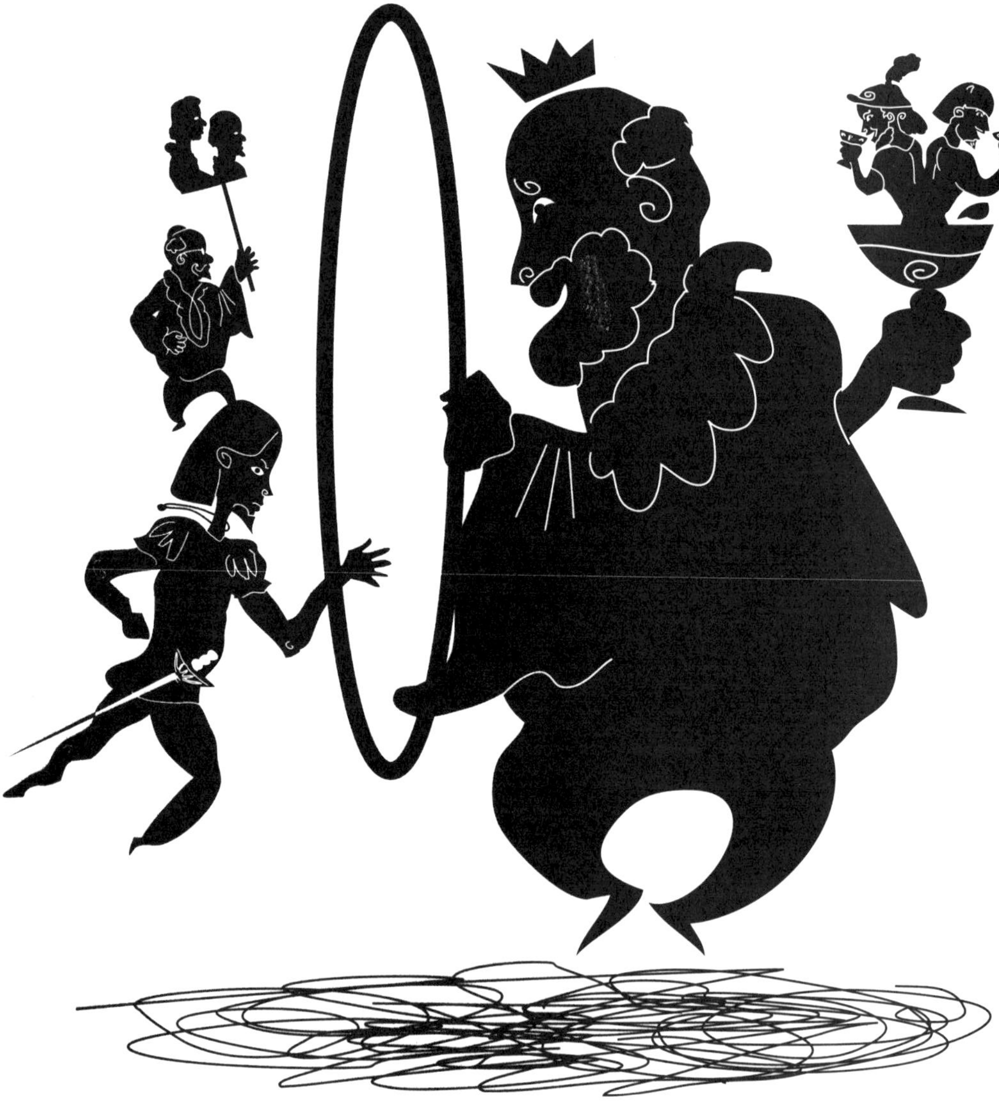

Claudius' power base is more complex.

BEING KING, Claudius has more resources at his disposal. Note also that Laertes is *not* controlled by his father, Polonius, as would be natural to surmise. Instead, Laertes resurfaces late in the play after the death of his father and is used by Claudius in the king's power struggle against Hamlet.

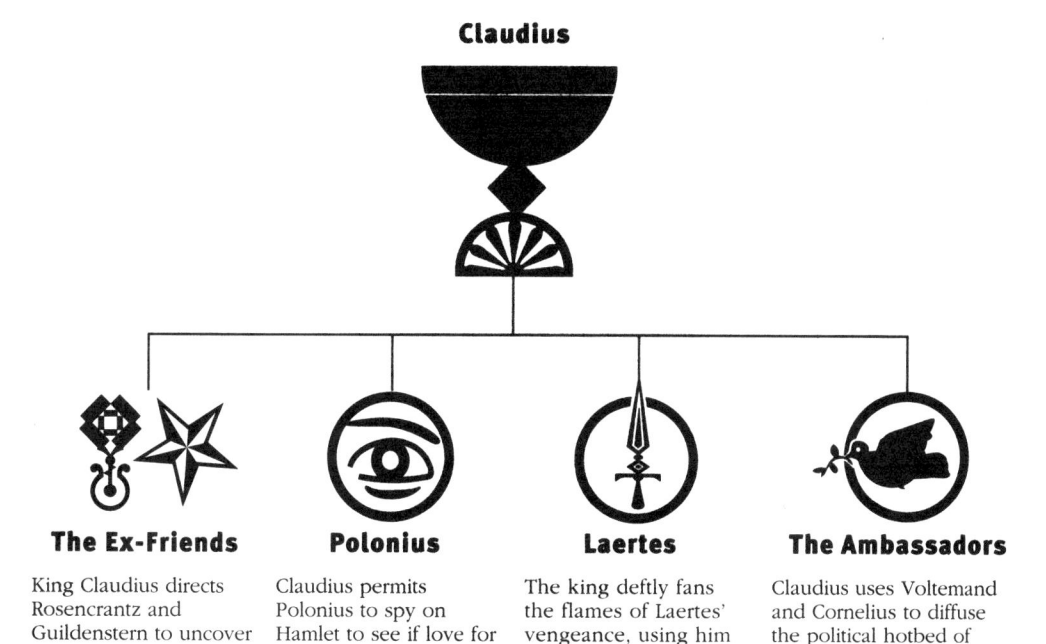

Claudius

The Ex-Friends	Polonius	Laertes	The Ambassadors
King Claudius directs Rosencrantz and Guildenstern to uncover the origins of Hamlet's madness	Claudius permits Polonius to spy on Hamlet to see if love for Ophelia is the cause of Hamlet's madness.	The king deftly fans the flames of Laertes' vengeance, using him as an assassin to kill Hamlet.	Claudius uses Voltemand and Cornelius to diffuse the political hotbed of Fortinbras' military buildup in Norway.

Mobilized against Hamlet   *Mobilized against Fortinbras*

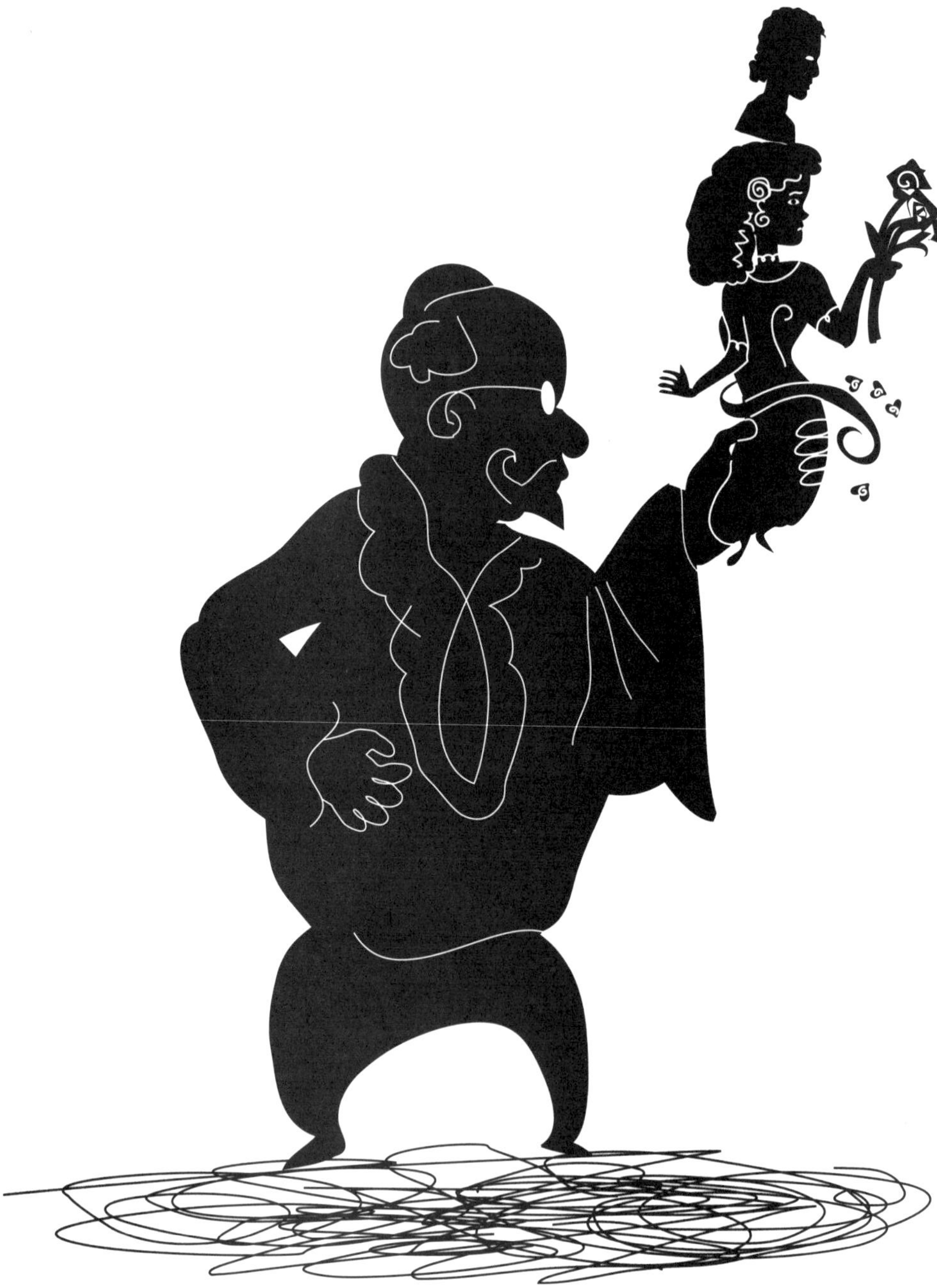

Polonius controls his own power base.

ALTHOUGH IT IS a minor power base, Polonius' control of Ophelia and Reynaldo is telling. Ophelia's obedience to her father, for instance, angers Hamlet. Also, Reynaldo's commission builds credibility to Polonius' penchant for spying—which leads to the old counselor's death.

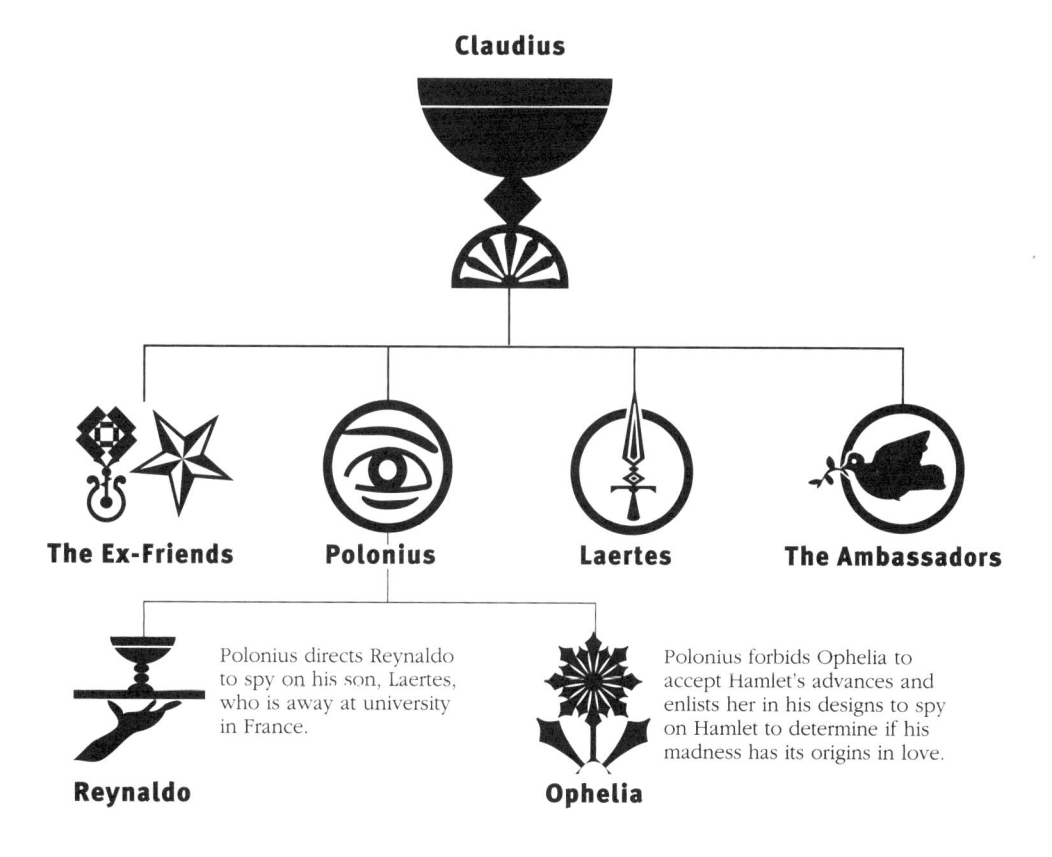

Claudius

The Ex-Friends | **Polonius** | **Laertes** | **The Ambassadors**

Reynaldo
Polonius directs Reynaldo to spy on his son, Laertes, who is away at university in France.

Ophelia
Polonius forbids Ophelia to accept Hamlet's advances and enlists her in his designs to spy on Hamlet to determine if his madness has its origins in love.

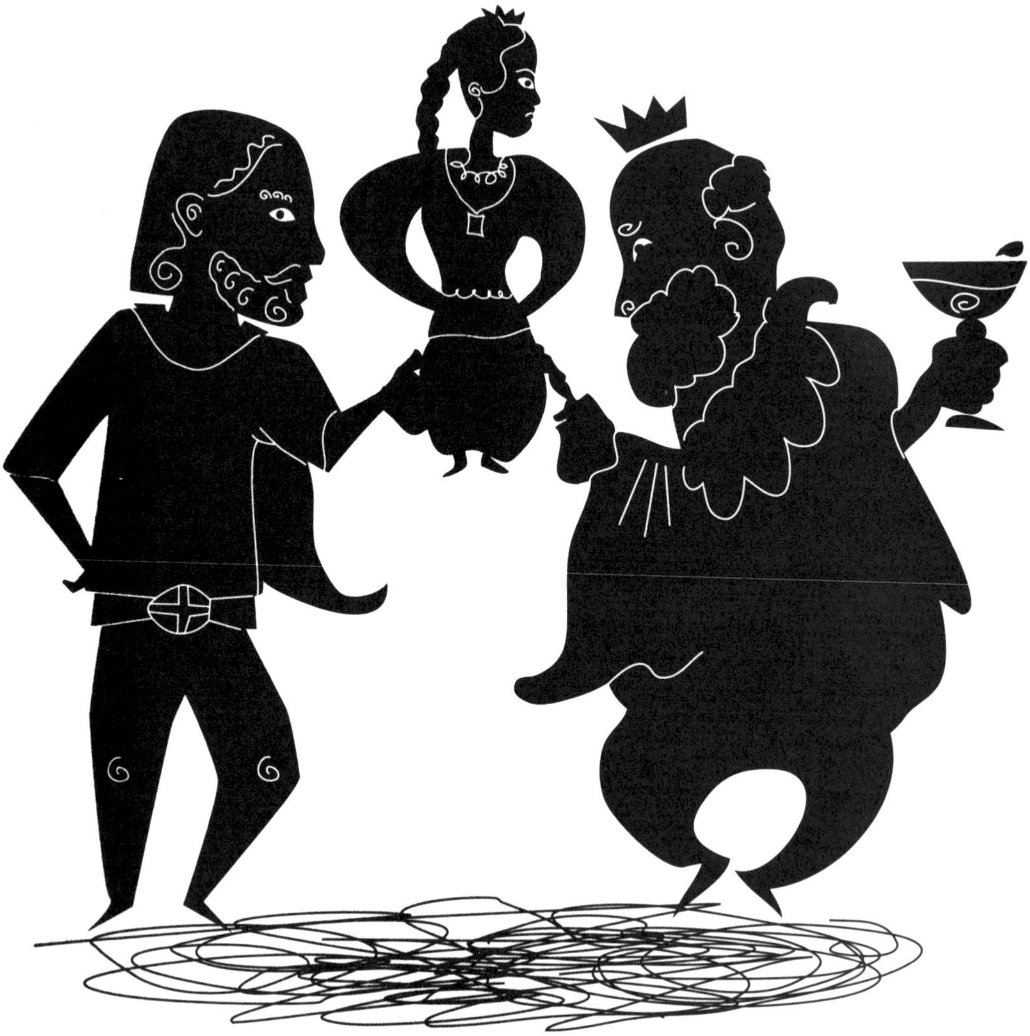

Gertrude is actually a wild card in the power struggle.

THE QUEEN IS TORN between the two power bases. Sometimes she is seen as being part of Claudius' power base; sometimes she is part of Hamlet's. For instance, at the end of the play, Hamlet successfully directs her to repent and refuse Claudius' advances. She can be thought of as being pulled between the two power bases controlled by her son and her new husband. Her connection is depicted with two arrows.

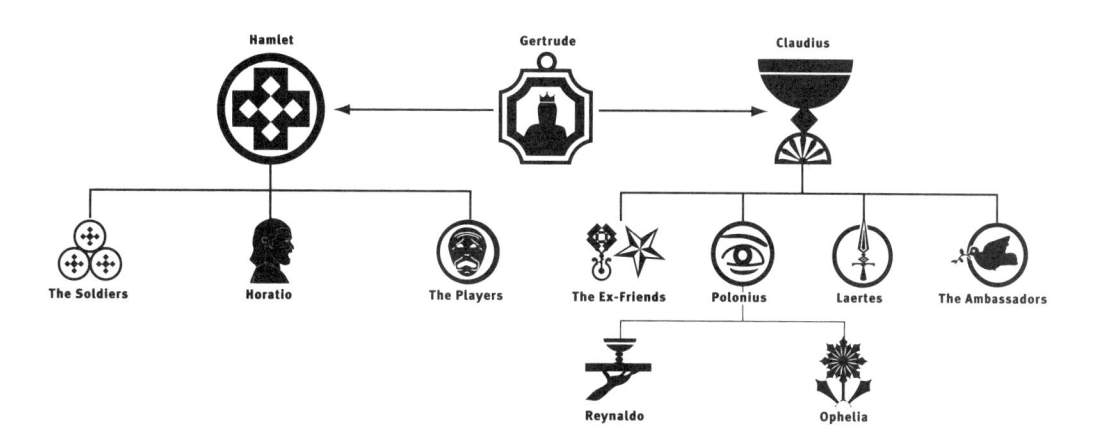

POWER BASES | Gertrude's Ambivalence

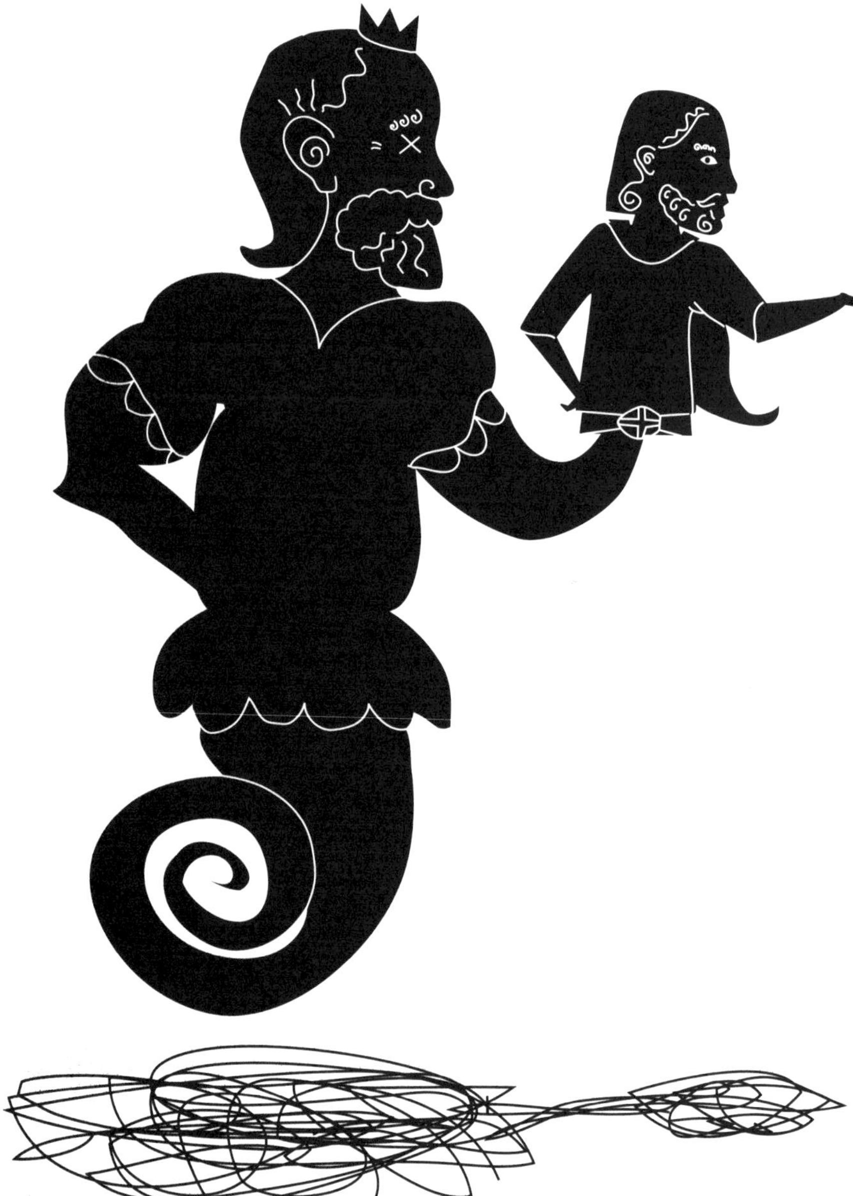

Hamlet's actions are motivated by the ghost of Old Hamlet.

THE GHOST of Old Hamlet can be thought of as the origin of Hamlet's motivation, as he calls for the prince to avenge his murder. Since the ghost's identity is in question—is it an omen? a devil? Old Hamlet's spirit? a hallucination?—we'll keep the connection a dashed line.

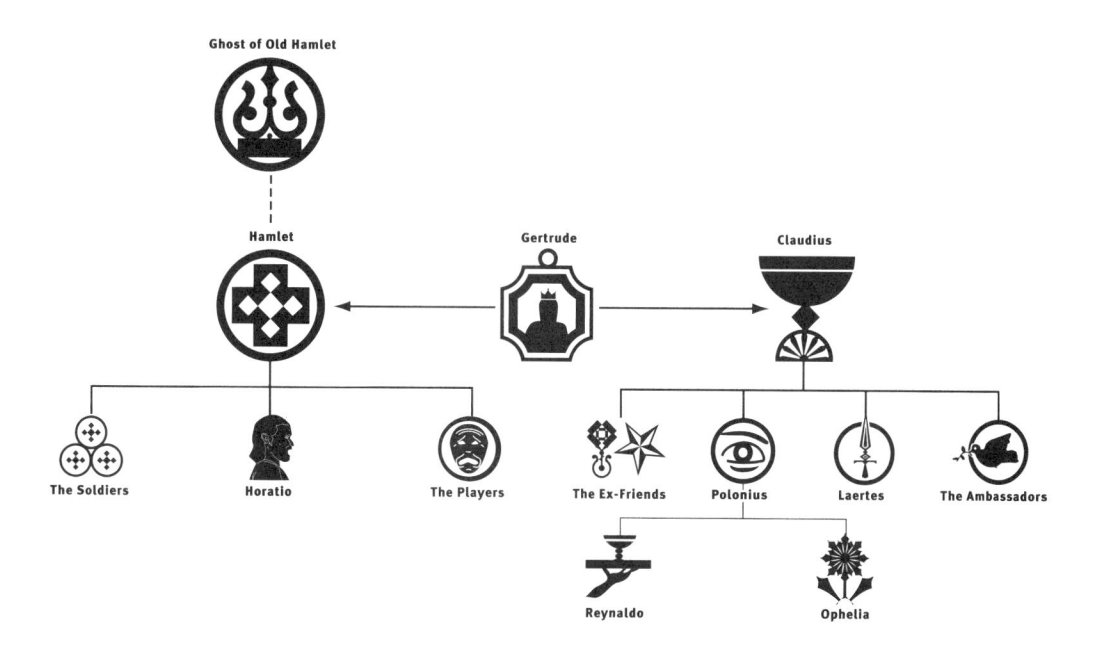

1 Ghost of Old Hamlet

2 Gertrude

3 Claudius

Hamlet

The Soldiers · Horatio · The Players

The Ex-Friends · Polonius · Laertes · The Ambassadors

Reynaldo · Ophelia

4

Let's review our completed power base diagram.

SPLITTING THE DIAGRAM down the middle, the protagonist's (Hamlet's) power base is depicted on the left; the antagonist's (Claudius') power base is depicted on the right. Claudius' sphere of influence is more complex, requiring two tiers, while Hamlet's is simpler.

1. Old Hamlet can be said to indirectly motivate the actions of Hamlet. His ghost appears to the prince, demanding vengeance for his murder.

2. Gertrude, the power base wild card, is shown straddling the two camps of her son and her new husband. She has loyalties to each at different times in the play.

3. Laertes is not controlled by his father, but reappears later in the play to be coaxed into action by Claudius.

4. Polonius controls his own minor power base comprised of Reynaldo and Ophelia.

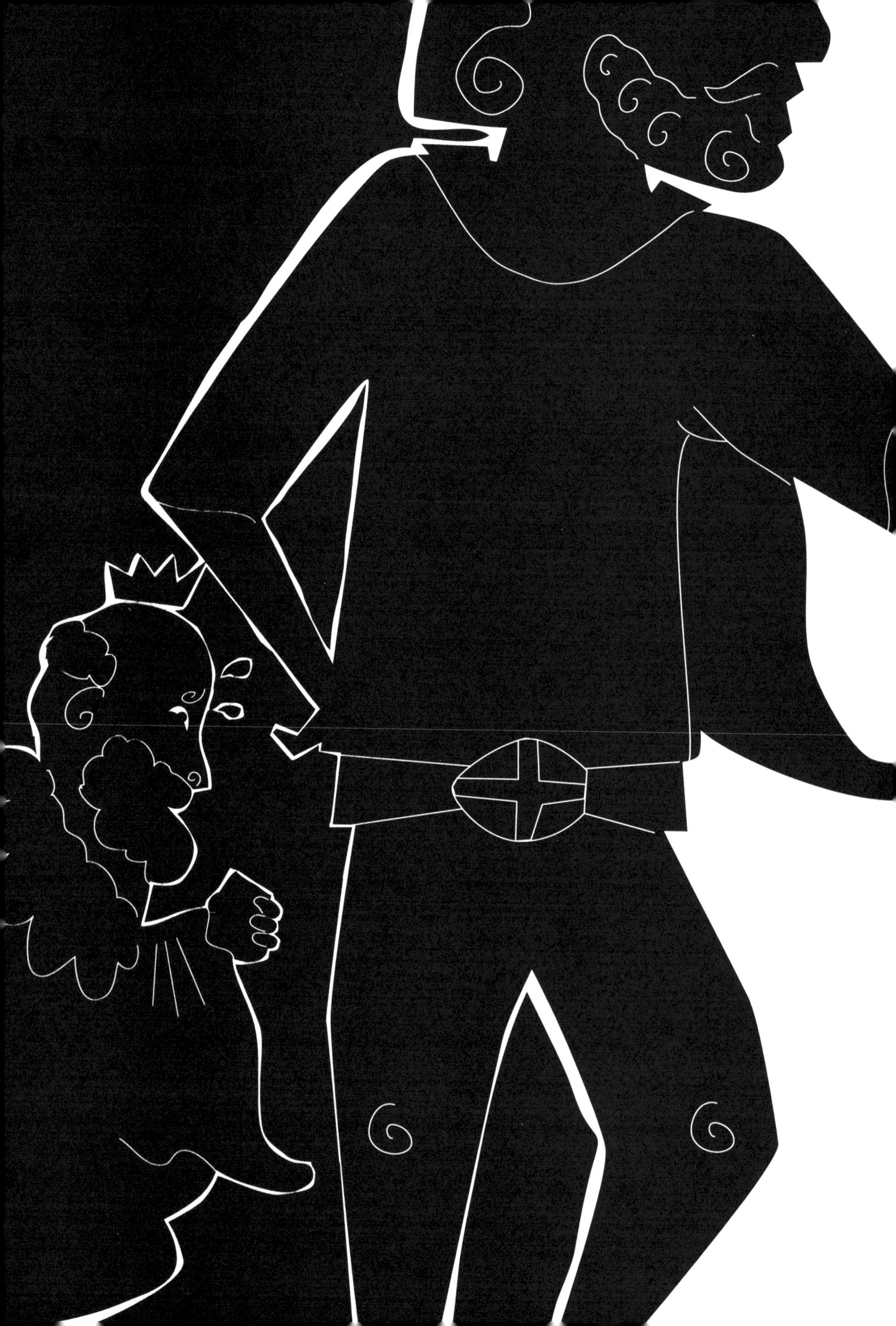

Main *plot*

Vengeance is the backbone of Hamlet. *It is the fear of Claudius, the drive of Laertes and the chief concern of Denmark's prince. Correspondingly, each event relating to the prince's vengeance—that of Old Hamlet's murder—can be considered an element of the main plot. All other events are subsidiary, no matter how important—the play must focus on the chief concern of the main character. When viewed in this light, the play reduces to a rather simple structure, made significantly deeper by its soul-searching and, above all, deeply human soliloquies. We'll examine this structure in the next few pages before moving on to the embellishments of subplot.*

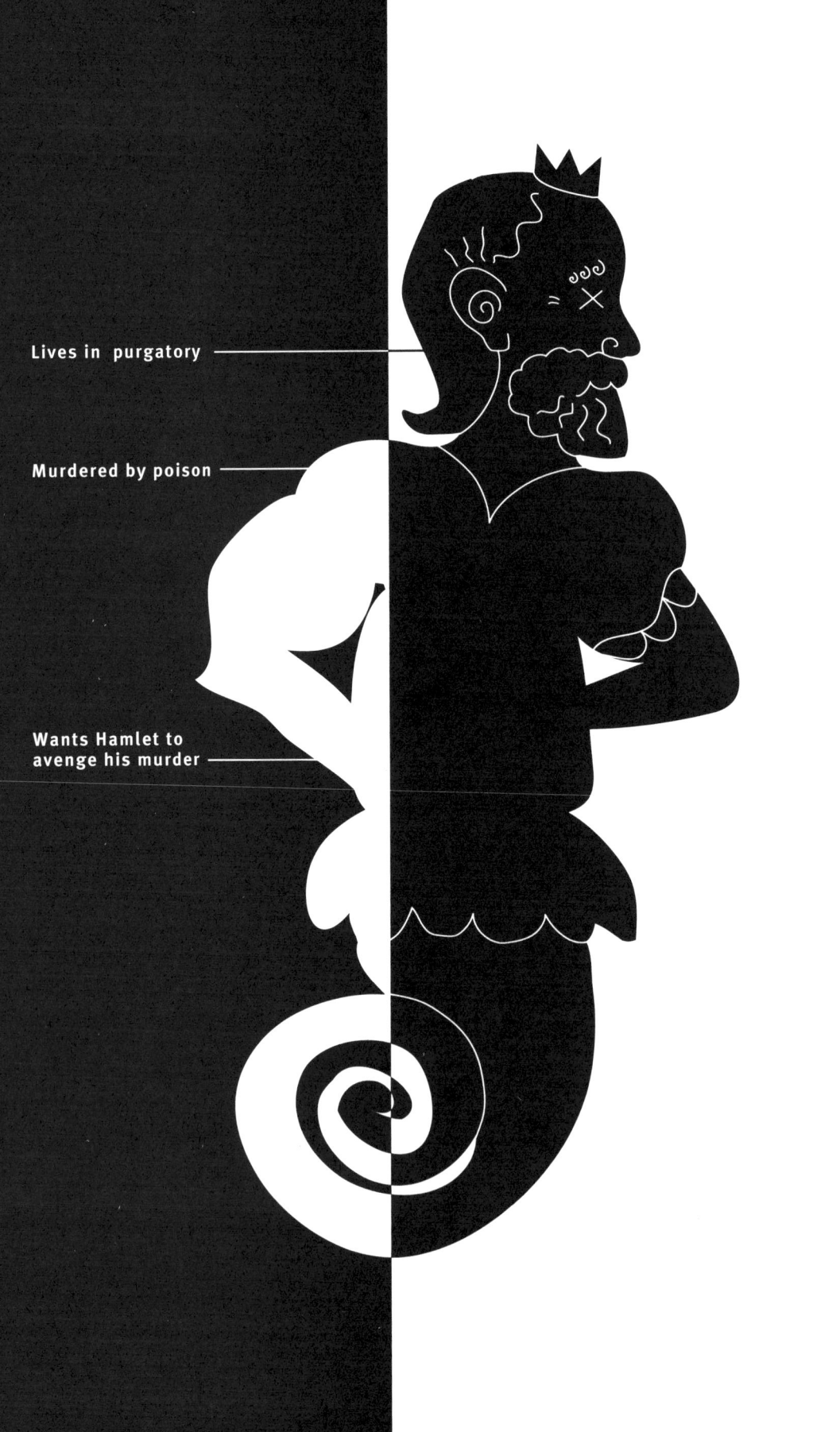

- Lives in purgatory
- Murdered by poison
- Wants Hamlet to avenge his murder

The main plot of Hamlet is simple: ghost, play, revenge.

GHOST. First, the ghost of Old Hamlet appears to the prince and relays the details of his murder by King Claudius—his brother and Hamlet's uncle.

PLAY. Then, to test the truthfulness of the ghost, Hamlet arranges to have the players stage a reenactment of this murder as entertainment for the royal court. King Claudius is overcome and runs out, causing the play to stop, thereby confirming his guilt.

REVENGE. When the right moment arises, Hamlet stabs the king and forces him to drink poison, at last avenging his father's murder.

- Lives in purgatory
- Murdered by poison
- Wants Hamlet to avenge his murder

This is how it might look on a timeline of the play.

We'll lay it out on a line, with regular divisions for each scene. This will help give you a big-picture view of the main plot.

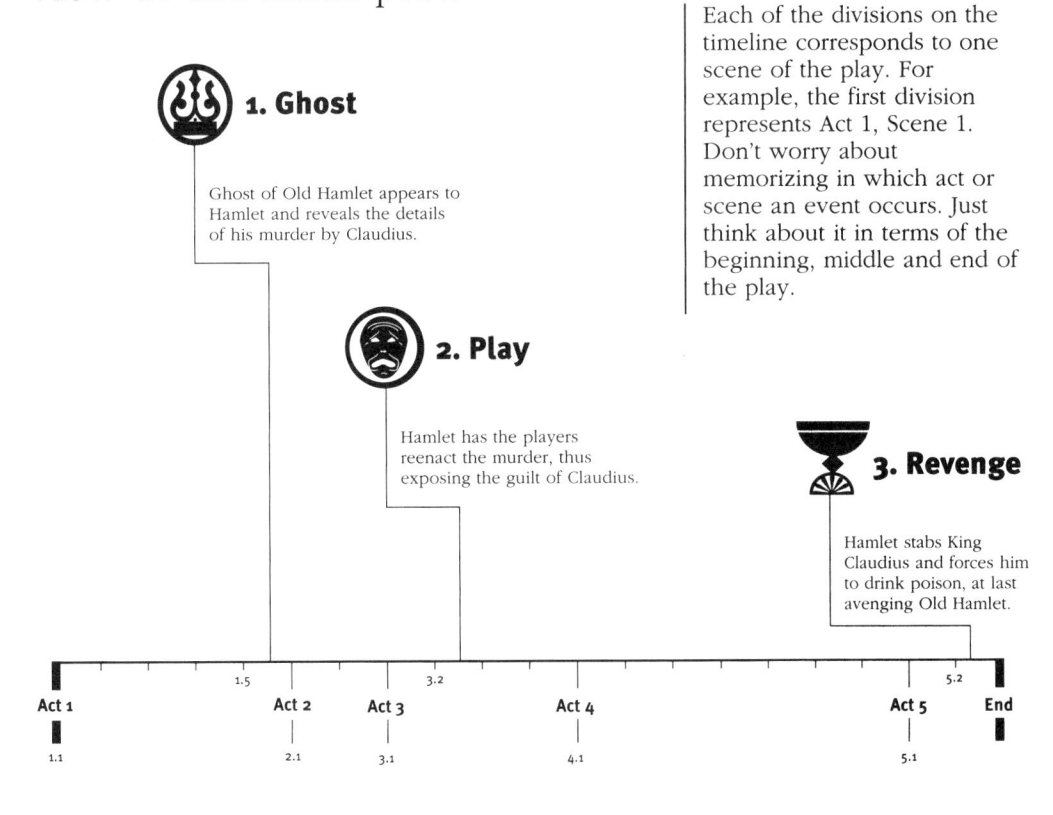

Each of the divisions on the timeline corresponds to one scene of the play. For example, the first division represents Act 1, Scene 1. Don't worry about memorizing in which act or scene an event occurs. Just think about it in terms of the beginning, middle and end of the play.

1. Ghost
Ghost of Old Hamlet appears to Hamlet and reveals the details of his murder by Claudius.

2. Play
Hamlet has the players reenact the murder, thus exposing the guilt of Claudius.

3. Revenge
Hamlet stabs King Claudius and forces him to drink poison, at last avenging Old Hamlet.

Act 1 — 1.1 — 1.5 — Act 2 — 2.1 — Act 3 — 3.1 — 3.2 — Act 4 — 4.1 — Act 5 — 5.1 — 5.2 — End

MAIN PLOT | Timeline

Pretends to be crazy

Speaks in antic fashion
that most shrug off
as nonsense

Uses madness
as a means to keep
Claudius' camp in
a state of confusion

Now, let's add Hamlet's madness to our simplified plot.

ANTIC DISPOSITION. Right after Hamlet vows to avenge his father's murder, he tells Horatio and the soldiers that he may pretend to be mad. Hamlet refers to it as an "antic disposition." He dresses strangely and begins talking nonsensically (actually, his wordplay shows keen insight, but most of the characters see it as the ramblings of a madman).

WHY DOES HAMLET PRETEND TO BE MAD? To begin with, a superstition existed in Hamlet's day that anyone killing a lunatic would catch the victim's lunacy. Surviving princes often relied on this ruse. Hamlet makes use of this strategy because he is naturally concerned for his own life. Further, Hamlet's feigned madness allows a bit of freedom to plot and move within the castle without raising the suspicions of his enemies. Finally—and perhaps the strongest reason supported by the text—Hamlet's madness keeps his opponents confused and off-guard, hopelessly sifting through layers of veiled insult, cynicism and misinformation.

- Pretends to be crazy
- Speaks in antic fashion that most shrug off as nonsense
- Uses madness as a means to keep Claudius' camp in a state of confusion

Here is how our timeline looks now.

The first element of our timeline, *Ghost*, has now been appended to read: *Ghost/Madness*. Not a big change to our timeline, but most definitely a key element of the plot. Hamlet will pretend to be mad until the last act.

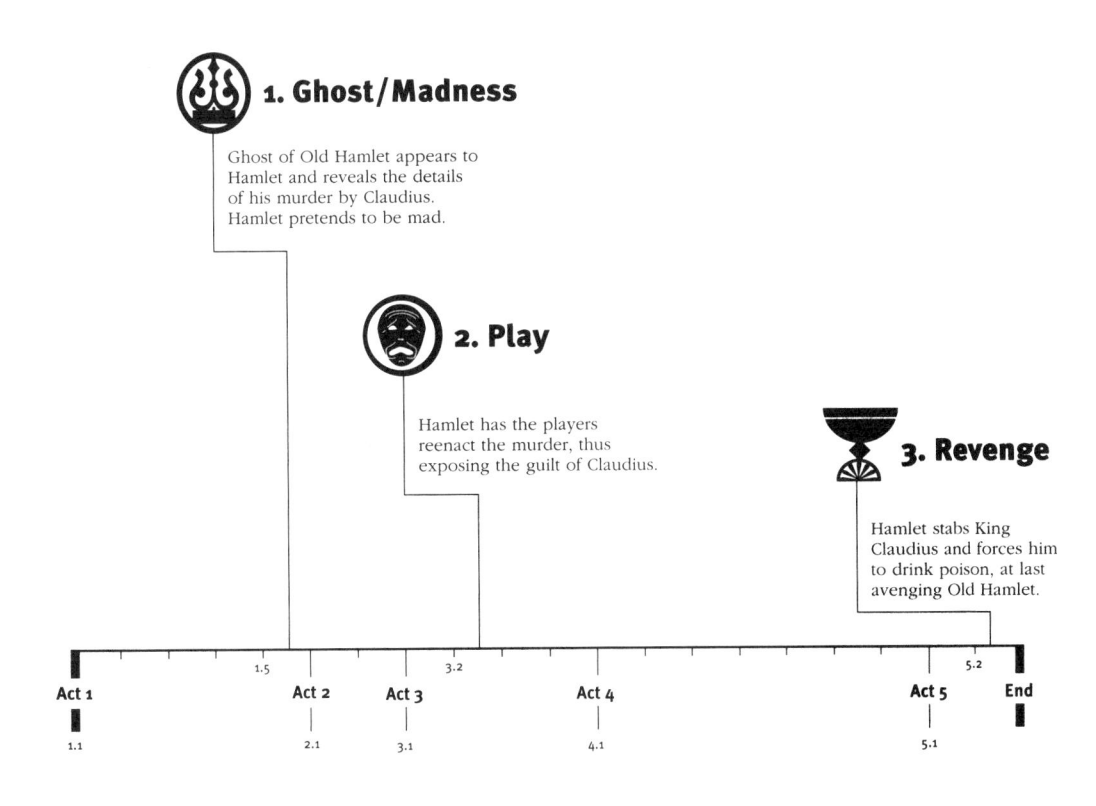

1. Ghost/Madness
Ghost of Old Hamlet appears to Hamlet and reveals the details of his murder by Claudius. Hamlet pretends to be mad.

2. Play
Hamlet has the players reenact the murder, thus exposing the guilt of Claudius.

3. Revenge
Hamlet stabs King Claudius and forces him to drink poison, at last avenging Old Hamlet.

Act 1 — 1.1 — 1.5 — Act 2 — 2.1 — Act 3 — 3.1 — 3.2 — Act 4 — 4.1 — Act 5 — 5.1 — 5.2 — End

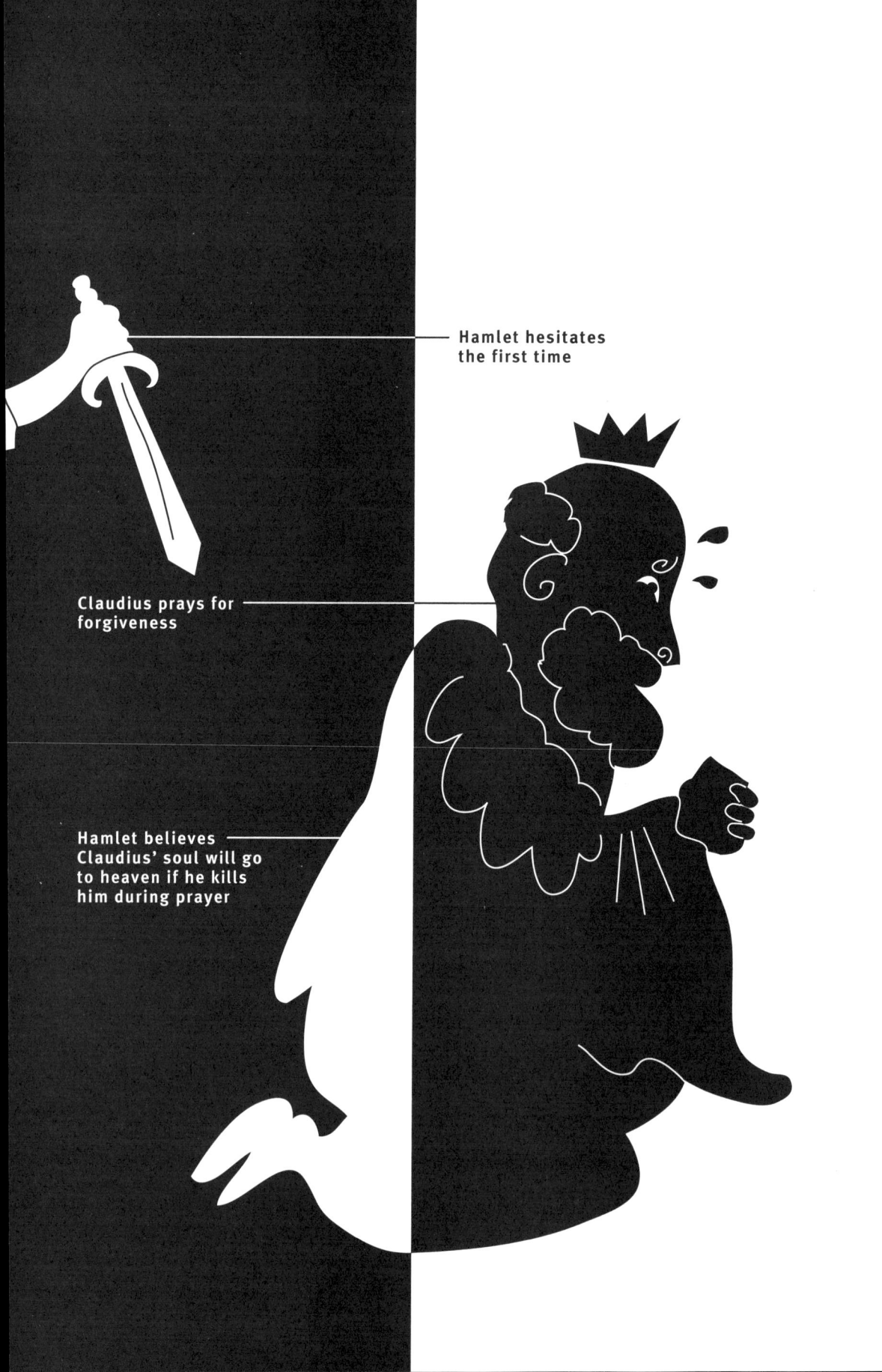

Hamlet hesitates the first time

Claudius prays for forgiveness

Hamlet believes Claudius' soul will go to heaven if he kills him during prayer

Why doesn't Hamlet kill Claudius right after his ingenious play?

If you're wondering why Hamlet doesn't kill Claudius in Act Three, just after the play-within-the-play exposes the king's guilt, then you're asking the right question. The short answer is: he begins to, but then hesitates. Why? When Hamlet comes upon Claudius, the king is on his knees praying for forgiveness (or at least making an effort to pray). Hamlet believes that if he kills the praying Claudius, then Claudius' soul will immediately go to heaven, which is counter to Hamlet's purpose. Therefore, he waits for a future opportunity—a decision which later proves fatal.

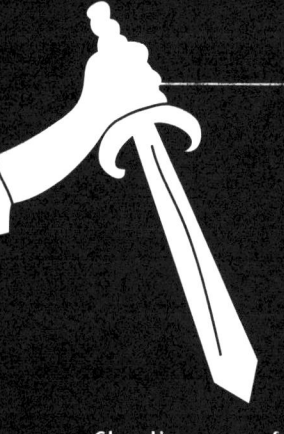

- Hamlet hesitates the first time
- Claudius prays for forgiveness
- Hamlet believes Claudius' soul will go to heaven if he kills him during prayer

Now our main plot is shaping up.

We now see the flow of the main plot: 1. The ghost of Old Hamlet appears to Hamlet; 2. Hamlet stages a play to expose his father's murderer; 3. Claudius runs out and prays for forgiveness, causing Hamlet to hesitate; 4. Hamlet eventually exacts his revenge. Think of this as the backbone of the play. We'll fill in more details later, but first we need to talk about the subplots.

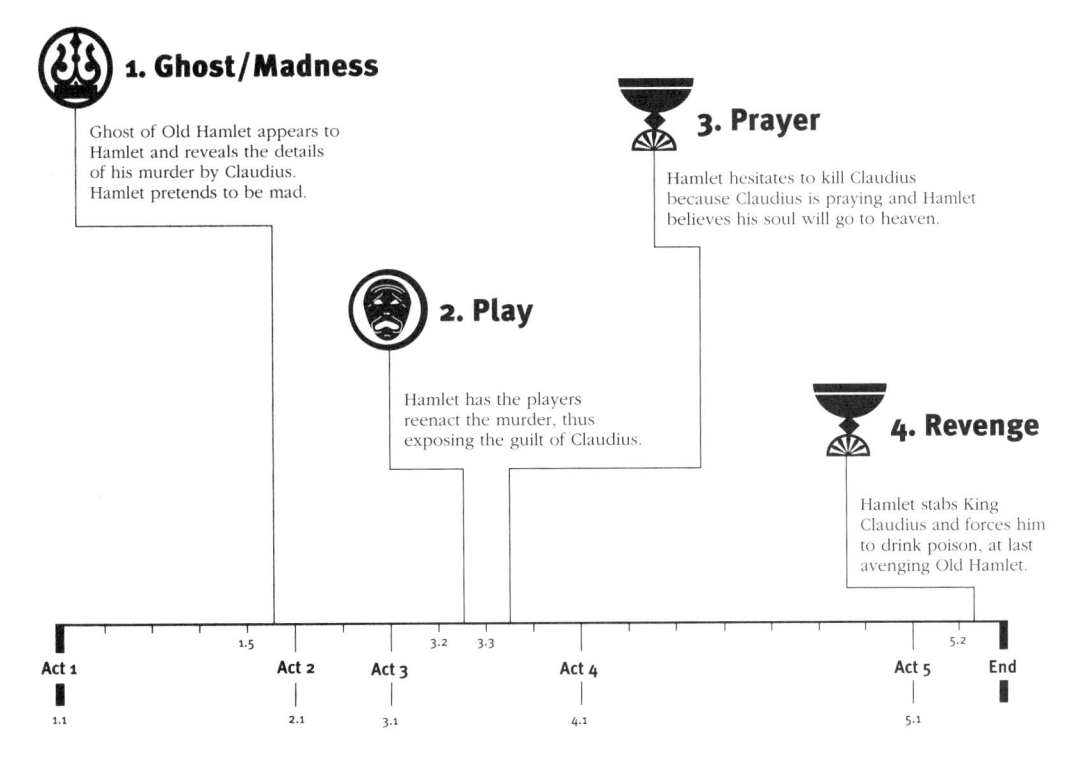

1. Ghost/Madness
Ghost of Old Hamlet appears to Hamlet and reveals the details of his murder by Claudius. Hamlet pretends to be mad.

2. Play
Hamlet has the players reenact the murder, thus exposing the guilt of Claudius.

3. Prayer
Hamlet hesitates to kill Claudius because Claudius is praying and Hamlet believes his soul will go to heaven.

4. Revenge
Hamlet stabs King Claudius and forces him to drink poison, at last avenging Old Hamlet.

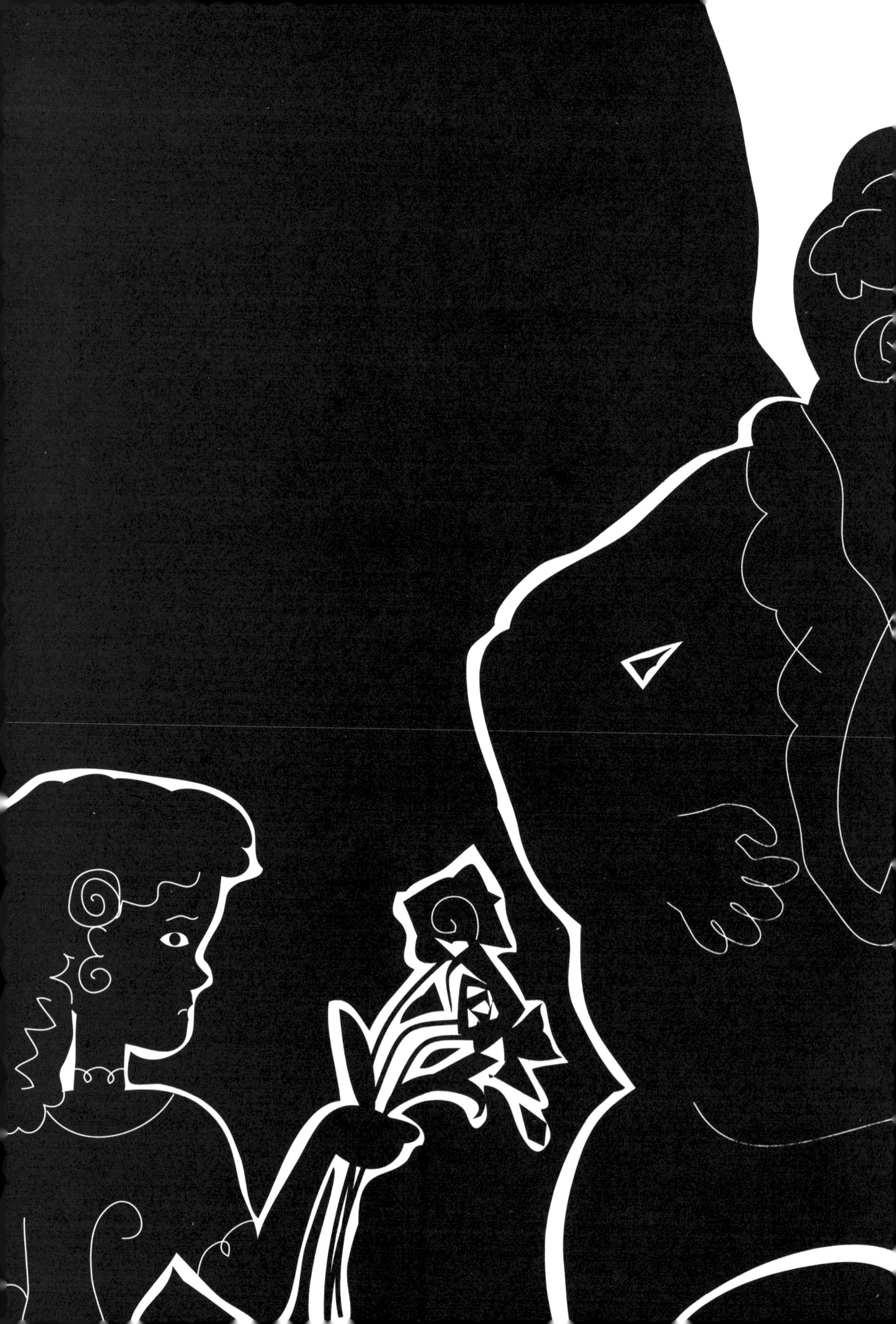

The *subplots*

What are subplots? Loosely speaking, any action that takes place outside of the protagonist's chief concern can be thought of as a subplot. The chief concern of Hamlet is the vengeance of his father's murder, so there is substantial material in the play that can be categorized as subordinate to the main plot. We'll first take a look at Ophelia, Hamlet's girlfriend, who is caught between the opposing social forces of her father and her boyfriend. Next we will examine Polonius and his predilection for clandestine activities. Finally, we will look at Rosencrantz and Guildenstern, who concern themselves more with garnering the king's favor than with any loyalty to their childhood friend, the prince.

Ophelia — She will go mad and die by drowning

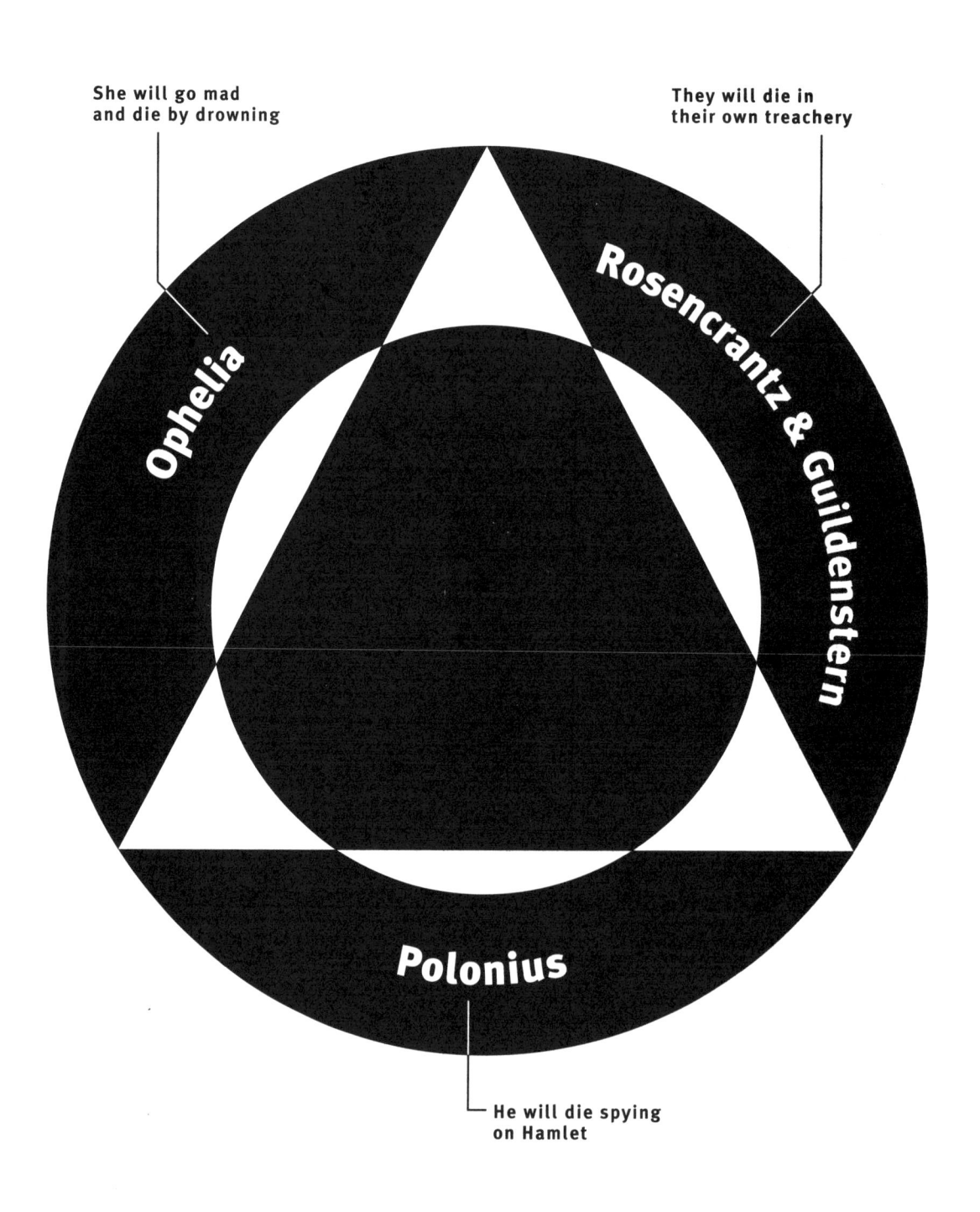

Rosencrantz & Guildenstern — They will die in their own treachery

Polonius — He will die spying on Hamlet

There are three primary subplots in Hamlet.

One of the most rewarding features of Shakespeare's writing is the depth he achieves through the use of subplot. Some plays, such as *Macbeth,* make limited use of subplot and do not extend far beyond the boundary of main action. Others, like *A Midsummer Night's Dream,* rely heavily on more loosely woven subplots that intersect the main action at critical nodes. The plot of *Hamlet*—with its main preoccupation being the revenge of Old Hamlet's murder—lies somewhere in between.

    The three dominant subplots involve Hamlet's girlfriend, Ophelia; Hamlet's ex-friends, Rosencrantz and Guildenstern; and Ophelia's father, Polonius. These three subplots eventually reenter the main action at dynamic points of intersection. In doing so, the subplots add depth to the main characters while simultaneously motivating action that would not be credible in their absence.

- Obedient daughter
- Caught between her love for Hamlet and obedience to her father
- Drowns hanging flower garlands

Ophelia's subplot: refusal, confusion, madness and death.

REFUSAL. We first see Ophelia as she receives strict instruction from her father, Polonius, to refuse Hamlet's attentions. He believes the prince is not serious about his relationship with Ophelia, who is not royalty. He is, of course, wrong.

CONFUSION. Hamlet's feigned madness confuses Ophelia, who believes he has gone insane because she has obediently refused his attentions. Hamlet also shows anger at her willingness to help her father spy on him. Hamlet's anger is another source of confusion for the genuinely good-hearted Ophelia.

MADNESS. Ophelia goes mad after the death of her father and the voyage of Hamlet to England. It is a genuine contrast to Hamlet's calculated insanity.

DEATH. In her madness and depression, Ophelia drowns as she reaches to hang garlands over the brook. There is an element of suicide in her death that is left deliberately unresolved.

- Obedient daughter
- Caught between her love for Hamlet and obedience to her father
- Drowns hanging flower garlands

Let's see her subplot on the timeline.

Looking at Ophelia's subplot on the timeline, we can see her positioning relative to the main plot. For instance, her confusion occupies the space between the Ghost's appearance and the players' performance.

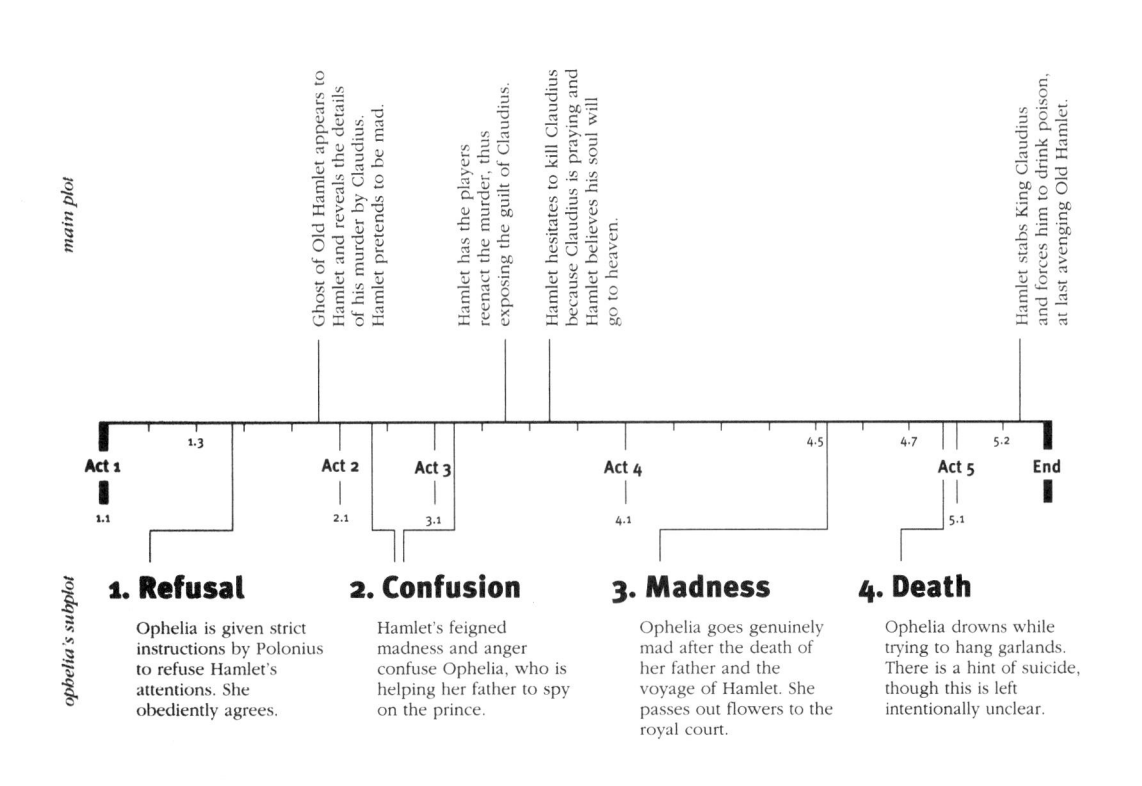

main plot

- Ghost of Old Hamlet appears to Hamlet and reveals the details of his murder by Claudius. Hamlet pretends to be mad.
- Hamlet has the players reenact the murder, thus exposing the guilt of Claudius.
- Hamlet hesitates to kill Claudius because Claudius is praying and Hamlet believes his soul will go to heaven.
- Hamlet stabs King Claudius and forces him to drink poison, at last avenging Old Hamlet.

Act 1 — 1.1 — 1.3 — Act 2 — 2.1 — Act 3 — 3.1 — Act 4 — 4.1 — 4.5 — 4.7 — Act 5 — 5.1 — 5.2 — End

ophelia's subplot

1. Refusal
Ophelia is given strict instructions by Polonius to refuse Hamlet's attentions. She obediently agrees.

2. Confusion
Hamlet's feigned madness and anger confuse Ophelia, who is helping her father to spy on the prince.

3. Madness
Ophelia goes genuinely mad after the death of her father and the voyage of Hamlet. She passes out flowers to the royal court.

4. Death
Ophelia drowns while trying to hang garlands. There is a hint of suicide, though this is left intentionally unclear.

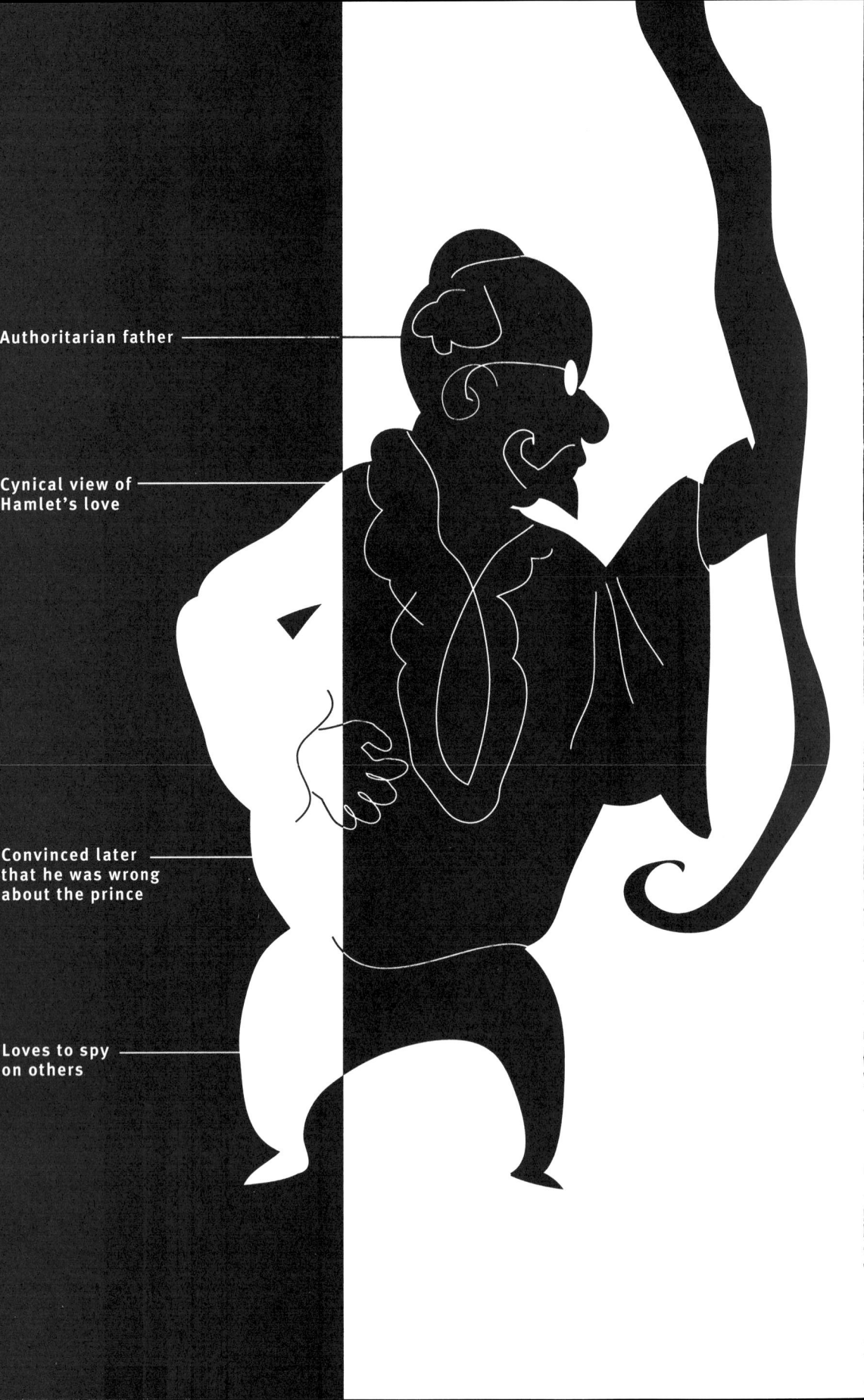

- Authoritarian father
- Cynical view of Hamlet's love
- Convinced later that he was wrong about the prince
- Loves to spy on others

Polonius' subplot: advice, retraction, espionage, accident.

ADVICE. Polonius advises his two children, Laertes and Ophelia, in his first big scene. His advice to Ophelia has lasting repercussions: he forbids her to speak or meet with Prince Hamlet. Polonius feels that, like all young men, the prince's intentions are not honorable where love is concerned.

RETRACTION. Hamlet's apparent madness causes Polonius to rethink the prince's feelings for Ophelia. He misreads all of Hamlet's subsequent actions as originating in true, unrequited love and he retracts his original statement as a natural misjudgment.

ESPIONAGE. Polonius loves to spy. He spies on both Laertes and Hamlet. He recommends espionage to Claudius and Gertrude. He dies spying.

ACCIDENT. When in heated conversation with Gertrude, Hamlet mistakes the tapestry-hidden Polonius for Claudius and runs him through with a sword. He is buried hastily, but soon his murder becomes known to all.

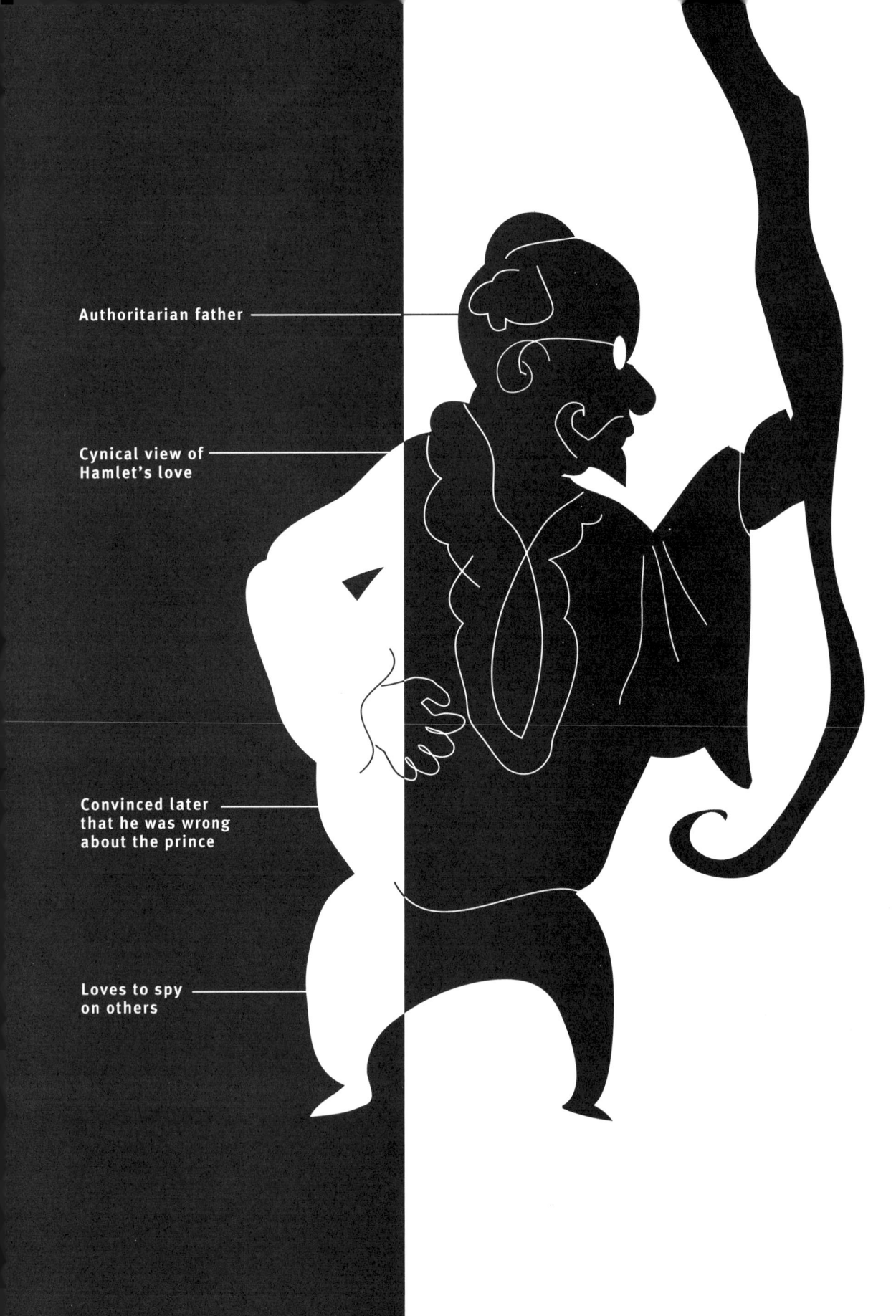

- Authoritarian father
- Cynical view of Hamlet's love
- Convinced later that he was wrong about the prince
- Loves to spy on others

Polonius has a more complex timeline.

Although Polonius' subplot is more complex to position on the timeline, if you remember to reverse a sequence of cause and effect, you won't have any trouble: Polonius' accidental death was caused by his espionage; his espionage was launched to prove the motive behind his retraction; his retraction was prompted by Hamlet's madness, which he believed refuted the validity of his initial advice to Ophelia.

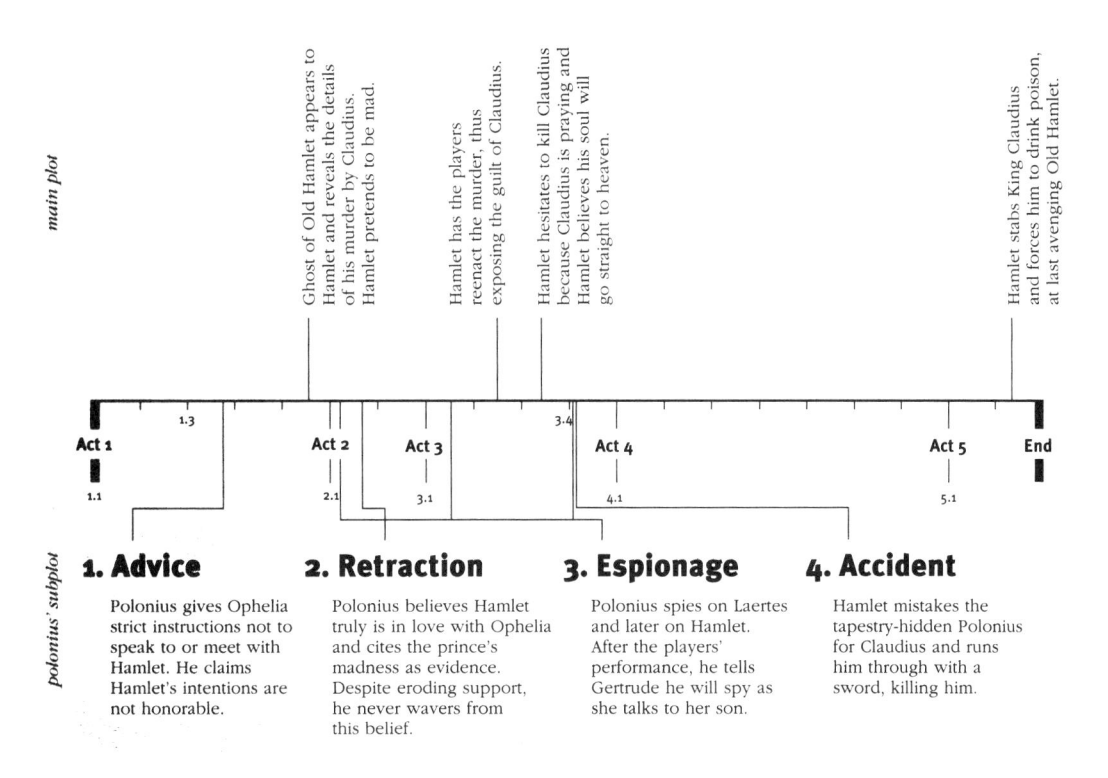

main plot

Ghost of Old Hamlet appears to Hamlet and reveals the details of his murder by Claudius. Hamlet pretends to be mad.

Hamlet has the players reenact the murder, thus exposing the guilt of Claudius.

Hamlet hesitates to kill Claudius because Claudius is praying and Hamlet believes his soul will go straight to heaven.

Hamlet stabs King Claudius and forces him to drink poison, at last avenging Old Hamlet.

Act 1 — 1.1, 1.3 | Act 2 — 2.1 | Act 3 — 3.1, 3.4 | Act 4 — 4.1 | Act 5 — 5.1 | End

polonius' subplot

1. Advice
Polonius gives Ophelia strict instructions not to speak to or meet with Hamlet. He claims Hamlet's intentions are not honorable.

2. Retraction
Polonius believes Hamlet truly is in love with Ophelia and cites the prince's madness as evidence. Despite eroding support, he never wavers from this belief.

3. Espionage
Polonius spies on Laertes and later on Hamlet. After the players' performance, he tells Gertrude he will spy as she talks to her son.

4. Accident
Hamlet mistakes the tapestry-hidden Polonius for Claudius and runs him through with a sword, killing him.

- Old school friends of Hamlet
- Called to court by Claudius and Gertrude to discover cause of Hamlet's madness
- Hamlet easily sees through their ruse
- Killed in England upon their arrival

Ex-friends' subplot: assignment, discovery, voyage and execution.

ASSIGNMENT. Rosencrantz and Guildenstern, old school friends of Hamlet, are called by Claudius and Gertrude to discover the root cause of Hamlet's madness. They are, essentially, spies for the king.

DISCOVERY. At their first meeting, Hamlet quickly discerns the nature of his old friends' visit. They never directly confess their mission, but when they continue in it, the prince quickly treats the pair as his *ex*-friends.

VOYAGE. After Polonius' murder, Hamlet is sent to England by Claudius, ostensibly on a mission of state. His ex-friends escort him, unknowingly carrying the order for Hamlet's execution.

EXECUTION. Once on the ship, Hamlet slyly switches the document with one he has forged, ordering the deaths of Rosencrantz and Guildenstern. A pirate ship conveniently kidnaps and returns Hamlet home. The ex-friends are immediately executed upon their arrival in England.

Old school friends of Hamlet

Called to court by Claudius and Gertrude to discover cause of Hamlet's madness

Hamlet easily sees through their ruse

Killed in England upon their arrival

The ex-friends are no match for Hamlet.

Rosencrantz and Guildenstern are dramatic foils to Hamlet's rational capabilities: neither of the ex-friends ever develops a plausible explanation for Hamlet's madness, admitting defeat before Claudius and Gertrude; Hamlet at once sees through the purpose of their visit; and, finally, Hamlet outwits them on the way to England—with deadly results—using only the simple materials in his luggage.

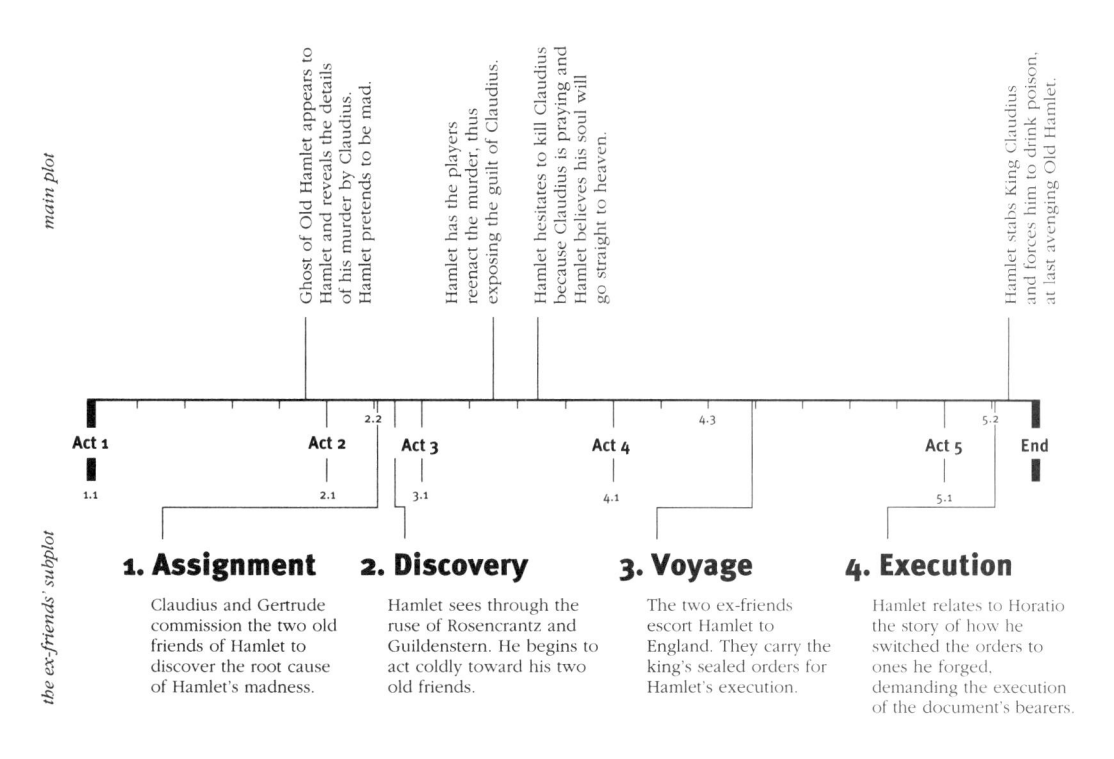

main plot

- **2.2** Ghost of Old Hamlet appears to Hamlet and reveals the details of his murder by Claudius. Hamlet pretends to be mad.
- Hamlet has the players reenact the murder, thus exposing the guilt of Claudius.
- Hamlet hesitates to kill Claudius because Claudius is praying and Hamlet believes his soul will go straight to heaven.
- **5.2** Hamlet stabs King Claudius and forces him to drink poison, at last avenging Old Hamlet.

Act 1 — 1.1 — Act 2 — 2.1 — Act 3 — 3.1 — Act 4 — 4.1 — 4.3 — Act 5 — 5.1 — End

the ex-friends' subplot

1. Assignment
Claudius and Gertrude commission the two old friends of Hamlet to discover the root cause of Hamlet's madness.

2. Discovery
Hamlet sees through the ruse of Rosencrantz and Guildenstern. He begins to act coldly toward his two old friends.

3. Voyage
The two ex-friends escort Hamlet to England. They carry the king's sealed orders for Hamlet's execution.

4. Execution
Hamlet relates to Horatio the story of how he switched the orders to ones he forged, demanding the execution of the document's bearers.

SUBPLOTS | Rosencrantz & Guildenstern: Timeline

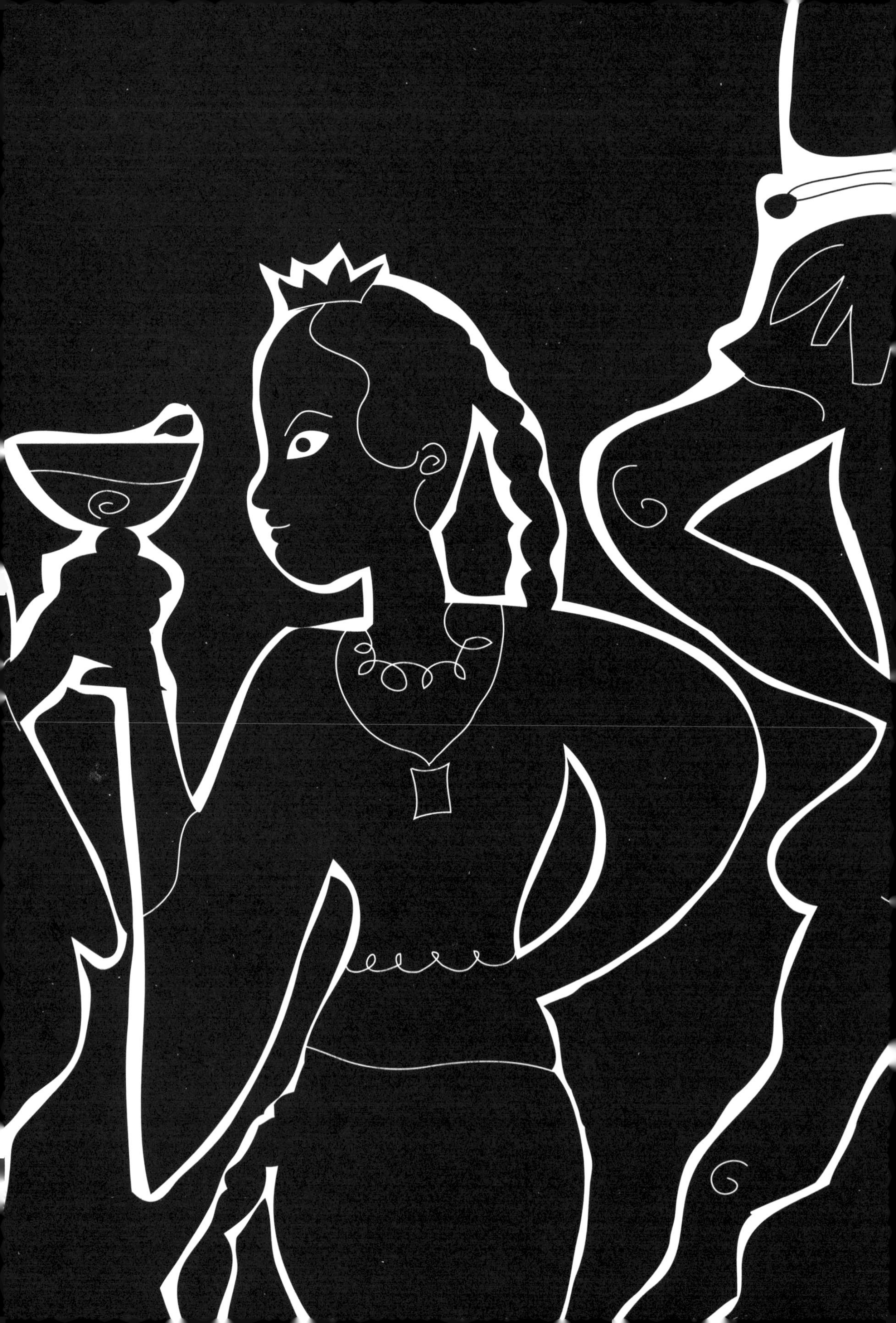

The finale

The subplots collide with the main at the funeral of Ophelia: returned from his voyage, Hamlet experiences grief over the death of his love and expresses it as anger; Laertes experiences hatred at seeing the face of the man who killed his father. What follows is a conspiracy between desperate king and bloodthirsty avenger—a double poisoning in the guise of a harmless fencing competition between Hamlet and Laertes. Before the match is over, four more major characters join Polonius and Ophelia in their deaths.

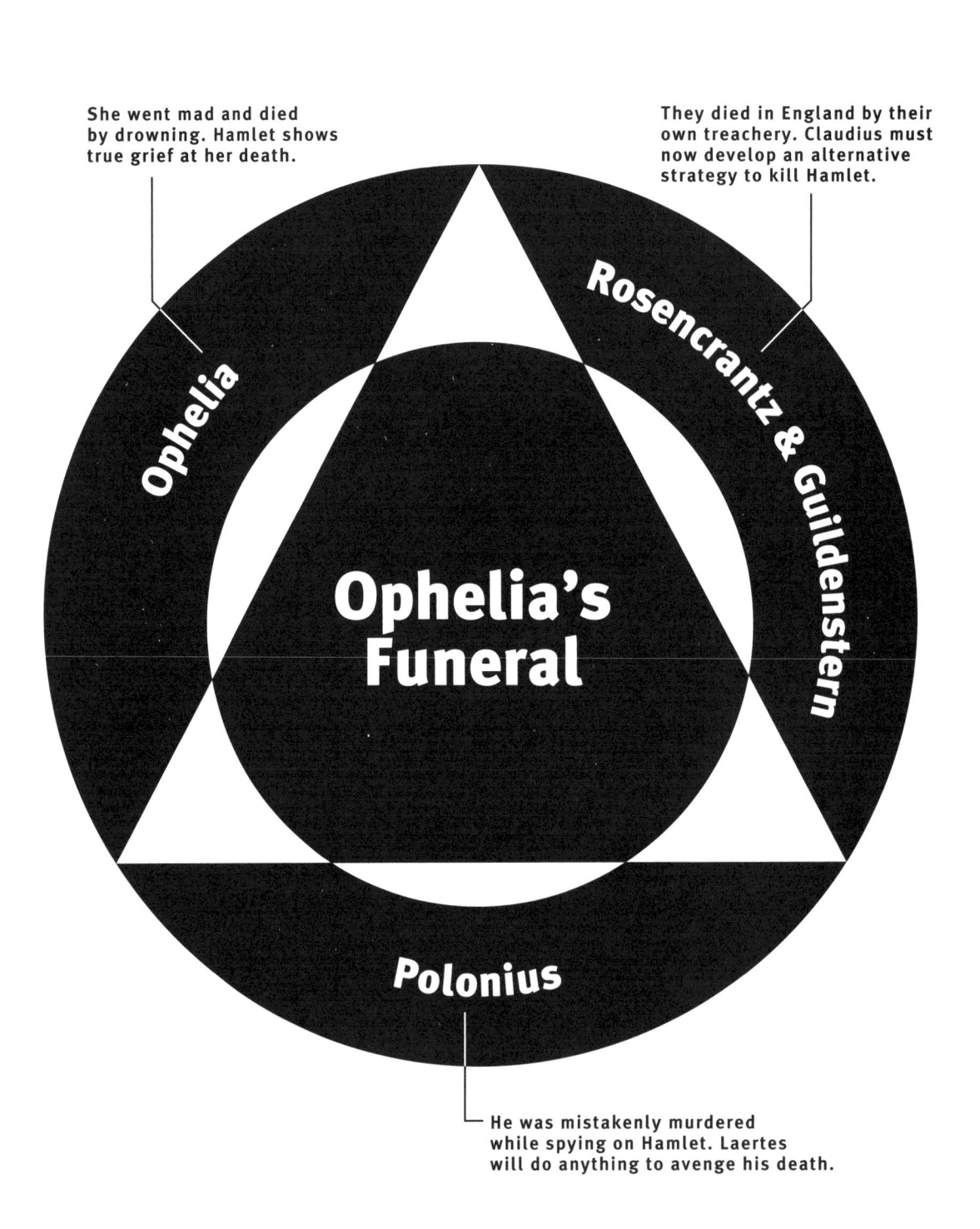

Ophelia
She went mad and died by drowning. Hamlet shows true grief at her death.

Rosencrantz & Guildenstern
They died in England by their own treachery. Claudius must now develop an alternative strategy to kill Hamlet.

Ophelia's Funeral

Polonius
He was mistakenly murdered while spying on Hamlet. Laertes will do anything to avenge his death.

The three subplots intersect the main plot at Ophelia's funeral.

All three subplots powerfully intersect the main action at the point of Ophelia's funeral. Newly returned from his voyage and unaware of Ophelia's death, Hamlet happens upon the funeral procession. There he meets Laertes and Claudius. The ensuing action propels the plot forward.

Hamlet is overcome by the surprise news of Ophelia's death. Enraged by Laertes' accusations, he says that no one, not even Laertes, loved Ophelia as much as he did. Laertes sees the man he believes is responsible for his father's death and, to some extent, his sister's. He must be held back from fighting Hamlet at the grave site. Claudius, previously fearful at the news of Hamlet's return, quickly begins constructing an alternative plan to kill him. The king convinces Laertes to join him in his plan and the two set a trap for the prince. They conspire to poison Hamlet during a fencing match.

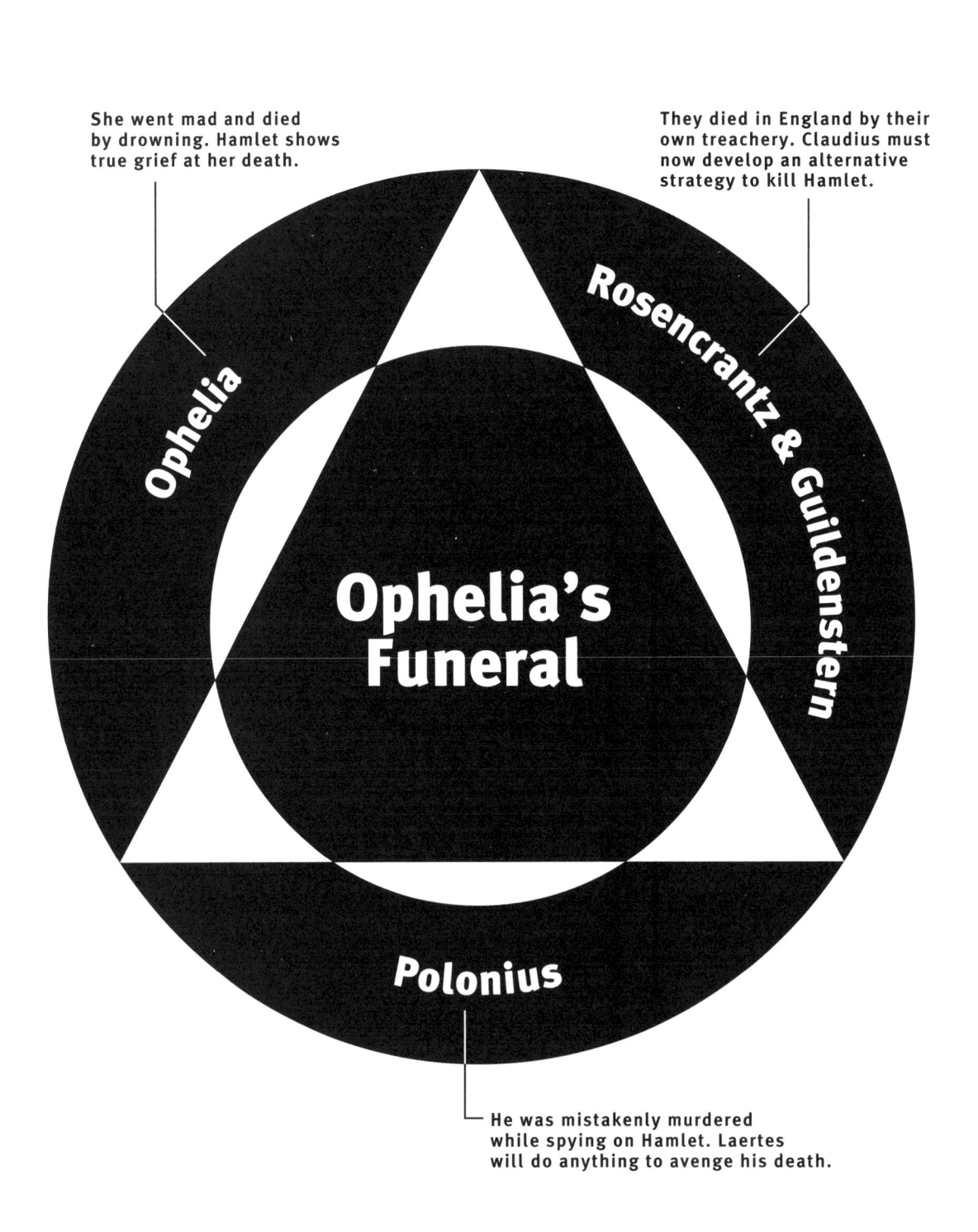

Ophelia's Funeral

Ophelia — She went mad and died by drowning. Hamlet shows true grief at her death.

Rosencrantz & Guildenstern — They died in England by their own treachery. Claudius must now develop an alternative strategy to kill Hamlet.

Polonius — He was mistakenly murdered while spying on Hamlet. Laertes will do anything to avenge his death.

The main plot and subplots are linked.

Here are the main plot and the subplots on one timeline. The intersection at Ophelia's funeral is highlighted to stress its significance as the bridge between main plot and subplots. All that follows is the fencing match.

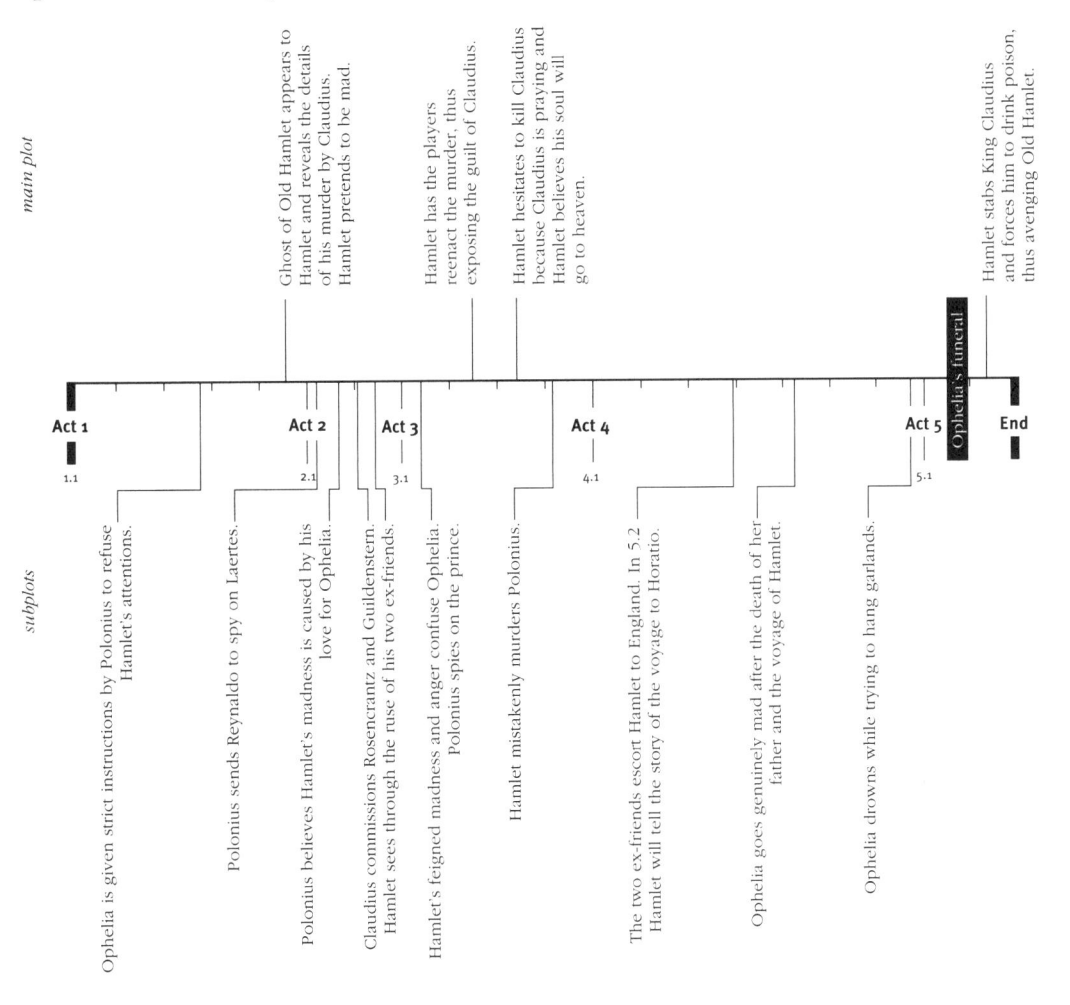

main plot

- Ghost of Old Hamlet appears to Hamlet and reveals the details of his murder by Claudius. Hamlet pretends to be mad.
- Hamlet has the players reenact the murder, thus exposing the guilt of Claudius.
- Hamlet hesitates to kill Claudius because Claudius is praying and Hamlet believes his soul will go to heaven.
- Hamlet stabs King Claudius and forces him to drink poison, thus avenging Old Hamlet.

Act 1 — 1.1
Act 2 — 2.1
Act 3 — 3.1
Act 4 — 4.1
Act 5 — 5.1 — **Ophelia's funeral** — End

subplots

- Ophelia is given strict instructions by Polonius to refuse Hamlet's attentions.
- Polonius sends Reynaldo to spy on Laertes.
- Polonius believes Hamlet's madness is caused by his love for Ophelia.
- Claudius commissions Rosencrantz and Guildenstern. Hamlet sees through the ruse of his two ex-friends.
- Hamlet's feigned madness and anger confuse Ophelia. Polonius spies on the prince.
- Hamlet mistakenly murders Polonius.
- The two ex-friends escort Hamlet to England. In 5.2 Hamlet will tell the story of the voyage to Horatio.
- Ophelia goes genuinely mad after the death of her father and the voyage of Hamlet.
- Ophelia drowns while trying to hang garlands.

FINALE | Subplots and main plot linked | 105

Easily manipulated by Claudius to kill Hamlet

Dips his sword in poison

Killed by his own poisoned swordtip

Exchanges pardons with Hamlet before dying

The play ends with a fencing match and multiple deaths.

A DEADLY MATCH. Claudius and Laertes conspire to kill Hamlet. Their plan: a double poisoning. They remove the safety button from Laertes' sword and dip the point in poison. Also, after each round, Claudius is to offer Hamlet a poisoned cup of wine.

The match begins and Hamlet has the upper hand after two rounds. Hamlet refuses the cup each time Claudius offers it to him, preferring to drink after the match. Queen Gertrude, ignorant of the conspiracy, drinks from the cup in Hamlet's honor. Laertes scratches Hamlet in an illegal parry. After a scuffle in which the weapons are exchanged, Hamlet cuts Laertes with the poisoned sword.

Saying she has been poisoned, Gertrude suddenly dies. Remorseful, Laertes confesses the conspiracy. Hamlet quickly stabs Claudius and forces him to drink the rest of the poisonous cup. Laertes and Hamlet exchange pardons, then Laertes dies.

With his last breaths, Hamlet asks Horatio to tell his story and then gives Denmark to Fortinbras, who has just arrived from his conquests in Poland.

- Easily manipulated by Claudius to kill Hamlet
- Dips his sword in poison
- Killed by his own poisoned swordtip
- Exchanges pardons with Hamlet before dying

The final scene: a succession of death.

Thus we arrive at the final timeline, showing the major events in Hamlet. The final vengeance scene, bloody and bittersweet, is listed out in detail. You can refer to it if you need to remember the sequence of events.

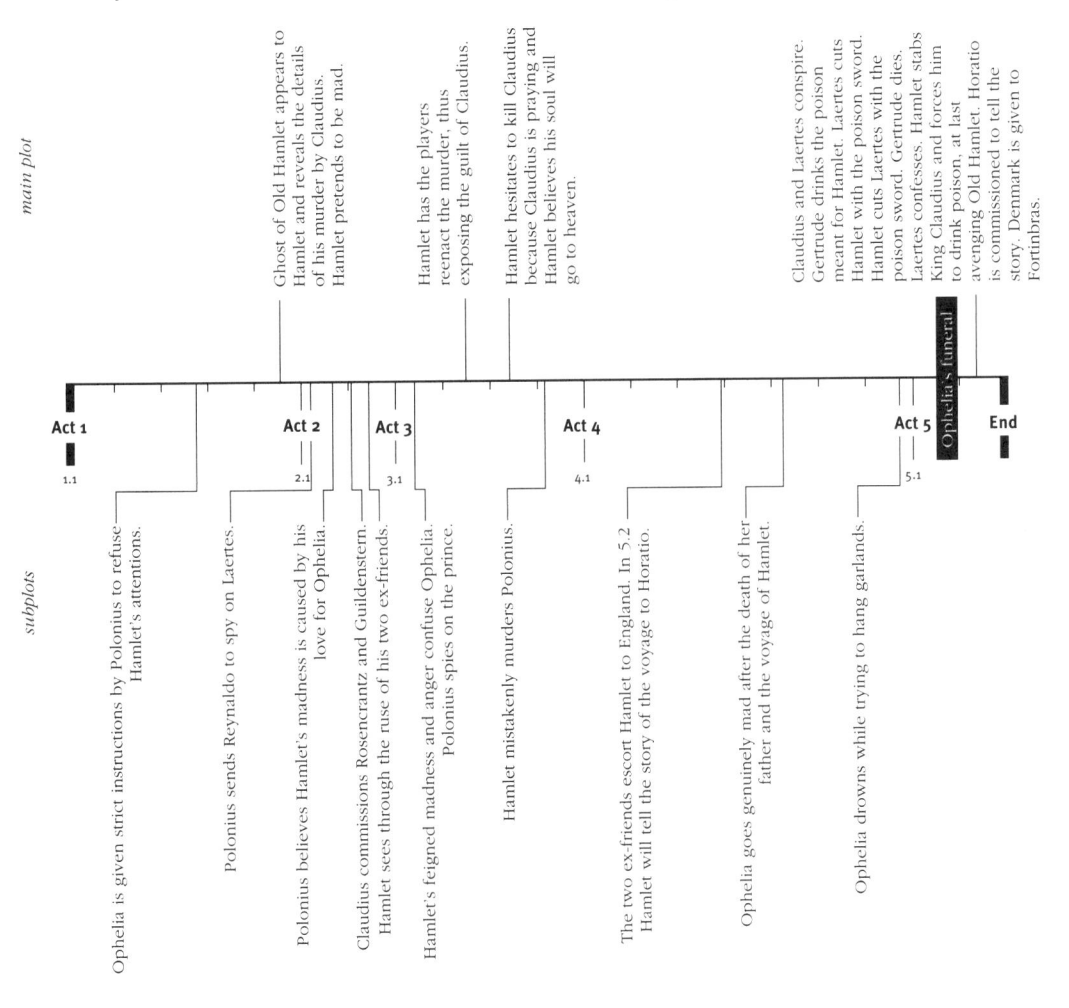

main plot

- Ghost of Old Hamlet appears to Hamlet and reveals the details of his murder by Claudius. Hamlet pretends to be mad.
- Hamlet has the players reenact the murder, thus exposing the guilt of Claudius.
- Hamlet hesitates to kill Claudius because Claudius is praying and Hamlet believes his soul will go to heaven.
- Claudius and Laertes conspire. Gertrude drinks the poison meant for Hamlet. Laertes cuts Hamlet with the poison sword. Hamlet cuts Laertes with the poison sword. Gertrude dies. Laertes confesses. Hamlet stabs King Claudius and forces him to drink poison, at last avenging Old Hamlet. Horatio is commissioned to tell the story. Denmark is given to Fortinbras.

Act 1 (1.1) — **Act 2** (2.1) — (3.1) **Act 3** — **Act 4** (4.1) — **Act 5** (5.1) — *Ophelia's funeral* — **End**

subplots

- Ophelia is given strict instructions by Polonius to refuse Hamlet's attentions.
- Polonius sends Reynaldo to spy on Laertes.
- Polonius believes Hamlet's madness is caused by his love for Ophelia.
- Claudius commissions Rosencrantz and Guildenstern. Hamlet sees through the ruse of his two ex-friends.
- Hamlet's feigned madness and anger confuse Ophelia. Polonius spies on the prince.
- Hamlet mistakenly murders Polonius.
- The two ex-friends escort Hamlet to England. In 5.2 Hamlet will tell the story of the voyage to Horatio.
- Ophelia goes genuinely mad after the death of her father and the voyage of Hamlet.
- Ophelia drowns while trying to hang garlands.

FINALE | Subplots and main plot linked | 109

Polonius
Stabbed mistakenly

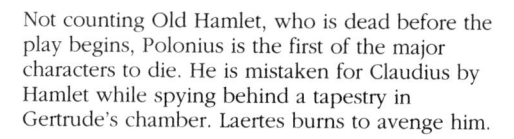

Not counting Old Hamlet, who is dead before the play begins, Polonius is the first of the major characters to die. He is mistaken for Claudius by Hamlet while spying behind a tapestry in Gertrude's chamber. Laertes burns to avenge him.

Ophelia
Drowns

After her father's death and during Hamlet's voyage, Ophelia dies while hanging flower garlands over the brook. Her lack of struggle to swim lends a suicidal element to her death which is intentionally left unresolved.

Rosencrantz and Guildenstern
Executed in England

Acting as escorts and messengers, Rosencrantz and Guildenstern sail with Hamlet to England. The ex-friends are outwitted by the prince. Their letter calling for Hamlet's execution is switched with a forgery calling for their own execution.

Gertrude
Drinks poison

Unaware of Claudius' conspiracy with Laertes to poison Hamlet, Gertrude drinks from the cup of poisoned wine meant for her son. Her death interrupts the fencing match, the first in the bloody final scene of the play.

Claudius
Stabbed and forced to drink poison

Laertes, dying, confesses the criminal plan. Hamlet uses the poisoned sword to stab Claudius, then grabs the remaining poisoned wine and forces it into the king's mouth. Thus, Hamlet avenges the deaths of his father, his mother and himself.

Laertes
Poisoned cut

After scratching Hamlet with the poisoned swordtip, the contestants scuffle and exchange swords. Laertes is then cut by the poisoned sword. Before dying, he confesses the conspiracy and the two forgive one another.

Hamlet
Poisoned cut

Hamlet's vengeance, arguably successful, brings about the deaths of all the major characters, including his mother, his girlfriend, and possibly his future father-in-law and brother-in-law. Hamlet's death throws the country into chaos, resolved with its possession by an aggressive, opportunistic rival—Prince Fortinbras of Norway.

The only remaining major character— the storyteller.

CIRCLES. There is a recursive aspect to *Hamlet* in that the play's only surviving major character, Horatio, is given the task of telling the very story we have just seen. When the curtain closes, we almost expect it to reopen, as Horatio goes about fulfilling his duty to the prince.

It is also no coincidence that the storyteller remains standing; *Hamlet* is widely regarded as Shakespeare's most personal drama—for example, his deceased son was named "Hamnet" and the great central soliloquy ("To be or not to be...") closely mirrors language from his sonnets. Thus, in the character of Horatio, the role of storyteller is given a sense of immortality.

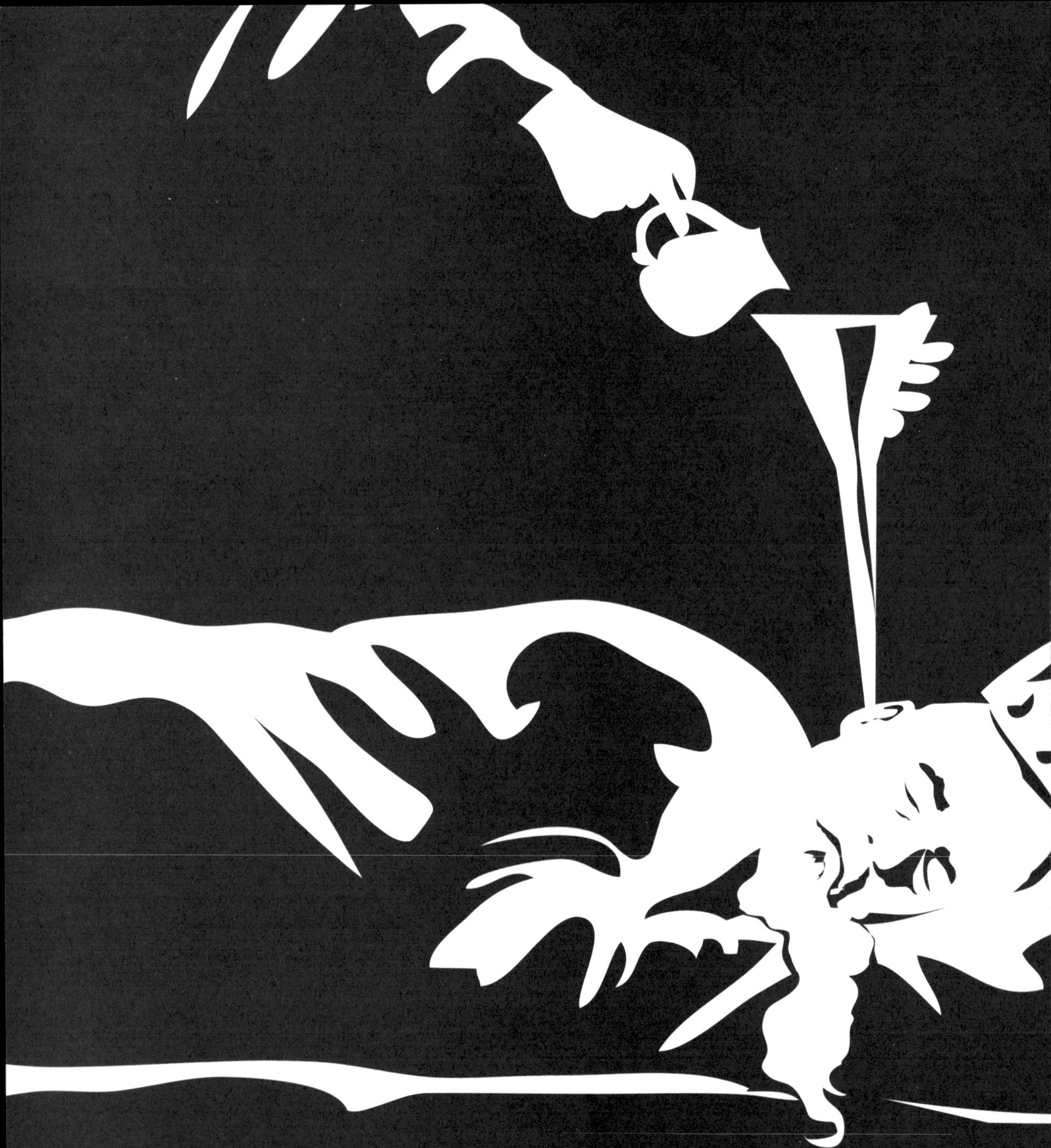

Scene *by scene*

This chapter serves as a summary of the action and dialogue in each scene of the play. The scene breaks in Shakespeare's plays are arbitrary—they were not noted in the original documents—but, except in rare instances, they occur when the stage completely clears. Some are short, as in 4.6, when a message from Hamlet is delivered to Horatio by the pirates. Others are quite lengthy, as in 2.2, which is over 500 lines. Read this chapter in one or two sittings, if time allows, to gain a sweeping panoramic view of Hamlet, *before tackling the actual text of the play.*

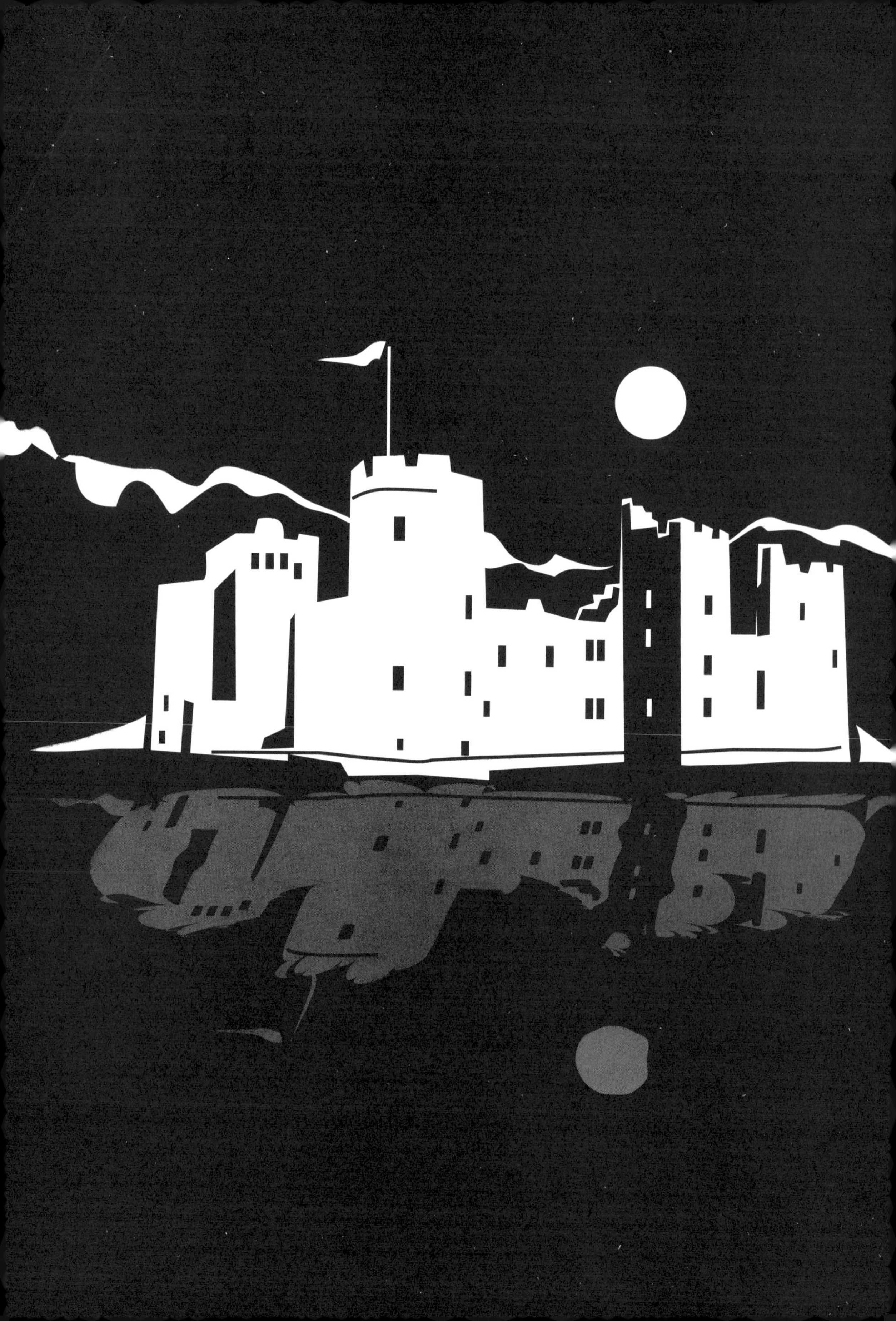

BEFORE THE PLAY BEGINS

The Norwegian dispute; Old Hamlet's death; Claudius' succession and marriage; Hamlet and Ophelia.

BEFORE THE CURTAINS PART, several important events have already taken place. To begin with, Old Hamlet was king of Denmark—Europe's oldest monarchy—and had positioned his castle at Elsinore, a coastal town in the east. He was a good, strong king and his subjects thought well of him. Norway, their northern rival, was ruled by King Fortinbras. He was an ambitious ruler who either overestimated his own abilities or underestimated those of his adversaries.

King Fortinbras challenged Old Hamlet to a deadly fight—one-on-one—with the winner to receive substantial landholdings from the loser. It was not an action of unbridled virulence, rather they drew up contracts for this purpose, ensuring that everything was done legally. Old Hamlet was the victor, killing King Fortinbras and winning the lands, which were the inheritance of Prince Fortinbras. Old Norway, the brother of King Fortinbras, then succeeded to the throne—presumably because Prince Fortinbras was still too young to rule. Prince Hamlet was born that very day.

Prince Hamlet grew up happy, often playing games with his father's court jester, Yorick and his childhood schoolmates, Rosencrantz and Guildenstern. He adored his father and believed his mother did as well, feeling that Gertrude's love for Old Hamlet only grew stronger with the passing of time. The prince then went away to university in Wittenberg, Germany, where he met his loyal best friend, Horatio.

While he was away, the prince's uncle, Claudius, brother to Old Hamlet, became bitterly jealous of his brother's success. He fell in love with his sister-in-law, Gertrude, and he felt that she was encouraging him in his affection. He yearned to exchange places with his brother. Then, one day, he stopped yearning. When Old Hamlet was sleeping in the garden, Claudius poured poison into his ear, killing him. He released a story that the king had been bitten by a poisonous serpent. He secured the Danish council's approval to succeed his brother to the throne and to marry his sister-in-law after less than two month's bereavement.

Hamlet, who had returned home for his father's funeral, was shocked to be attending his mother's wedding. He sought solace from his loving girlfriend, Ophelia, the daughter of Claudius' chief counselor, Polonius.

INCEST
In England, marriage to a sister-in-law was considered incestuous under canon law. Since man and wife are one flesh, they reasoned, a sister-in-law is as closely related as a brother. The act also became illegal under English civil law in 1835, and was not repealed until 1907.

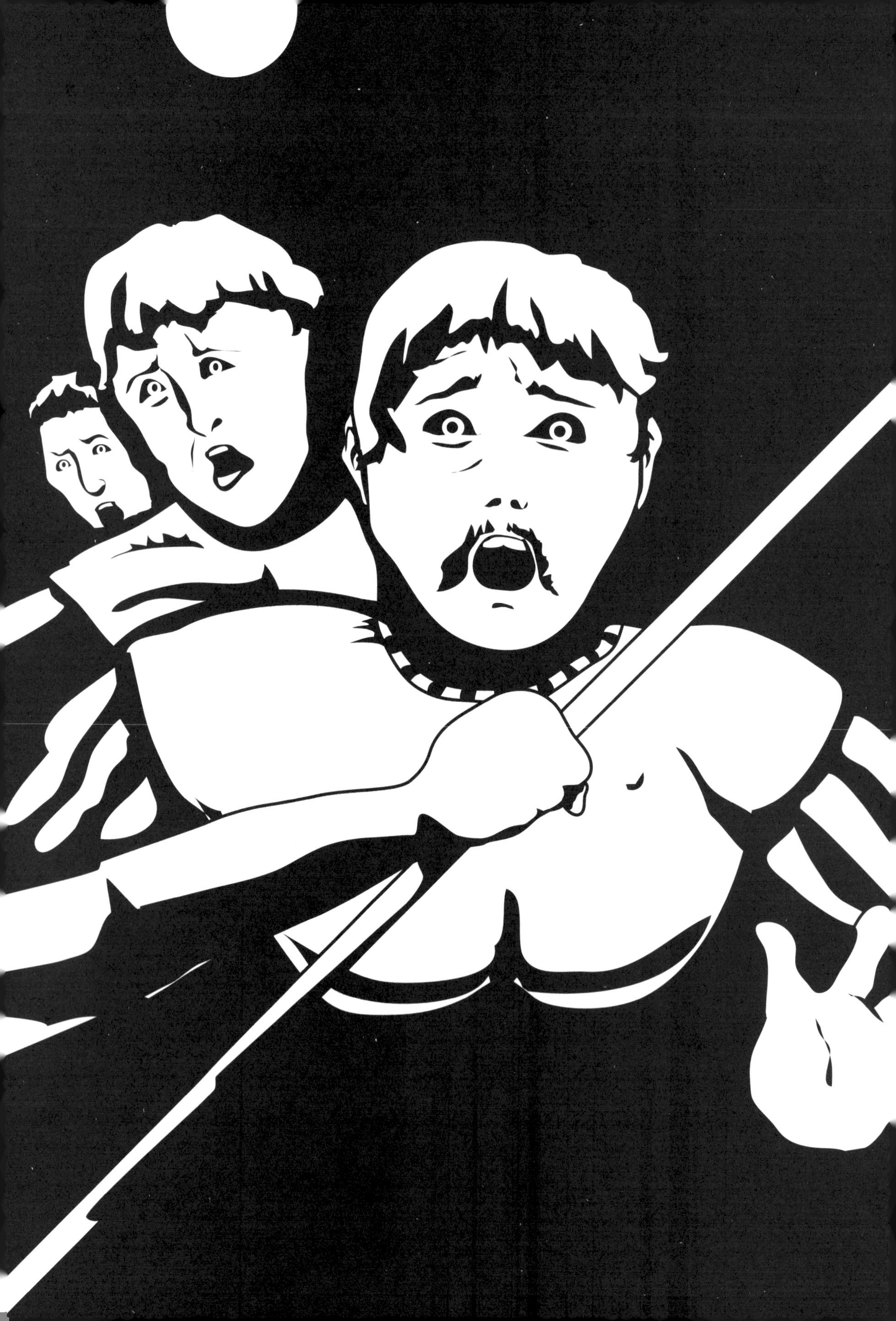

ACT 1, SCENE 1

The ghost appears to the soldiers and Horatio outside the castle.

THE PLAY OPENS outside the castle walls at Elsinore, Hamlet's hometown. On the guard tower stands the soldier, Francisco. He is promptly relieved of his watch by Barnardo, followed by Marcellus and Horatio. They soon begin talking about a strange apparition they saw on two previous nights while on guard duty: the ghost of Old Hamlet dressed in his war gear. Horatio claims it is simply a fantasy—the result of an overactive imagination.

As they discuss the circumstances of the visitations, suddenly the ghost appears, as before. Frightened, the soldiers urge Horatio to speak to it. He does, but the ghost simply moves away and then vanishes. Marcellus says that the ghost has appeared at this same hour for the past two nights. Horatio quickly retracts his earlier comment about the ghost's origins. He now believes that the apparition must forebode some terrible calamity for Denmark. Confused, Marcellus asks if anyone knows why the king has placed a 24-hour guard on the castle in the first place.

Horatio surmises that the guard has been ordered because Prince Fortinbras of Norway—their rival to the north—has been seen building a large army. Horatio tells the soldiers the story of the late King Fortinbras' challenge to Old Hamlet: a one-on-one combat to the death, the winner to receive substantial landholdings from the loser. Old Hamlet won the contest, killing King Fortinbras and gaining the lands. Now that Old Hamlet is dead, rumor has it that Fortinbras is coming to Denmark to reclaim his lost inheritance.

Once Horatio's story is finished, the ghost appears again. Marcellus strikes at it with his spear, to no avail. One moment the apparition appears in one spot, only to reappear in another. Finally, the ghost makes as if it is about to speak—but the cock crows and it vanishes from sight for the remainder of the evening.

Marcellus says some believe that the cock crows all night at Christmas time so no evil or witchcraft can be performed during the holy season. Horatio agrees. He says that dawn is quickly approaching and he recommends they find Prince Hamlet to inform him of the strange happenings of these past three nights.

As the scene closes, Marcellus says he knows where Hamlet can be found. The men exit the stage: rattled, confused and looking as if they have just seen a ghost.

IDENTITY
The identity of the ghost is in question from the beginning of the play. In 1.1, we get two possibilities: an overactive imagination or an evil portent of calamity for Denmark.

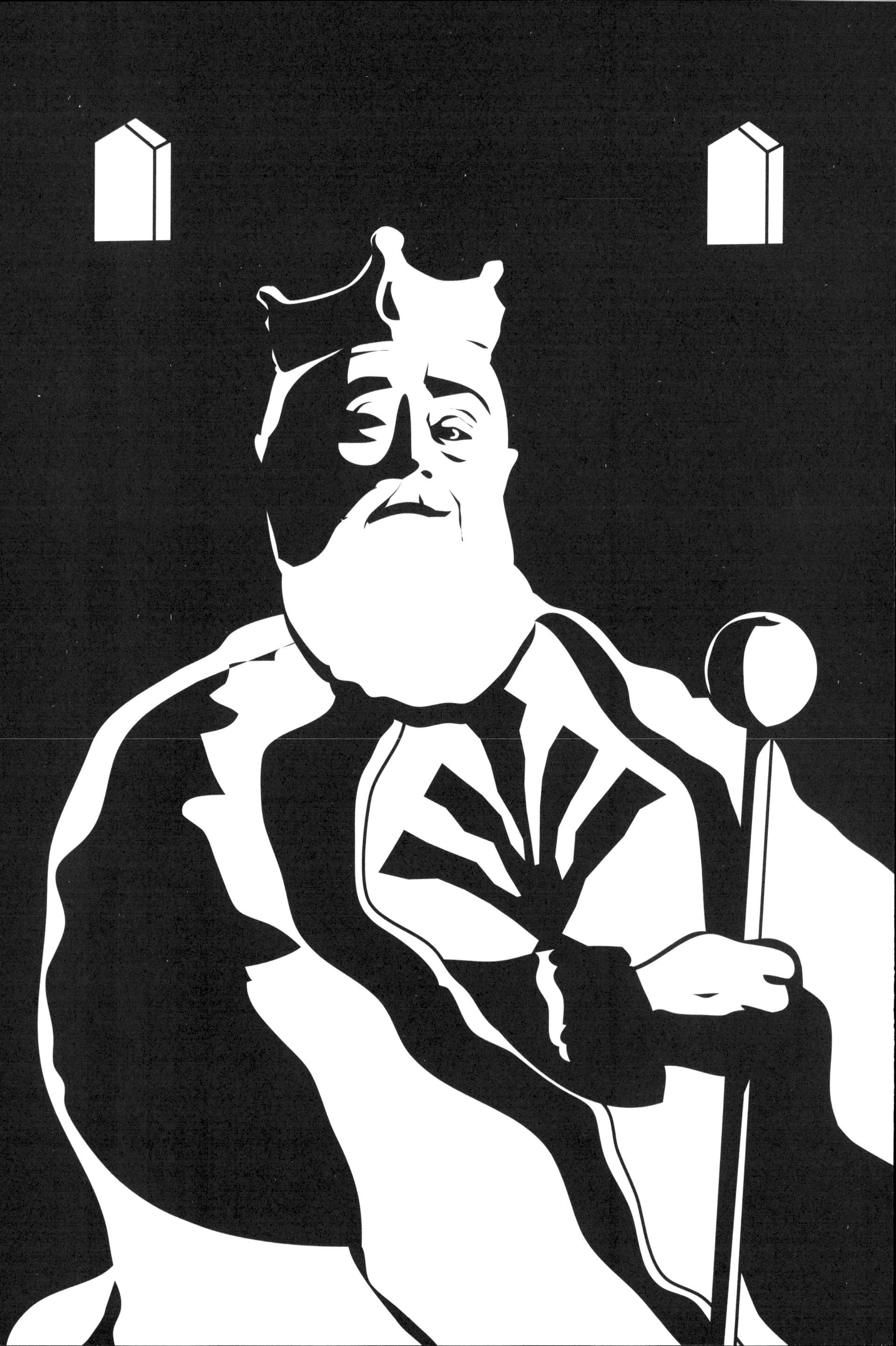

ACT 1, SCENE 2

Claudius holds court and Hamlet is told of his father's ghost.

CLAUDIUS, GERTRUDE, HAMLET, Polonius and his son, Laertes, enter the court, followed by the council and ambassadors. Hamlet is dressed in black, still mourning his father who has been dead less than two months. Claudius, Hamlet's uncle, is the new king of Denmark and has recently married Hamlet's mother, Gertrude. There is a flourish of trumpets as the characters take their places and Claudius prepares to address the court.

Claudius handles two major issues: his hasty marriage to his former sister-in-law and a request from Prince Fortinbras of Norway for the return of lands lost by his father. Claudius admits that the death of Old Hamlet was a great loss to Denmark. He reminds the council, however, that he obtained their prior approval for the marriage and it is in the nation's best interest that it has taken place. He then dispatches the ambassadors to Fortinbras' uncle, Old Norway, asking him to restrain his nephew. Finally, Laertes obtains permission to return to school in France.

The attention then turns to Hamlet. Claudius and Gertrude urge him to end his mourning. Hamlet speaks dismissively to Claudius, but to his mother he defends his extended bereavement. The king and queen request that he not return to university in Wittenberg and he relents. As the king and queen leave, Claudius proclaims that Hamlet's decision to stay has made him so happy he will fire cannons after his evening toasts.

Hamlet is left alone to brood. In a soliloquy of despair, he decries the sinfulness of suicide. His life has become weary and without meaning. Using mythological figures, he contrasts the superlative, high-minded Old Hamlet with the inferior, lustful Claudius. He remembers his mother's seemingly insatiable love for his father and criticizes the speed at which she married her brother-in-law. He proclaims the frailty of all women. The speech closes with Hamlet's frustration at his own inability to change any of these situations.

Horatio, Marcellus and Barnardo enter the court, interrupting the soliloquy. Horatio is in Denmark, Hamlet discovers, for the King's funeral and the royal wedding. Horatio describes the visitation of the ghost the previous night. Hamlet is amazed by the news and questions Horatio intently, hanging on every detail.

At the close of the scene, Hamlet plans to join Horatio and the soldiers on their watch that same night. He charges them to tell no one.

DIPLOMAT
Claudius is an accomplished diplomat. His resourcefulness will serve him well throughout the play, allowing him to turn situations to his own advantage and mobilize his power base.

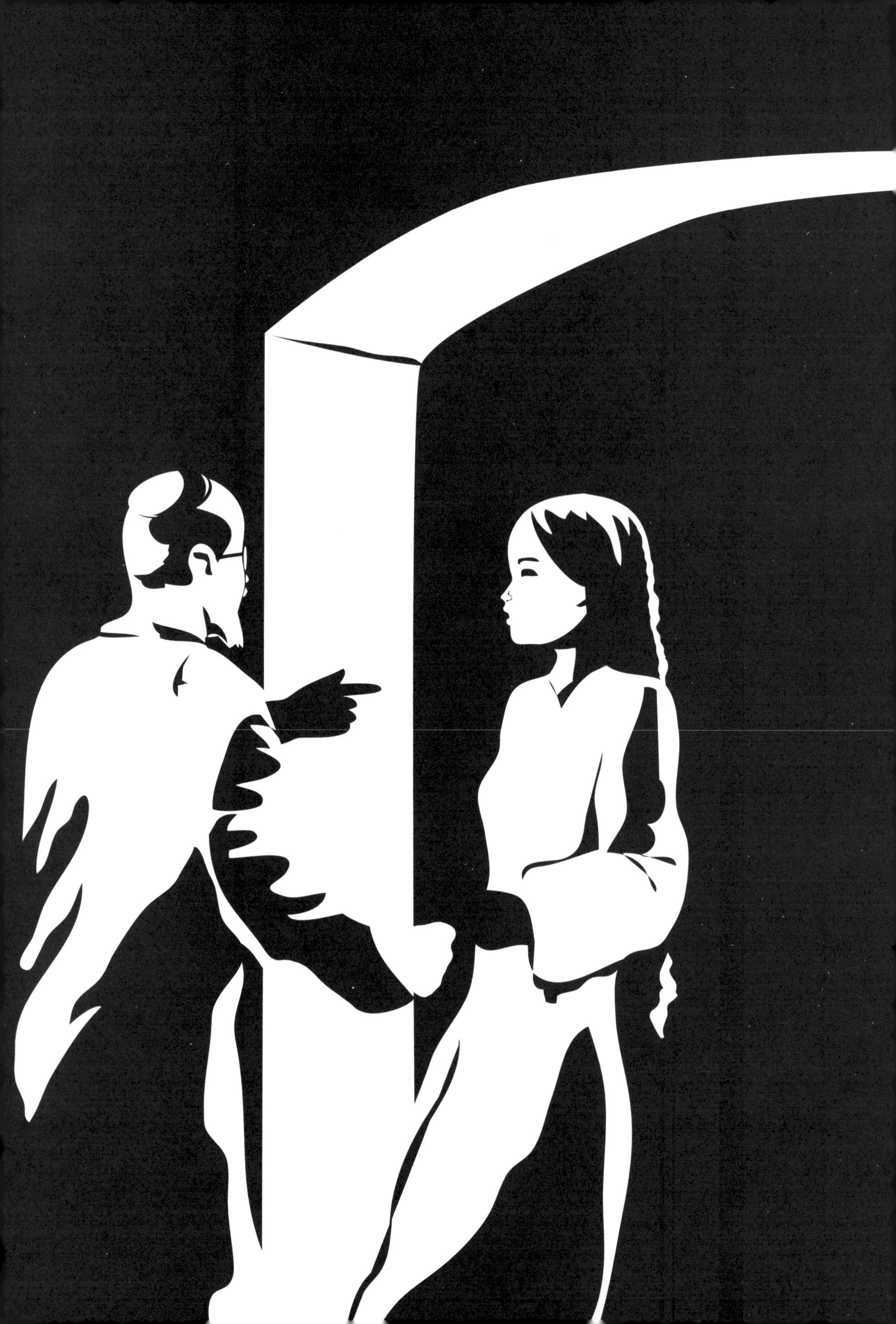

ACT 1, SCENE 3

Laertes departs for France and Ophelia is forbidden to see Hamlet.

THE LOCATION FOR this domestic scene, while not specified, is generally taken by most directors to be the house of Polonius, chief counsel to Claudius. Having obtained the King's approval to depart in the previous scene, Laertes has his bags packed for France, where he is to continue his university education (interestingly enough, a privilege denied Hamlet). Later, in 2.1, Polonius will send his servant, Reynaldo, to spy on Laertes.

First, Laertes is alone with his sister, Ophelia. He bids her farewell, asking her to write often, to which she agrees. He then counsels her to be wary of Hamlet. In language charged with sexual innuendo, Laertes describes Hamlet's overtures as a passing fancy, at best, and a princely conquest, at worst. He warns her to fear the prince's desires, weighing carefully what damage would be done to her reputation should she be wooed by his advances. Ophelia cunningly agrees to keep her brother's advice as long as he does likewise while in France.

Their father, Polonius, interrupts their goodbyes to impart some long-winded, equivocal and, somehow, prudent advice. This is where we find the great line, "To thine own self be true." The fatherly farewell has an upbeat, even humorous tone. Some directors go so far as to have Laertes and Ophelia steal glances—with rolled eyes and knowing smirks—toward one another.

Laertes then leaves, but not before reminding Ophelia to remember his advice. She responds, saying she has locked it away in her memory and given him the only key.

The secretive language is too much for Polonius; as Laertes rides away, Polonius asks Ophelia what was said between them. The tone of the scene changes here, becoming more serious. Ophelia tells her father that she and Laertes were discussing Hamlet's recent overtures.

Polonius asks what has transpired between her and Hamlet. Ophelia replies that Hamlet has tendered his affections. Polonius then presumes to instruct Ophelia on the ways of men. He wrongly proclaims that Hamlet's intentions toward her are not honorable. Ophelia begins to defend the prince's actions, but quickly defers to her father's cynicism. Finally, Polonius forbids Ophelia from receiving Hamlet's letters or from talking with the prince at all. She reluctantly obeys.

What began as a light-hearted scene now ends with this intolerant demand.

CONTROLLED
Shakespeare, imposing Elizabethan values on Ophelia, makes her a possession of her father until married, upon which she would belong to her husband. This controlling social norm is used as an ingredient of dramatic tension and ultimately produces negative results for Ophelia.

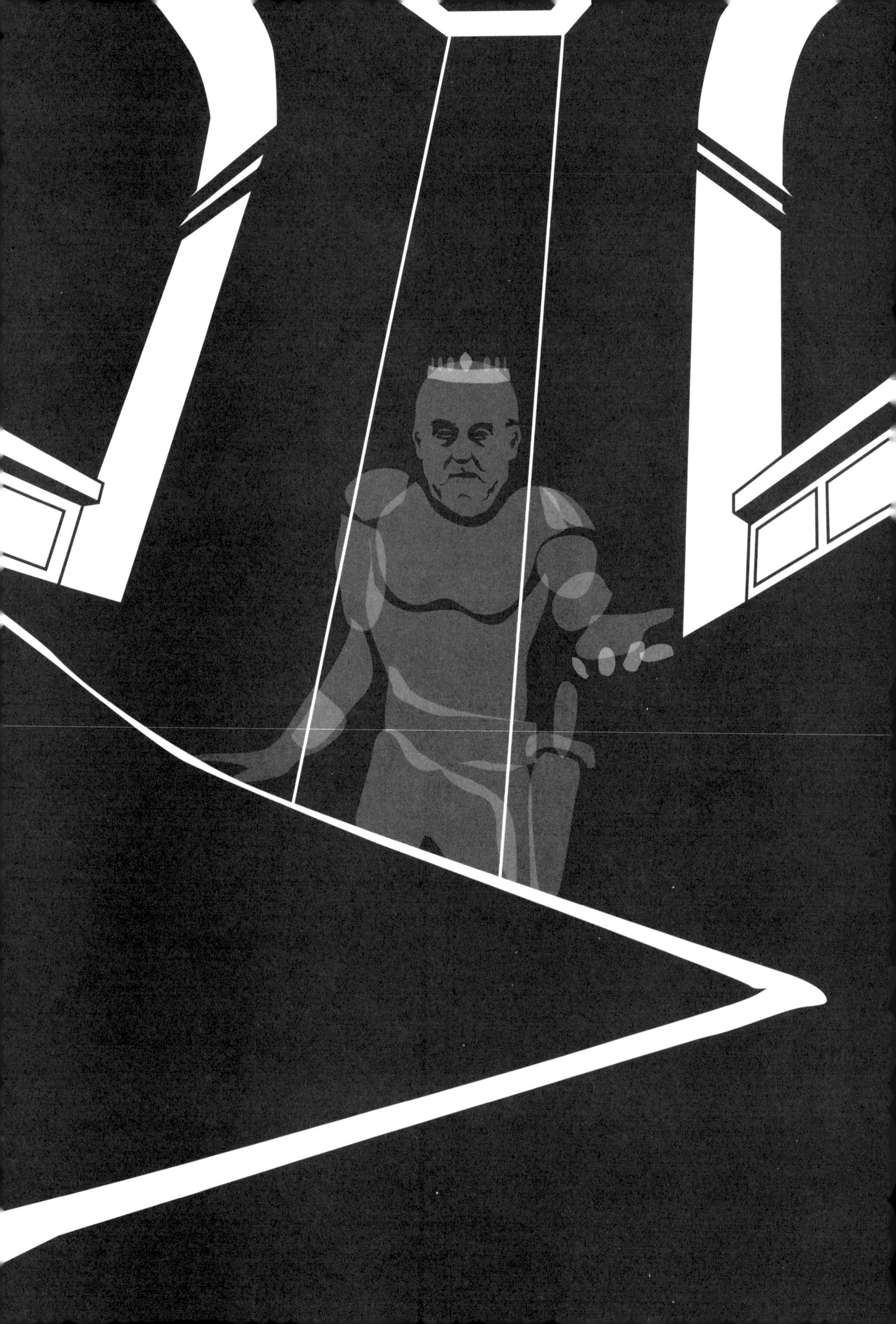

ACT 1, SCENE 4

Claudius carouses as the ghost beckons to Hamlet.

ON THE CASTLE battlements, Prince Hamlet joins Horatio and Marcellus on the night watch. It is midnight—the same hour the ghost of Old Hamlet appeared on the past three consecutive evenings. In fact, the scene itself appears to the audience as a replay of the opening scene, with the substitution of Prince Hamlet for Barnardo. The air is bitingly cold and the friends make nervous small talk in the darkness.

From within the castle, a flourish of trumpets is sounded, followed by two cannon blasts. Horatio questions the prince, "What does this mean, my lord?" Hamlet answers that King Claudius is carousing, engaged in undignified drinking and dancing. Each time Claudius makes a toast and drinks it down, the cannons are fired to signify he has kept his pledge (Claudius promised to do so in 1.2). Horatio asks if this behavior is customary of the royalty in Denmark. Hamlet responds that it is, although he asserts it is a custom whose observance would best be neglected.

The ghost enters as suddenly as before. Horatio is the first to notice and calls it to the attention of the prince. Hamlet is electrified by what he sees. He prays that angels defend them, whether the ghost turns out to be a good spirit or a demon from hell. He speaks to the ghost, saying that he will call it Hamlet, King and father, in deference to the shape it has assumed.

Hamlet questions his father's ghost as to why he has come back from the dead to haunt the world of the living. The ghost will not speak, however, but only beckons Hamlet to follow him.

Horatio surmises that the ghost wishes a private audience with Prince Hamlet, away from the hearing of the others. Marcellus advises the prince not to follow and Horatio concurs. Hamlet scoffs at their counsel, saying he has nothing to fear, since he does not place a high value on his own life.

Horatio and Marcellus try to restrain him further, appealing to his reason. Horatio proposes that the ghost may be setting a trap for Hamlet, tempting him to a precipice and then—depriving the prince of his wits—causing him to plunge to his death. Hamlet eventually threatens the two, saying he will kill any man who tries to stop him from going with the ghost.

Hamlet bravely follows the ghost and after some consideration, the two friends follow after him.

CONTRAST
The intemperate, carousing uncle is set against the silent, tortured spirit of the father. This juxtaposition heightens the emotional payoff, when in the next scene Old Hamlet tells the prince of his murder at the hands of Claudius.

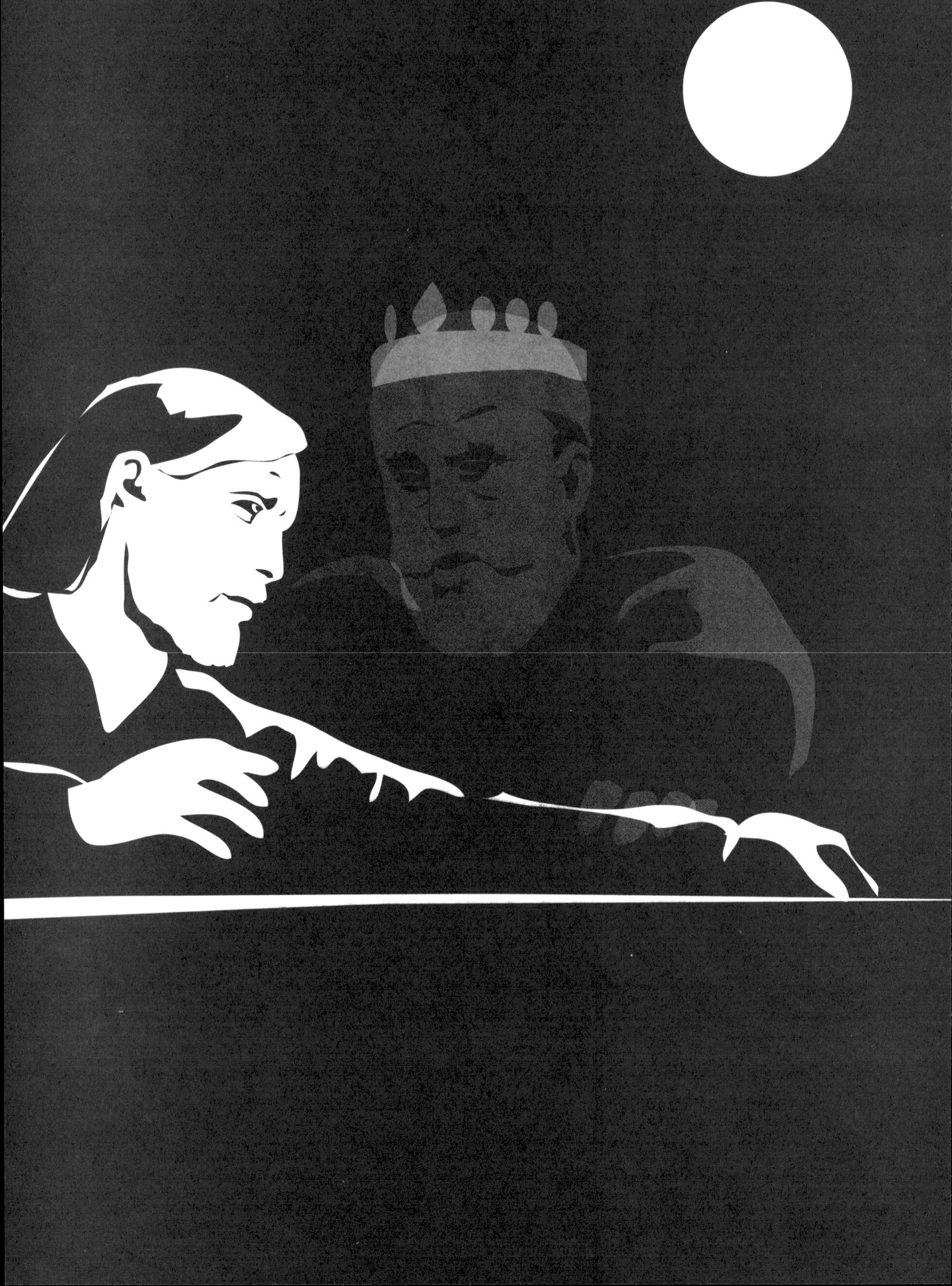

ACT 1, SCENE 5

Hamlet hears the ghost's story and swears to avenge the murder.

SOME DISTANCE AWAY from Horatio and Marcellus, the ghost of Old Hamlet stops and speaks to the prince. The ghost begins by telling Hamlet of his identity and condition—that he is indeed the spirit of Old Hamlet, who is confined by day to Purgatory as penance for his earthly sins, but allowed to walk the earth at night. Though he is forbidden to divulge any secrets of the afterlife, he hints at a horrific tale. Hamlet is deeply moved.

The ghost then tells Hamlet he was murdered and asks for vengeance. Hamlet is shocked and promises swift revenge. The ghost says that the people of Denmark are deceived—he was not, as the official report went, bitten by a snake. Instead, Claudius poured poison into Old Hamlet's ear while he was asleep in his orchard. Hamlet is aghast, but not disbelieving, as he already felt a keen distrust toward Claudius. After relating more details of the murder, the ghost gives Hamlet two directives concerning his vengeance: don't contaminate your mind and leave your mother's punishment to God. The ghost then vanishes, admonishing Hamlet, "Remember me."

In the ensuing soliloquy, Hamlet reaffirms his commitment to vengeance and declares he will cast off all other thoughts from his mind. From this point on, Hamlet claims his attentions will be completely focused on revenge. In writing, Hamlet ascribes his uncle a villain. He closes with a vow to remember his father.

Horatio and Marcellus enter, calling desperately for Hamlet. They question him about the encounter with the ghost. Twice Hamlet begins to tell them, but stops himself, saying they'll reveal it to others.

Hamlet's answers, however, are circular, his behavior borders on giddy. Horatio is confused by Hamlet's responses and tells the prince as much. Hamlet apologizes for any offense. When Horatio says there is none, Hamlet emphatically corrects him, saying there is offense (speaking of his father's murder) and much offense at that.

Hamlet then swears Horatio and Marcellus to secrecy. Many directors have Hamlet turn his sword upside-down, forming the shape of a cross, and having the others place their hands on it as they swear. The men swear in three different locations on the battlements, following the ghost's disembodied proclamation, "Swear!"

Lastly, Hamlet tells them that hereafter he may pretend to be mad and they promise to reveal this fact to no one.

RE-MEMBER
The ghost's final request for Hamlet to *remember* is thought by some to be a subtle wordplay—it can be taken to mean re-member, or reconstruct, me. In other words, Hamlet's mind may be reassembling the memory of his father, rather than experiencing an actual ghostly visitation.

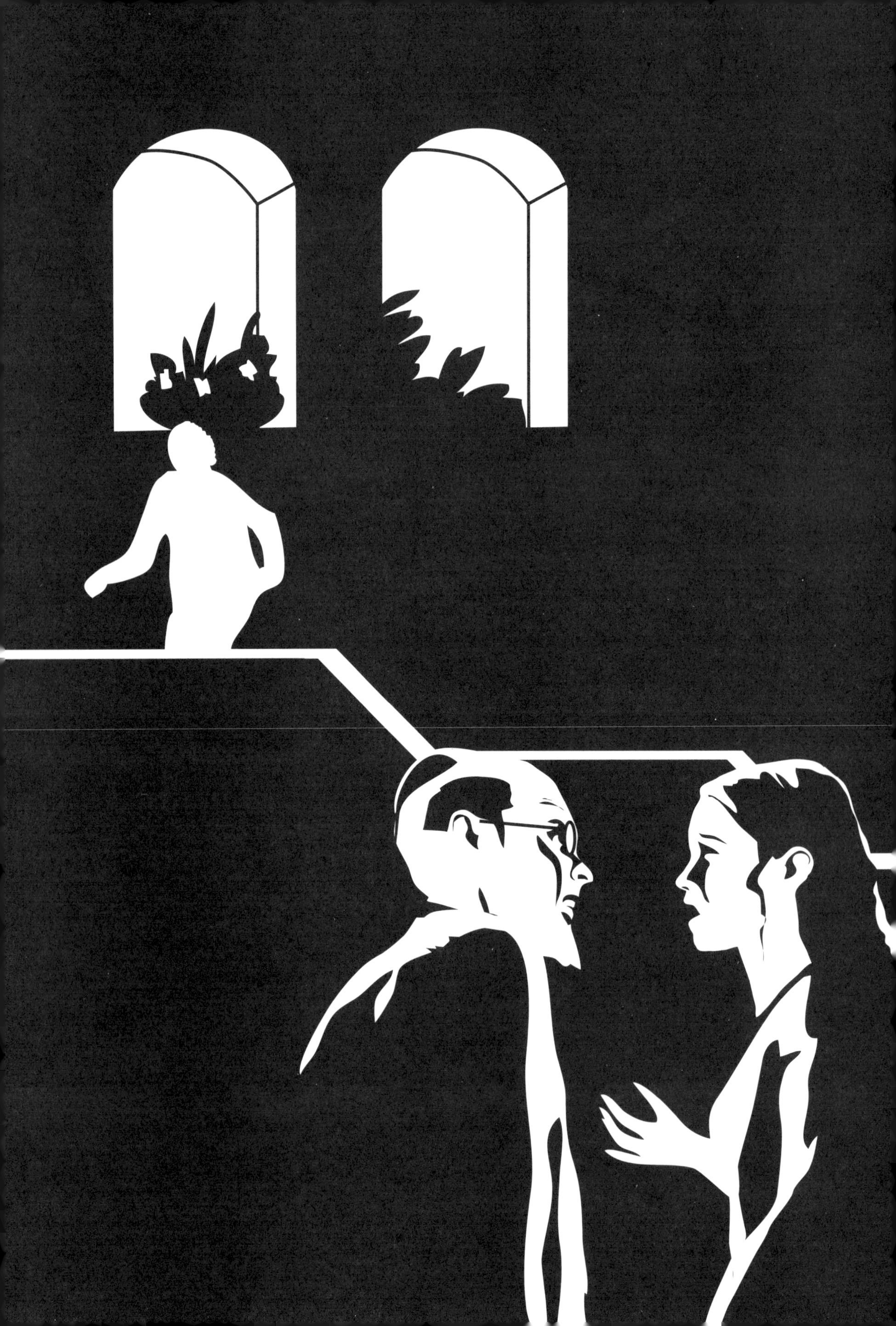

ACT 2, SCENE 1

Reynaldo is sent to spy on Laertes; Ophelia relates Hamlet's madness.

SOME TWO MONTHS LATER, we find Polonius sending his servant, Reynaldo, to spy on Laertes, who is away at university in France. Although no location is indicated, this scene is sometimes considered to take place in Polonius' house. Overtly, Reynaldo's task is to give money and some letters to Laertes; covertly, however, his assignment is to report back on Laertes' behavior. Polonius, true to form, is long-winded and overly specific in his instructions.

The first part of Polonius' strategy is for Reynaldo to seek out other Danes in Paris. He is to act as though he knows Laertes only through acquaintance with his father and friends. Next, Reynaldo is to bait these informants with false stories of Laertes' wild behavior. Polonius is careful to tell Reynaldo to qualify these accusations with the statement that this behavior is expected of a red-blooded young man on his own. Finally, Reynaldo is to keep quiet as the Danes either corroborate or refute his deceptions.

As Reynaldo exits, Ophelia bursts in, shaken. She tells of a frightening encounter with Hamlet, which just occurred in her room, She describes Hamlet's appearance in great detail: his vest was unbuttoned, he was without a customary hat, his stockings were unwashed and drooping around his ankles. She continues, saying he was white as a sheet, his knees were knocking together and his expression was so horrifying that he reminded her of a man newly-released from hell.

Polonius urges her to continue. Ophelia says that Hamlet held her tightly by the wrist, all the while staring at her face, studying it intently. Hamlet then wailed and released his grip. He departed slowly, without ever taking his eyes off of her.

Polonius pronounces his conclusion: This is the very ecstasy of love. Polonius now believes that Hamlet's madness has been brought about by the depth of his true feelings for Ophelia. He is anxious for Ophelia to accompany him as he goes before the king with this news.

Polonius asks Ophelia if lately she has spoken harshly to the prince. She emphatically states that she has not—she has only been obedient to his admonition not to speak with Hamlet or receive his letters. At this, Polonius confides that his advice was evidently misdirected; he believes now that Hamlet's love was true. He mitigates his error, however, saying that his concern was fitting a father and a man of his age. They leave to see the king.

MADNESS
It is important to remember that while Hamlet's unkempt appearance can be assigned to *feigned* madness, his very real depression has been deepened by Ophelia's rejection of his affections. The feigned sloppy dress makes the prince seem worse off than he really is—but it does not mean he doesn't have true feelings for Ophelia.

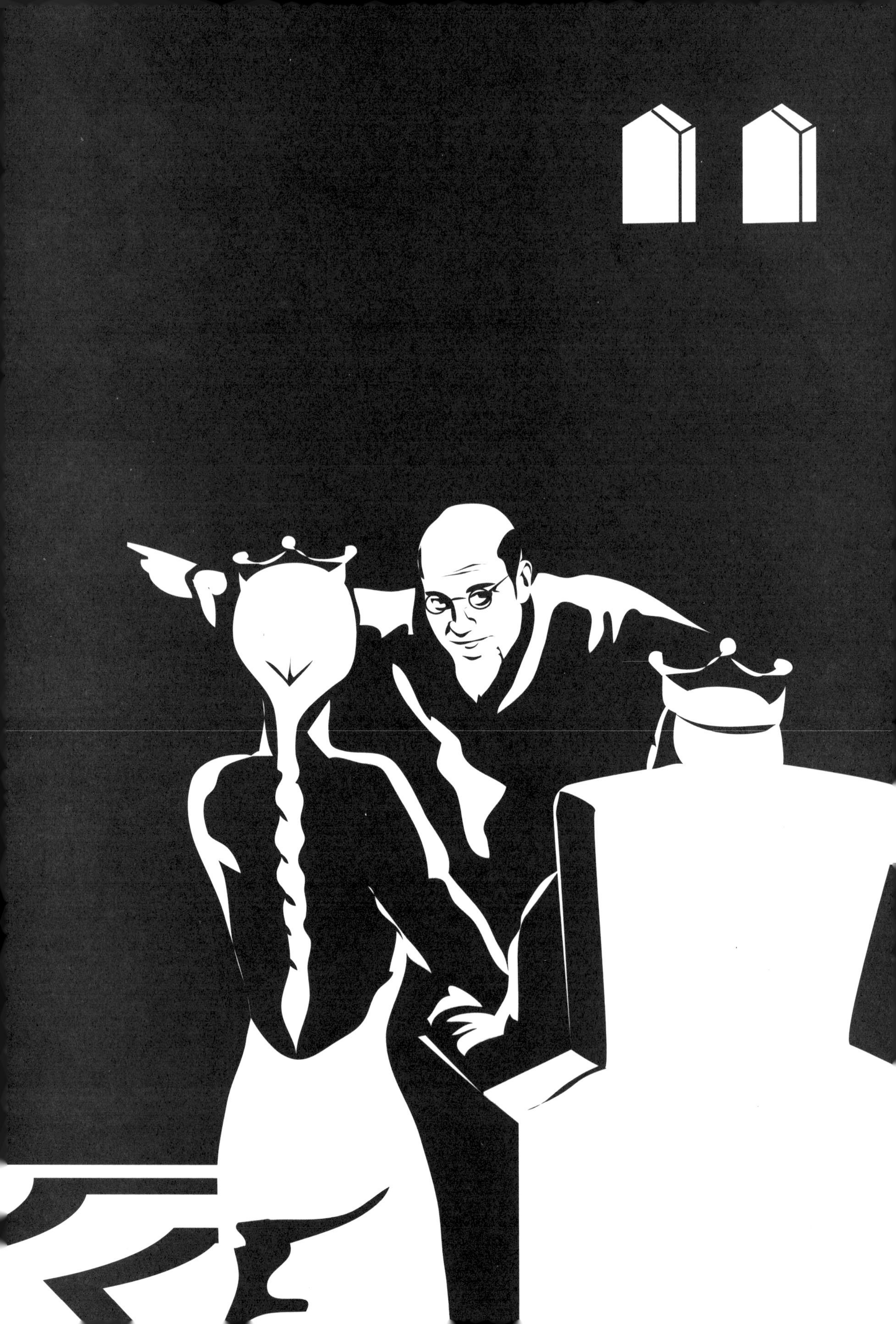

ACT 2, SCENE 2 PART 1

Claudius employs the ex-schoolmates; Polonius presents his theory at court.

THE ACTION SHIFTS to Claudius and Gertrude. Rosencrantz and Guildenstern have been summoned before the king and queen, who now employ them to talk to Hamlet in an effort to uncover the cause of the prince's "madness" and to determine—ostensibly, at least—if a suitable remedy is available. Rosencrantz and Guildenstern are quite pleased with their assignment: it looks easy enough to perform and it brings the promise of a healthy reward.

As they are led out, Polonius enters. He has brought with him Voltemand and Cornelius, whom he claims have successfully completed their diplomatic mission. Polonius continues that he has also discovered the root cause of Hamlet's "madness." Claudius eagerly asks for the details. Polonius, perhaps wishing to prolong the suspense, says the ambassadors should first be heard. The ambassadors convey that Old Norway was unaware of Fortinbras' belligerence and upon hearing of it, convinced him to redirect his aggression toward Poland.

As the ambassadors conclude, they relate that young Fortinbras has requested safe passage for his army through Denmark, *en route* to Poland. Claudius is pleased to provide this and the ambassadors depart.

True to character, Polonius launches into one of his long-winded speeches, concluding tediously that Hamlet is indeed mad. Gertrude urges Polonius to come to a less obvious point, but despite the queen's impatience, he continues in the same wearisome manner. Eventually, however, he makes progress by reading a love letter from Hamlet to Ophelia. The letter is a heartfelt affirmation of Hamlet's love for her—an exhortation to transcend even the smallest temptation to doubt his sincerity.

The king and queen are excited at the news, thinking it may well be the key to Hamlet's mental collapse. Claudius asks how Ophelia has responded to Hamlet's overtures. Polonius tells the royal couple of his instruction for her to refuse Hamlet's advances. He then makes a verbose defense of his decision to forbid the romance. Ultimately, however, he concedes that his decision set in motion a chain of events leading to Hamlet's insanity.

The king and queen accept the plausibility of Polonius' theory and ask how they can put it to test. It is agreed that Claudius and Polonius will hide behind a tapestry in the lobby as they spy on Ophelia and the prince, who is known to walk the halls for hours on end.

DECEPTION
At first, Prince Fortinbras appears to have a one-to-one correlation to Prince Hamlet: both fathers have been killed and both uncles have succeeded to the throne. In this scene, however, we notice an inversion of their comparison. Fortinbras is engaged in subterfuge by marching the army to Denmark. In Hamlet's case, his uncle was engaged in subterfuge by murdering Old Hamlet. Other differences are accentuated in 4.4.

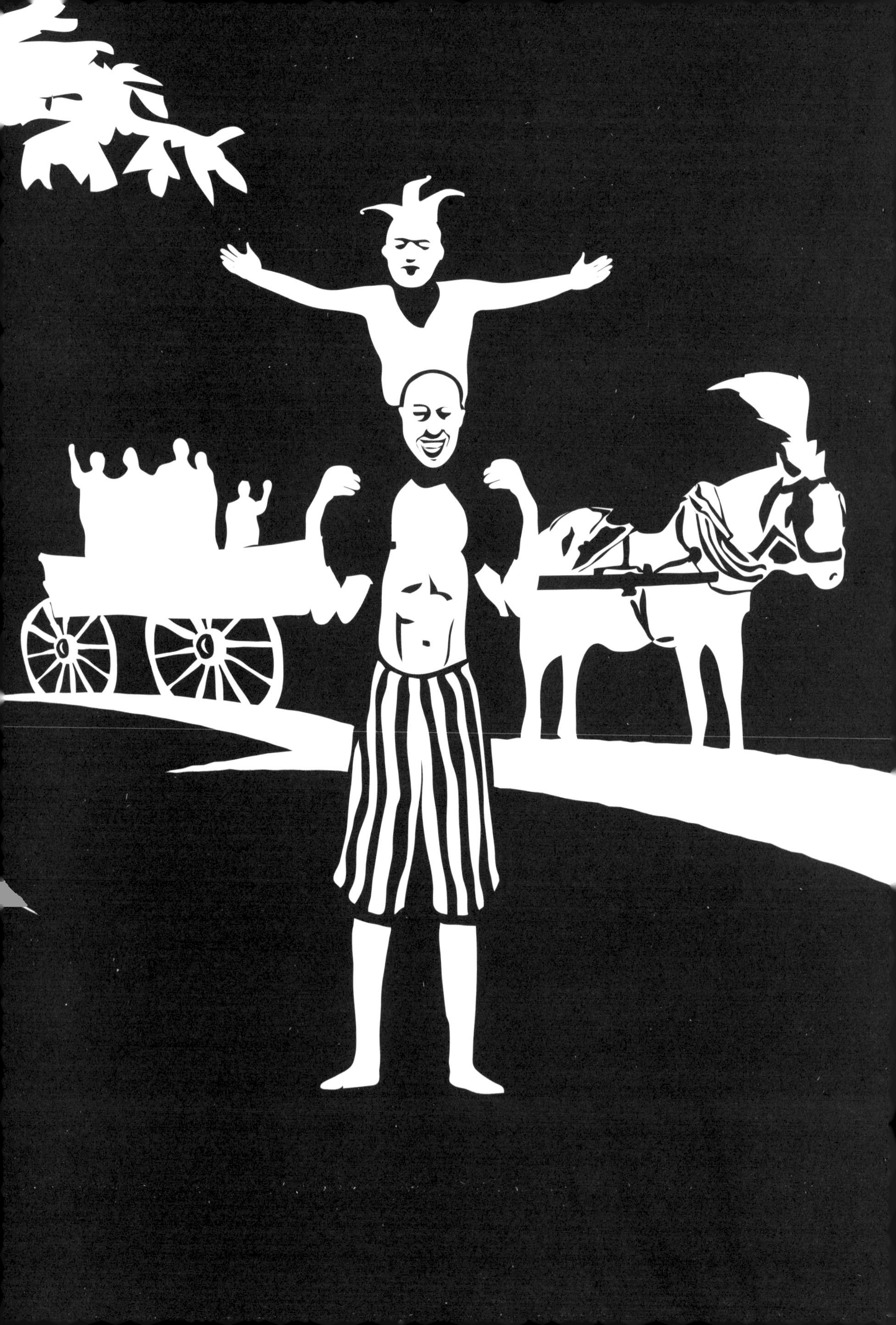

ACT 2, SCENE 2 PART 2

Hamlet with Polonius, Rosencrantz and Guildenstern; the players arrive.

THE KING AND QUEEN EXIT, as Hamlet enters, reading a book. Polonius speaks to him and Hamlet's ensuing responses move from delightfully abstruse to bitingly sarcastic. Though feigning insanity, Hamlet's speech has an undercurrent of lucidity—taken one way, his answers appear ridiculous; taken another, they appear brilliant. The wordplay is outstanding: Polonius, himself, concedes, "Though this be madness, yet there is method in it."

Polonius leaves to set up an "accidental" meeting between Hamlet and Ophelia. As he does, Rosencrantz and Guildenstern make their entrance. The old schoolmates exchange exuberant greetings with the prince and engage in bawdy humor. The cheerfulness of the conversation takes a turn, however, when Hamlet asks what brings them to Denmark, referring to it as a prison. The two reply that Denmark is no prison to them, they have simply come to visit him. Hamlet then quickly determines that they have been sent for by the king and queen.

Rosencrantz and Guildenstern are embarrassed at being found out, admitting that they were, in fact, sent for. Hamlet goes on to correctly reveal their mission: namely, to discover the origins of his recent madness.

As Hamlet waxes philosophical about his current depression (which is *real*, as opposed to his feigned madness), Rosencrantz pounces on the opportunity to change the subject. Knowing the prince's fondness for theater, he tells Hamlet of a group of traveling actors (the players) they passed on their way to Elsinore.

Hamlet is delighted to hear of their approach. Rosencrantz tells Hamlet the actors have been forced to tour because their hometown favored a child acting company over them.

Hamlet welcomes the players. In an aside, Hamlet tells his ex-schoolmates that he is not mad as they might suppose (from this point, he considers the two as ex-friends). Polonius reenters and Hamlet again jests with him, referring to him as "Old Jephthah," a biblical judge who, by misfortune, felt compelled to sacrifice his daughter.

Hamlet asks the lead actor to recite from Virgil's *Aeneid* a speech of the fall of Troy, in which Pyrrhus must slay Priam. The actor recites it so passionately that Hamlet bemoans his own relative lack of passion in the ensuing soliloquy. Hamlet then arranges for a play the next day to entrap Claudius: *The Death of Gonzago*. The scene closes with Hamlet saying, "The play's the thing, wherein I'll catch the conscience of a king."

RIVALS
Shakespeare's reference to the child actors was actually a derisive remark aimed at the boy acting troupe, *Children of the Chapel*. They were a fad very much in vogue in 1600 and were formidable rivals to the other acting companies, including Shakespeare's own.

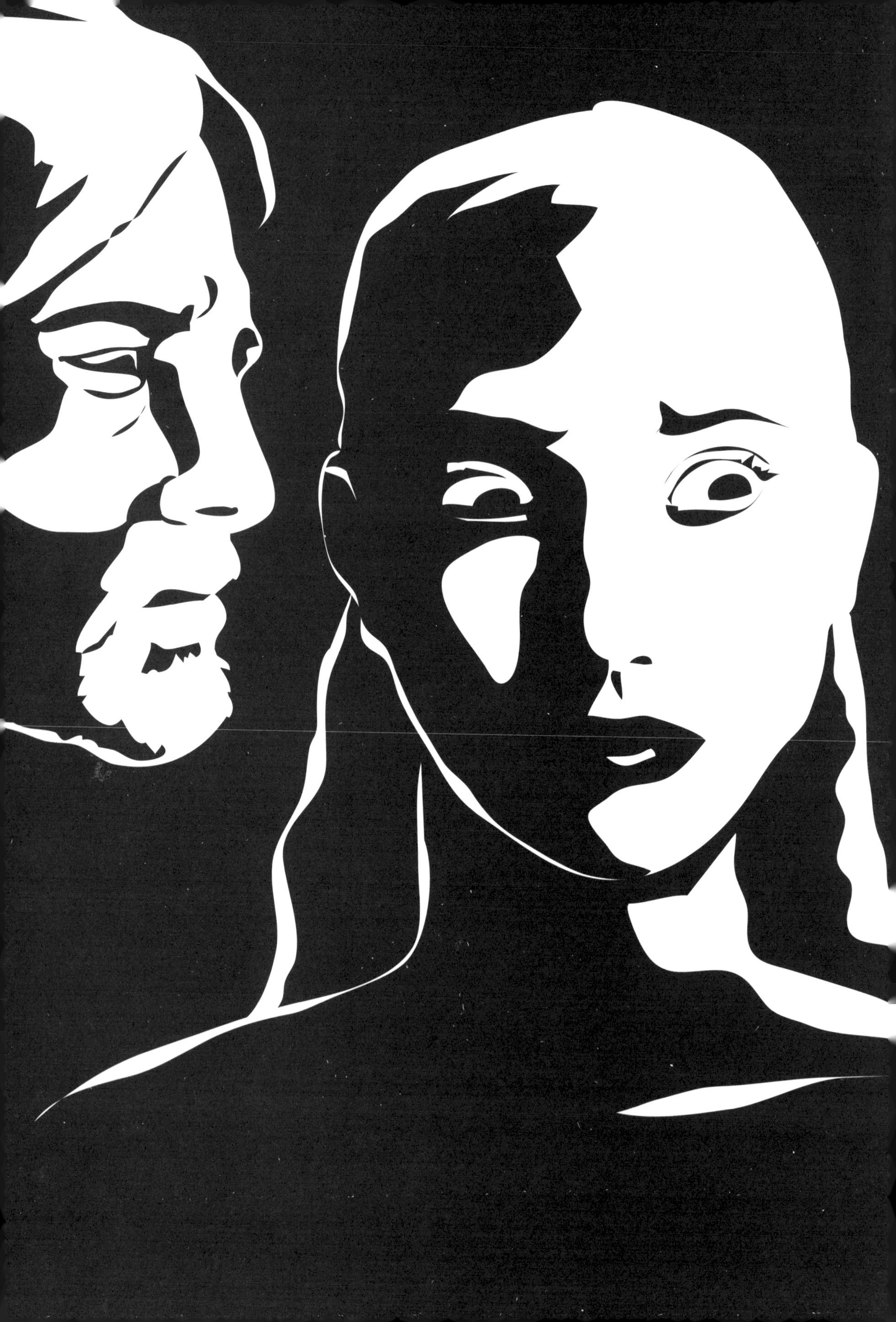

ACT 3, SCENE 1

Claudius and Polonius spy as Hamlet speaks with Ophelia.

THE NEXT DAY, Rosencrantz and Guildenstern stand before Claudius and Gertrude. They confess that, although Hamlet has admitted to a feeling of distraction, they have not been able to discover its cause because he is too aloof. They go on to tell the king and queen of Hamlet's joy at the arrival of the players. Polonius confirms this, saying the prince has invited the royal couple to witness a performance that night. Claudius and Gertrude brighten at the news.

Rosencrantz, Guildenstern and Gertrude leave as Polonius quickly prepares Ophelia for her encounter with Hamlet. He hands her a prayer book and tells her to pretend to read. Hamlet comes in and speaks what many consider the most brilliant lines in all of theater—the great central soliloquy beginning, "To be or not to be." Couched in a debate between suicide and perseverance, the soliloquy weighs the merits of rationality versus resolution. (Hamlet's position, however unenviable, is inescapably shared by all of us.) True to his nature, Hamlet only complicates the question, rather than reduce it to an *either/or* proposition.

Hamlet spies Ophelia reading and approaches her. She tells him she has some love tokens of his to return. Hamlet denies ever giving them to her and his responses become more and more puzzling. They appear to be talking *at* one another, rather than *to* one another.

Hamlet questions Ophelia's fidelity. This is confusing to Ophelia (and the audience, for that matter) until Hamlet follows the question with, "Where is your father?" Ophelia lies, saying Polonius is at home. Many directors have Hamlet deduce that Polonius is behind the tapestry by having the old man leave something in sight—his hat or other personal effect. In any case, it seems as if Hamlet *does* know because his speech grows more acrimonious.

Their conversation is punctuated by five directives from Hamlet for Ophelia to flee to a nunnery. It turns desperate as Hamlet launches on a personal attack and Ophelia pleads for God to help the prince and restore his mind. After Hamlet leaves, Ophelia mourns the loss of their relationship and Denmark's loss of what would have been a model king.

The men come out of hiding and Claudius says that Hamlet is definitely not mad *or* love-sick, but is brooding dangerously. He determines to send Hamlet to England to collect neglected tribute money. As the scene closes, Polonius convinces him to wait until evening, when Gertrude can speak more intimately with her son and Polonius can spy on their conversation.

CHASTITY
In this scene, Hamlet exhorts Ophelia to be chaste, in contrast to (his perception of) Gertrude's incestuous promiscuity. He tells her five times to get to a convent. Her symbolic chastity is reinforced by her father handing her a devotional book, providing an acceptable excuse for her unsupervised presence in the castle lobby.

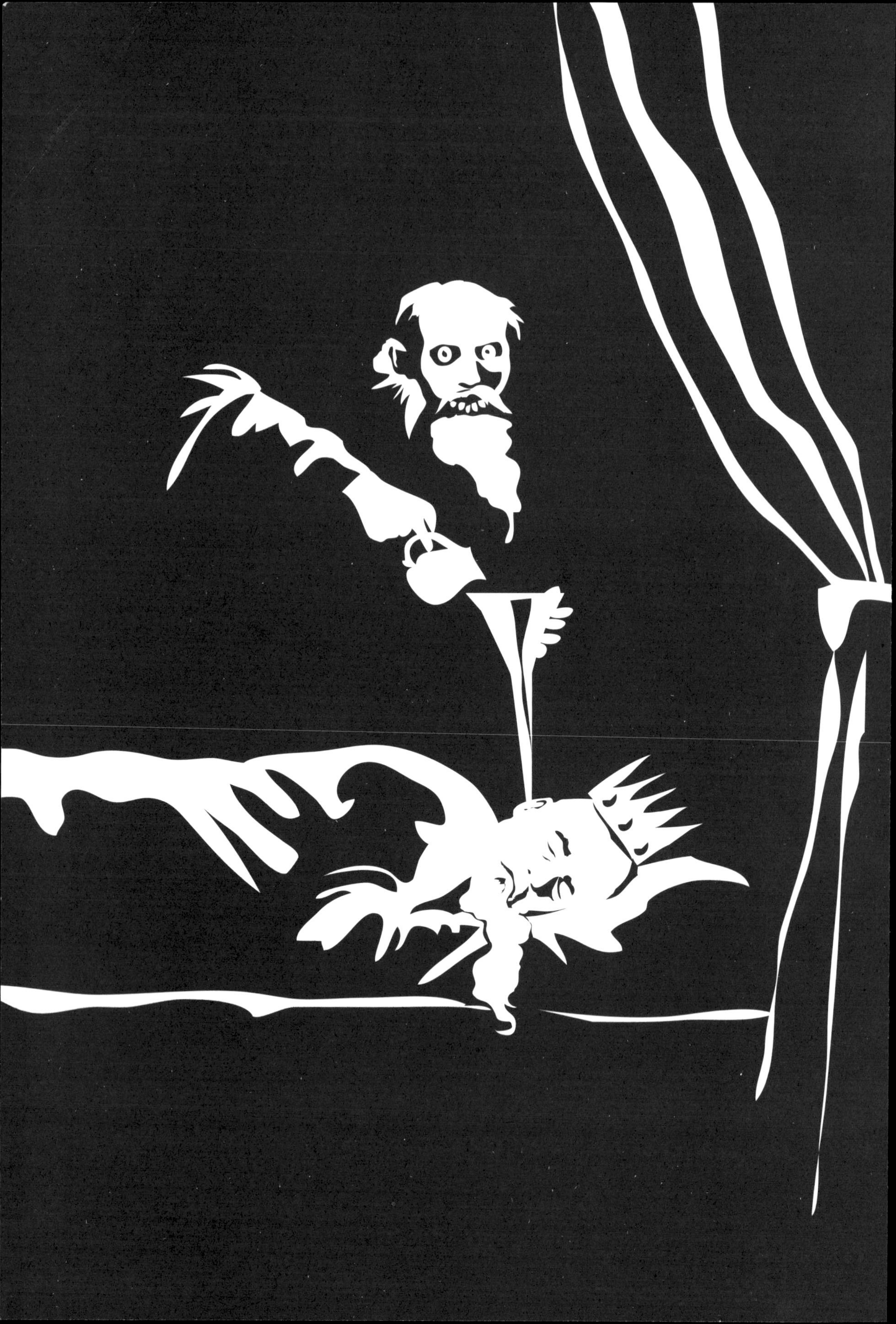

ACT 3, SCENE 2

Hamlet's play exposes Claudius' guilt; Gertrude sends for Hamlet.

HAMLET GIVES LAST-MINUTE coaching to the actors, admonishing them not to be either too melodramatic or too restrained with their lines. In kind, Hamlet takes Horatio aside and praises him for his even temper. He enlists Horatio to monitor Claudius' reaction to the play, which will reenact the circumstances of Old Hamlet's murder. The prince says that, if the king does not appear guilty, then they will know the ghost was sent from hell.

With a flourish, Claudius, Gertrude, Polonius, Ophelia, Rosencrantz and Guildenstern enter and take their seats. Hamlet jests at Polonius' expense and Gertrude invites Hamlet to sit by her. He declines, choosing to sit with Ophelia. He makes salacious comments to Ophelia, which she does not encourage. He throws verbal barbs at Gertrude as well, pointing out the quickness—or absence—of her mourning. The curtain opens and the players perform a pantomime of Old Hamlet's murder: a sleeping actor king is poisoned and the murderer seduces the actor queen.

Then the actors perform the play (ostensibly, *The Death of Gonzago*) with some additional dialogue written by Hamlet. The prince makes constant inappropriate comment during the play, mostly stabs at Gertrude and Ophelia. At one point, Claudius asks Hamlet what the play is called. Hamlet says it is called *The Mousetrap*. When the actor playing the murderer pours poison into the actor king's ear, Claudius loses composure, rising to his feet. Polonius, picking up on Claudius' panic, calls for the play to stop. Claudius, demanding more light in the theater, makes a fast exit.

Everyone follows except for Hamlet and Horatio. Hamlet gloats at the success of the play, maintaining that the ghost was a truthful spirit.

Rosencrantz and Guildenstern return to speak with Hamlet. They tell the prince that Claudius is distempered. Hamlet pretends they mean "drunk." Guildenstern tells Hamlet that Gertrude is astonished by his behavior. Hamlet pretends this is meant as a compliment. Rattled, the two appeal to their former friendship, begging Hamlet to tell them the reason for his antic behavior. In a powerful response, Hamlet hands Guildenstern a recorder, asking him to play. When Guildenstern says he hasn't the skill, Hamlet says that, yet, "you would play upon me."

Polonius returns with an invitation from Gertrude and—after more jesting at Polonius' expense—Hamlet leaves to go to her, urging himself to speak harshly but not act violently.

GONZAGO
In 1538, Francesco Maria della Rovere, the Duke of Urbino, was rumored to have been murdered by having poison poured into his ear. The name of Rovere's murderer was Luigi Gonzago, his barber-surgeon. Why Shakespeare's confused source reversed the murderer with the murdered is unknown.

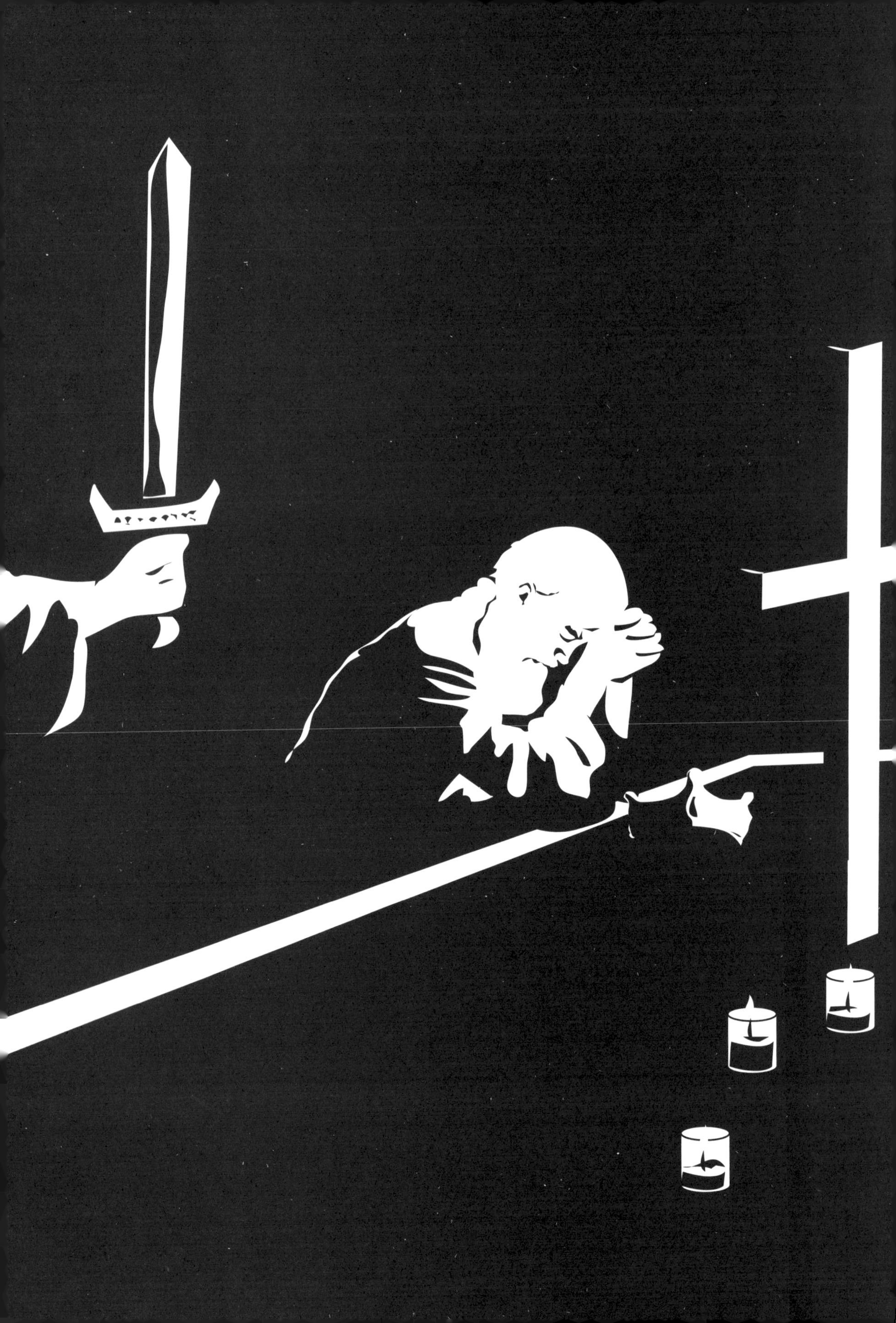

ACT 3, SCENE 3

Preparations are made for England; Hamlet refrains from killing Claudius.

KING CLAUDIUS DIRECTS Rosencrantz and Guildenstern to accompany Hamlet on his "diplomatic" mission to England. The king believes that Hamlet's behavior is too dangerous to leave unchecked. Hamlet's ex-friends accept the assignment enthusiastically, saying the king's safety is integral to the well-being of all. The idea of the kingship affecting nature and society is a recurring concept in Shakespearean drama.

Rosencrantz and Guildenstern leave to prepare for their journey and Polonius enters. Polonius informs the king that Hamlet is now on his way to Gertrude's room. As planned, Polonius says he will be spying from behind the tapestry—exactly as he and Claudius spied when Hamlet was speaking with Ophelia. Polonius justifies his spy tactics by virtue of his perceived impartiality. Polonius believes Gertrude, being Hamlet's mother, will certainly get to the source of the prince's madness, but by the same token will be overly sympathetic to her son.

After Polonius leaves, Claudius delivers an uncharacteristically moving soliloquy. He laments his crime of fratricide, which he believes has the curse of Cain upon it. Claudius feels as if he hovers between repentance and ambition, unable to act on either. He deeply philosophizes about the nature of mercy and forgiveness.

Claudius wrestles with the idea of praying, but feels unworthy to do so, since he'll not relinquish either of the rewards of his crime: his kingship or his queen. He considers the possibility of retaining these *and* still obtaining forgiveness. He concludes, however, that the way to heaven does not allow for both; his forgiveness must come with full repentance. He calls upon angels for assistance, begs his stubborn knees to bend and wills his heart to melt before God. Just then, Hamlet enters, sword drawn, behind the kneeling king.

Hamlet moves to kill him, but stops, believing that if Claudius dies while in prayer, he will go straight to heaven, rather than to hell. Hamlet recalls that his father is in Purgatory for his unconfessed sins. He believes if he kills Claudius at this moment, he will be doing his father an injustice and his vengeance will be circumvented. Hamlet leaves to go to his mother, vowing to save his revenge for a more opportune moment.

Once Hamlet has left, Claudius stands and says that while his words rise upward, his thoughts remain below and cannot reach heaven.

CLEANSING
In his spiritual crisis, Claudius asks if there is enough rain in heaven to wash his bloody hands white as snow. This concept resurfaces in *MacBeth* when Lady MacBeth cannot sufficiently cleanse the blood of regicide from her own hands.

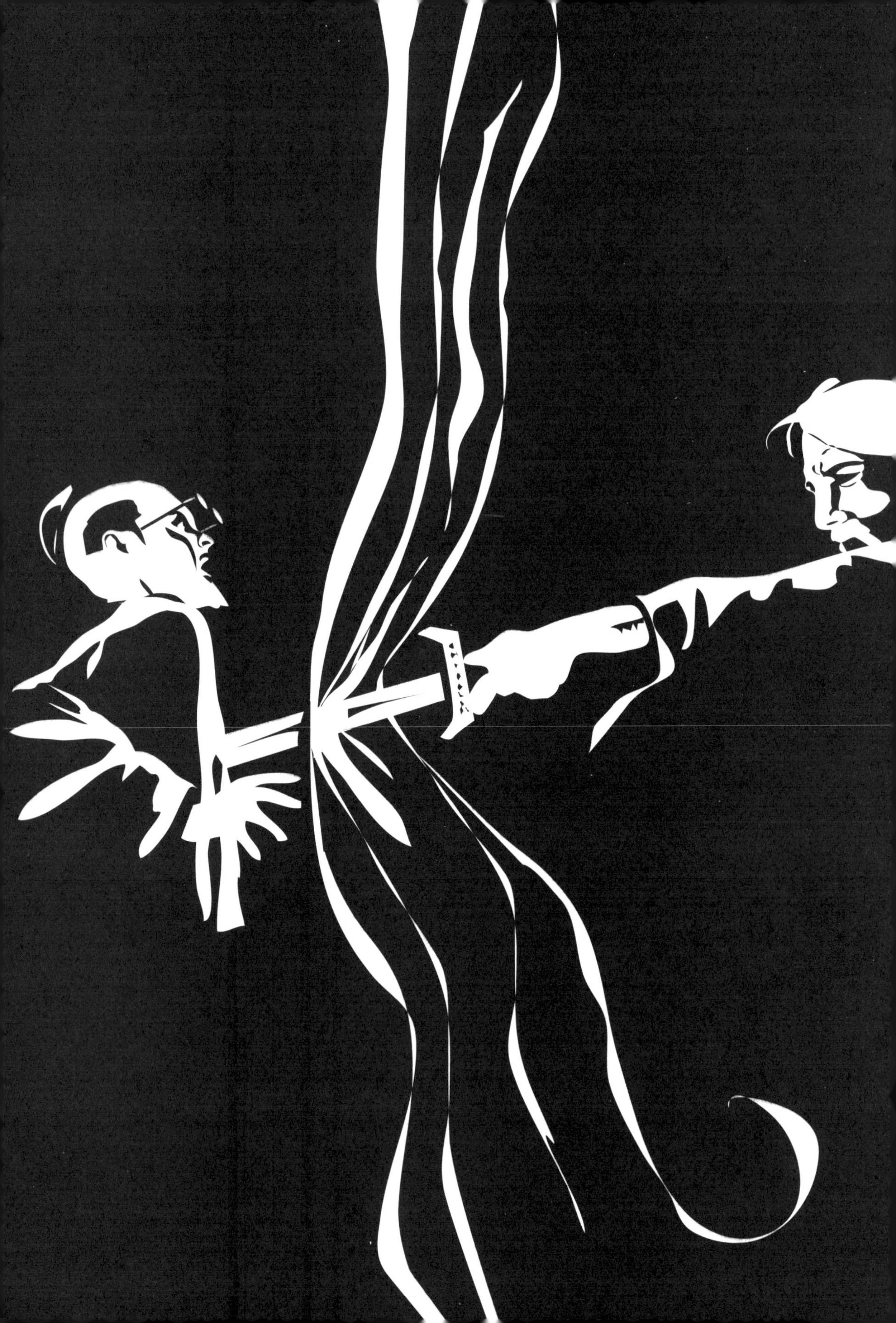

ACT 3, SCENE 4

Hamlet speaks with the queen; the slaying of Polonius.

Polonius and Gertrude are in her chambers. He gives her some last-minute advice before Hamlet's arrival: be firm and direct. The queen hears Hamlet coming and tells Polonius to hide. Polonius hastens behind the tapestry, in keeping with his plan. Hamlet and Gertrude immediately contend. She reprimands him for his offenses toward Claudius; he reprimands her for her offenses toward the memory of his father. He tells Gertrude he even wishes she weren't his mother.

Having had enough, Gertrude moves to leave but Hamlet sits her down, restraining her. Gertrude panics and calls for help. Behind the tapestry, Polonius panics as well and calls for help. Thinking him to be Claudius, Hamlet draws his sword and runs it through the tapestry, killing him. Gertrude exclaims her horror. Hamlet responds coolly, saying this is almost as bad as Gertrude's crime of murdering Old Hamlet and marrying his brother. Gertrude is confused by the assertion that Old Hamlet was murdered. She asks Hamlet what she has done to deserve this accusation.

In response, Hamlet calls her attention to two portraits: one of Old Hamlet, one of Claudius. He praises the portrait of Old Hamlet, comparing him to mythological gods. He denigrates the portrait of Claudius, comparing him to an infectious disease and a wasteland. Hamlet bullies Gertrude, calling her current marriage bed a pigsty.

As the intensity reaches a climax, the ghost appears—although only Hamlet can see him. Hamlet's barrage is silenced. The ghost says he has come to sharpen the prince's diminishing resolve. He then directs Hamlet to speak gently to his mother, who is distressed and thinks her son is talking to a hallucination.

As the ghost leaves, Hamlet defends his own sanity to Gertrude and begs her not to excuse her sin by assigning his accusations to madness. Hamlet apologizes for his impertinence and the conversation adopts a less confrontational tone. Gertrude admits that Hamlet's words have broken her heart in two. Hamlet suggests she throw away the evil half and live purely with the other. He directs her to conceal that he is only pretending to be mad and to refuse Claudius' bed, to which she agrees.

Hamlet reminds Gertrude that he must go to England. He says he suspects foul play from his two escorts—Rosencrantz and Guildenstern—but he assures her that their own devices will lead to their destruction. Hamlet then deals with the problem of Polonius. He drags the body out of the room as Act Three closes.

INNOCENCE
Although it is never quite resolved, Gertrude's culpability is to some extent exonerated in this scene. The degree of her innocence depends upon how genuine the audience accepts her surprise at Hamlet's disclosure that his father was murdered.

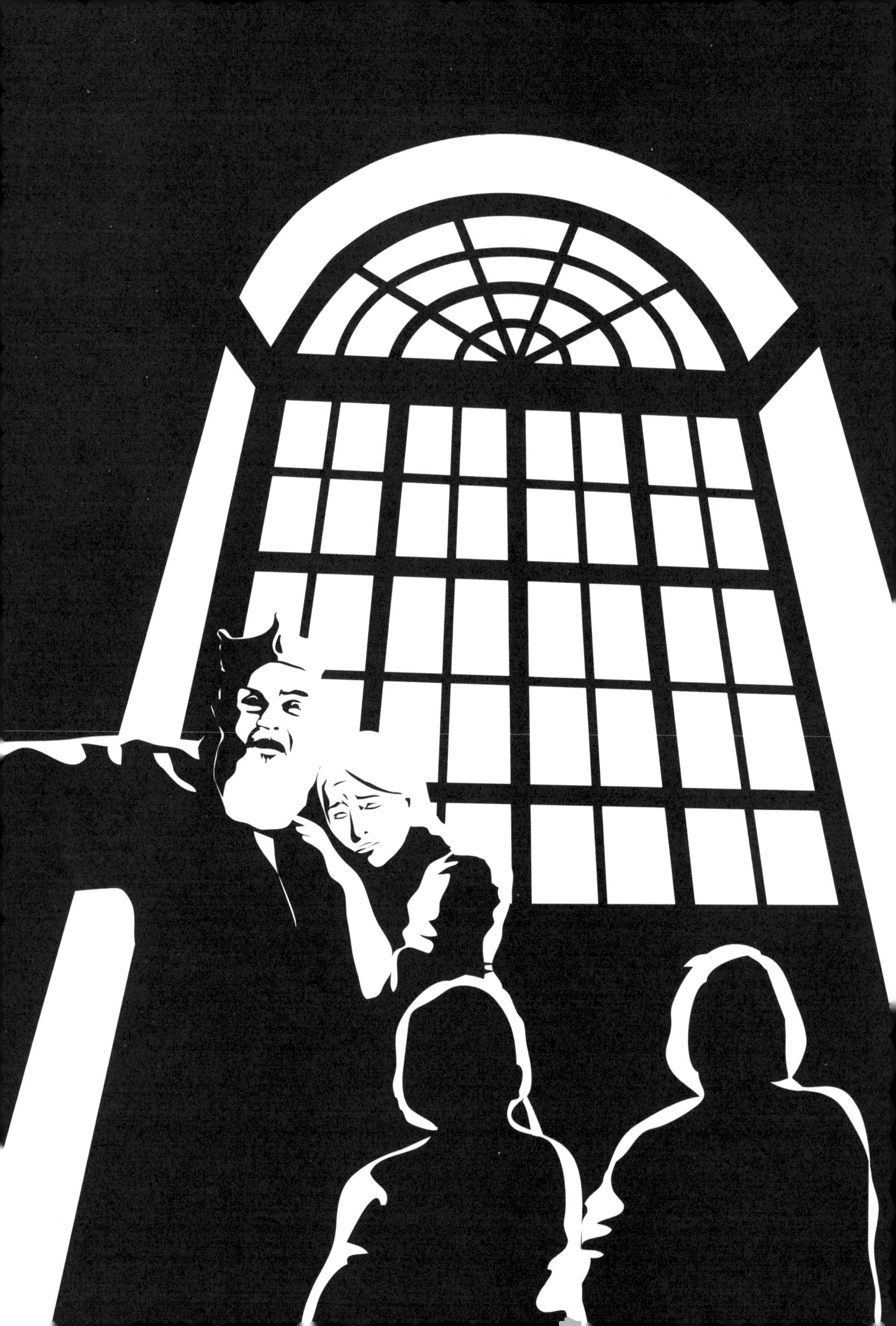

ACT 4, SCENE 1

Claudius learns of Polonius' death; the ex-friends are sent to Hamlet.

GERTRUDE, STILL IN her room, is joined by Claudius, Rosencrantz and Guildenstern. Immediately the queen dismisses her son's ex-friends and they wait just outside the door. She is visibly upset—sighing loudly. The king asks her why she is troubled and where the prince has gone. Gertrude evades the last question, perhaps intentionally, and says simply, "Ah, my good lord, what have I seen tonight!"

Making a show of concern, Claudius asks Gertrude, "How [is] Hamlet?" Gertrude says Hamlet is insane (either true to her son's request or actually believing him so). She tells Claudius of Polonius' death in succinct detail—the tapestry, the movement, the panic, the rapier and the result—and uses Hamlet's mental condition as an excuse for his actions. The news of Polonius' death sends Claudius into a pragmatic mindset, with his own safety at the center of his concern. From this point on, the king will mobilize his resources with great efficiency.

Claudius correctly realizes that Hamlet's rapier was meant for him. In an effort to ensure his own safety, the king points out that Hamlet's freedom has now become a threat not only to him, but to the queen and everyone else in the court.

He asks rhetorically how he and Gertrude are going to explain Polonius' murder. He speculates that others will blame him for not having the foresight to restrain the mad prince and remove him from general circulation. Claudius pretends his deep love for Hamlet clouded his judgment concerning the best course of action. He admits to covering up Hamlet's condition, ostensibly acting with the prince's best interests in mind.

Having made his pretense of concern, Claudius again asks Gertrude where Hamlet has gone. The queen, for her part, attempts to make her son seem more sympathetic than he really is. She says Hamlet has gone to remove the body of Polonius and that he weeps over it, despite the burden of his madness.

Claudius promises Gertrude that he will quickly send Hamlet away by sea and use all of his diplomatic skill to influence public opinion in the prince's favor. The king calls for Rosencrantz and Guildenstern. He directs them to find Hamlet and take Polonius' body to the chapel, without upsetting the prince. Finally, the king and queen leave to inform their friends and minimize the damage.

PROTECTION
Describing the murder to Claudius, Gertrude shrewdly omits one important detail. She does not mention Polonius echoing her cry for help—she simply mentions that Hamlet heard something stir. Gertrude's story makes it seem as if Hamlet was trying to protect his mother, rather than murder a spy.

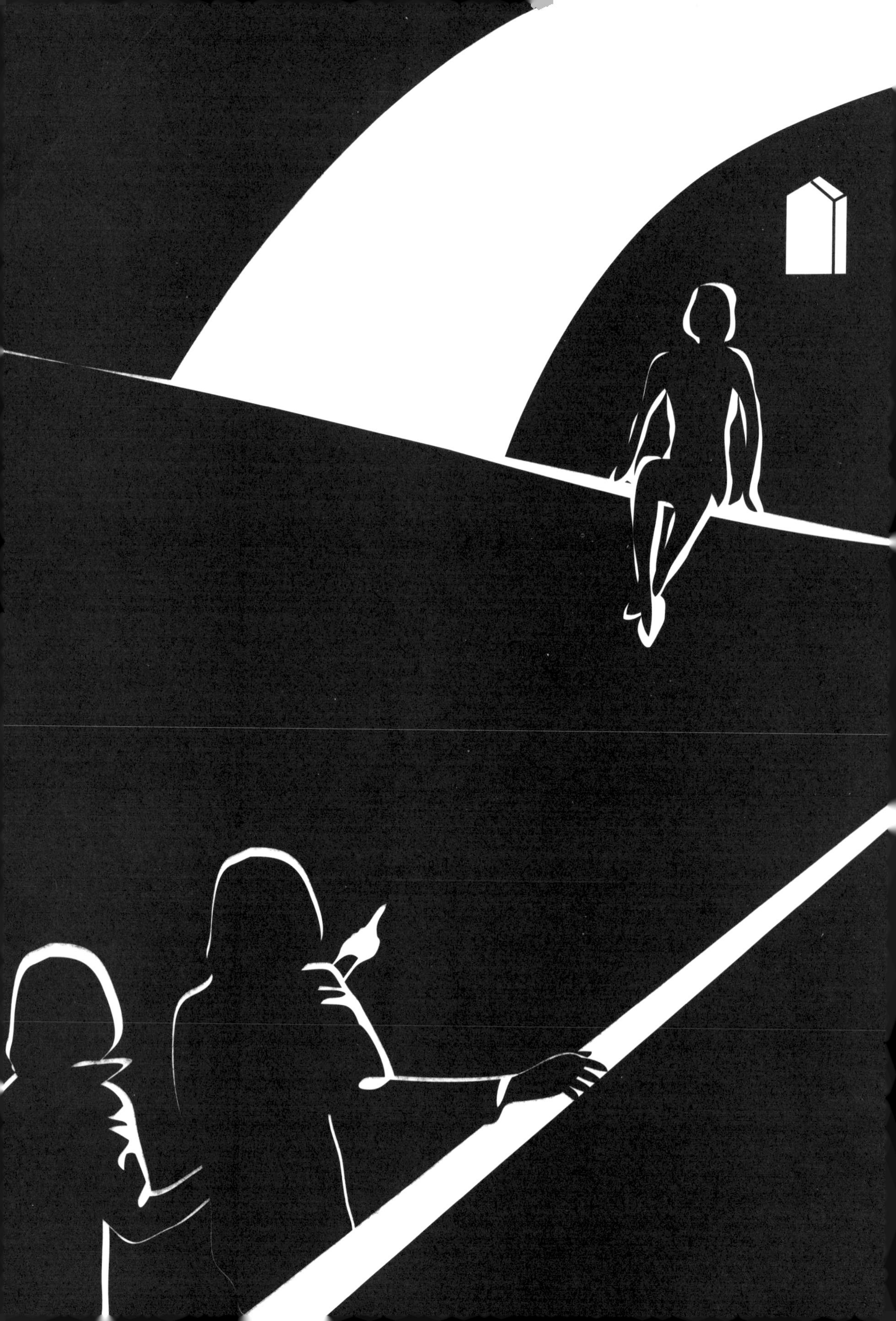

ACT 4, SCENES 2 & 3

Hamlet is found and brought before Claudius, who sends him to England.

JUST AS HAMLET safely stows the body of Polonius inside the castle, he hears the search party led by Rosencrantz and Guildenstern enter, calling for him. They meet and Rosencrantz asks him directly where he has stored the body. In antic form, he answers that he has mixed the body with dust. Rosencrantz continues to question him, saying they must take the body to the chapel. Hamlet sidesteps his questions and calls him a sponge.

Rosencrantz is confused and offended, but the prince explains his metaphor: Rosencrantz simply soaks up information which the king squeezes out of him when needed, leaving him bone dry. Hamlet adds another metaphor, saying the king is like an ape hiding an apple (Rosencrantz) in his mouth, which he will eat later. Rosencrantz is still confused and Hamlet—who has actually just given a useful warning to his ex-friend—says that it is just as well his words are misunderstood. Rosencrantz asks Hamlet to come with them to the king and he agrees.

Claudius, perhaps in soliloquy, perhaps to his lords, says Hamlet is dangerous, but well-liked by the slow-witted people of his country. He reasons that he must deal with the prince in a seemingly calm manner, appearing both rational and deliberative. Rosencrantz enters and tells Claudius they have Hamlet waiting outside, under guard, but they have been unable to discover where he has hidden the body. Claudius says for them to bring the prince before him.

They bring Hamlet inside and Claudius asks where he has hidden Polonius. As before, the prince responds in mordant riddle, saying the old man is at supper, where he is the main dish. He continues in antic fashion, confusing the king with his knavish description of how, after death, a king can eventually pass through the stomach of a beggar.

Claudius, having no time for foolishness, repeats his question. Hamlet's answers turn caustic, suggesting the king look for him in hell. Eventually, however, Hamlet names the place: under the lobby stairs. Claudius dispatches an attendant, then says he is sending Hamlet to England immediately, for Hamlet's own safety, escorted by Rosencrantz and Guildenstern.

Hamlet acts happy upon hearing the news and says, insultingly, "Farewell, dear mother." When Claudius corrects him, he defends his words, saying man and wife are one flesh. He leaves, calling, "Come, for England."

THREAT
As we find out in the closing soliloquy, Claudius now perceives Hamlet to be a threat. In his first attempt to kill the prince, Claudius arranges the voyage to England. He will provide papers calling for Hamlet's execution which will be carried by Rosencrantz and Guildenstern.

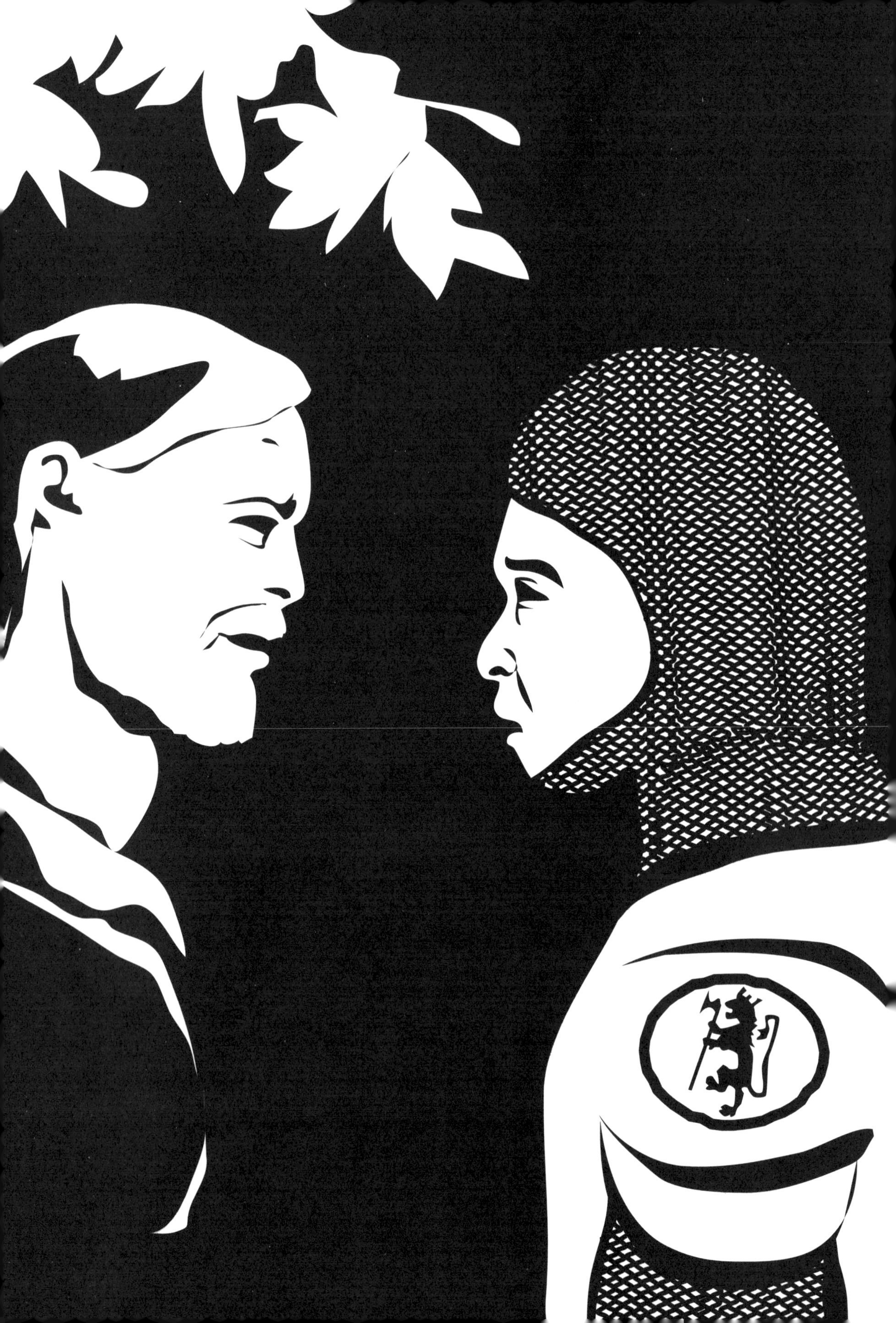

ACT 4, SCENE 4

Fortinbras marches against Poland; Hamlet speaks with their captain.

AT DENMARK'S BORDER, Prince Fortinbras addresses a captain of his army. He directs the captain to meet with King Claudius and remind him the Norwegian army will be passing through Denmark, as they had negotiated (in 2.2). Fortinbras tells him to convey that he will oblige his majesty with a meeting, should the king wish to speak with him face-to-face. He then dismisses the captain, ordering him to meet the army back at the rendezvous and to travel slowly while in Denmark.

Fortinbras exits and Hamlet enters, trailed by Rosencrantz and Guildenstern. Hamlet approaches the captain and asks him to identify the army, now marching through Denmark. The captain—perhaps recognizing the prince's royal insignia—answers that the army is from Norway, commanded by the nephew of Old Norway, Prince Fortinbras. Hamlet questions him further, asking why the army is marching. The captain answers that the army is marching against "some part" of Poland (which he later clarifies as meaning a portion of Poland's frontier).

Intrigued by the captain's odd qualification—"some part"—Hamlet asks him to explain further. The plain-speaking captain admits his army has been sent to gain a piece of land not worth five ducats a year to lease. In fact, he continues, the land would probably not raise that price if sold outright.

Hamlet says that since the land is worthless, surely the king of Poland will not defend it, but the captain maintains it has already been garrisoned. Hamlet is baffled and comments that now two thousand dead and twenty thousand ducats won't be enough to settle this insignificant dispute. He compares this situation to an undetected ulcer, that bursts and kills a person for no outwardly apparent cause.

Hamlet politely thanks the captain and they exchange farewells. Rosencrantz then approaches the prince and asks if he is ready to continue their journey to the ship. Hamlet tells him to go on ahead, saying he'll catch up with him in a few minutes.

Alone, the prince considers that he is constantly motivated forward in his revenge by the passionate examples of others. He laments his penchant for overthinking his charge and even assigns his hesitation to three-quarters cowardice and only one part wisdom. He reflects on Fortinbras' headstrong fervor that would risk lives for a worthless purpose when his own purpose is left unfinished. He resolves to focus entirely on vengeance from this moment on.

MOTIF
Hamlet's soliloquy in this scene is a simple restatement of that in 2.2, in which he chides himself for not having the same passion as the actor. The soliloquy here is omitted from the First Folio, 1623, and Quarto 1, 1603. Many feel it does not sufficiently advance the action to be included in the text.

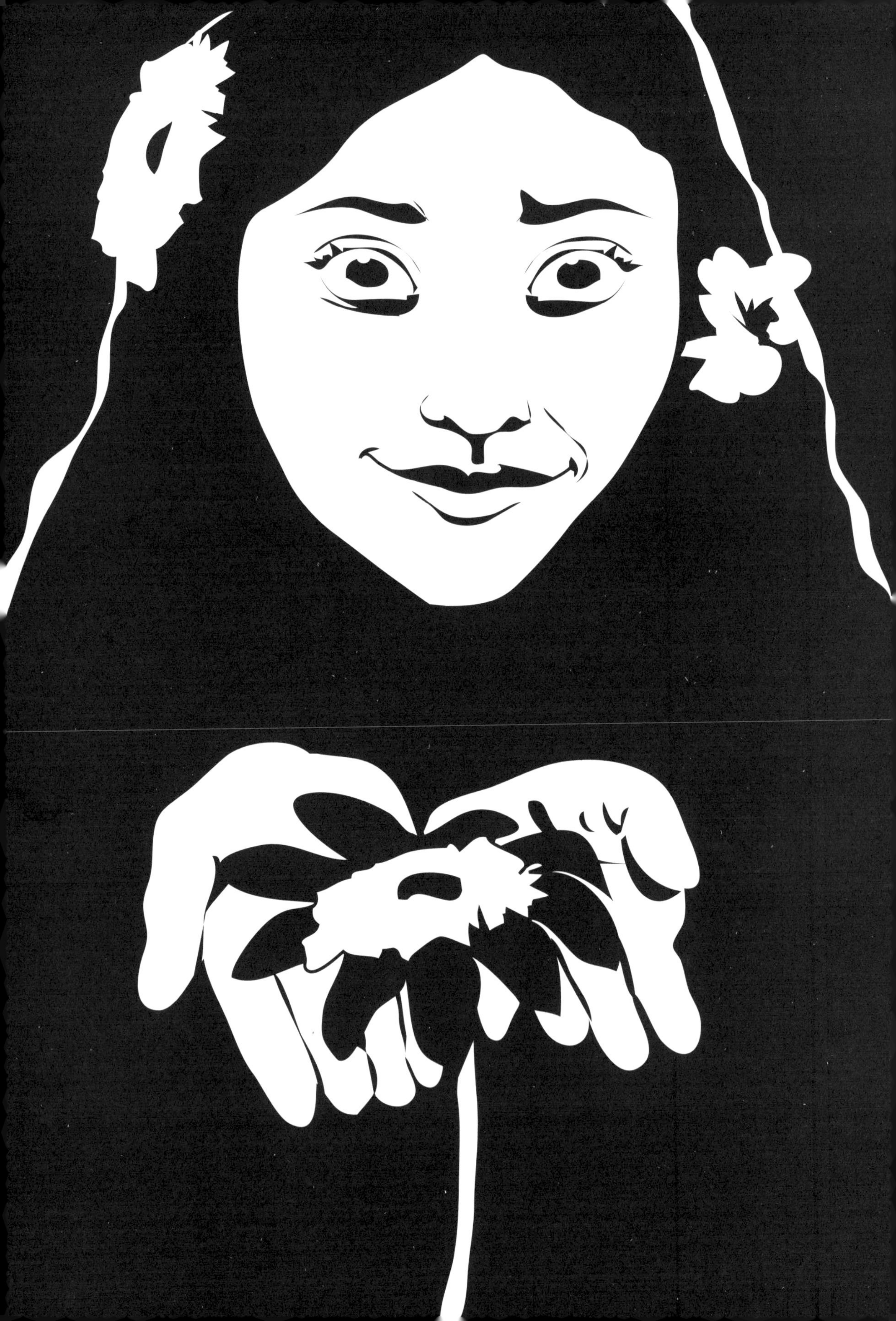

ACT 4, SCENE 5

Ophelia's madness; Laertes returns to avenge Polonius' murder.

ABOUT TWO MONTHS LATER, we enter a conversation between Queen Gertrude and Horatio, who tells the queen that Ophelia, who is now mad, wishes to speak with her. Gertrude, concerned Ophelia will be the cause of vicious rumors, agrees to see her and is saddened by the condition in which she finds her. Ophelia is incoherent—much like Hamlet's *feigned* madness—and she sings short verses about stolen virginity, unrequited love and funerals.

Claudius enters and the songs continue. He, too, is saddened by her condition, which he reasons is shock from the loss of her father. Ophelia then leaves and Claudius directs Horatio to watch after her. The king says the death and clandestine burial of Polonius has caused the people of Denmark to be very suspicious. Because of this, Laertes has returned, but has been aloof, listening to rumors and speculations that Claudius is responsible for the old man's death. These facts, he continues, along with Ophelia's madness and Hamlet's voyage have caused him much grief.

A commotion is heard outside. A messenger enters, announcing that Laertes has raised a mob, now at the gate, crying for Laertes to be made king. The mob breaks in and Laertes speaks accusingly to Claudius, demanding an explanation for his father's murder. Claudius asks if Laertes is going to indiscriminately seek his revenge, killing friends and enemies alike. This suggestion that Laertes is acting irrationally alters the tone of the exchange. Laertes becomes more receptive to reason and Claudius exploits this, saying he will prove himself innocent of any wrongdoing.

Ophelia enters again, singing. Laertes watches in disbelief as his transformed sister hands out flowers to those present. With each flower, she states its symbolic meaning to the recipient. Scholars differ as to which flower is meant for which character. She exits singing.

Claudius proposes that Laertes form a council of his wisest friends to judge the dispute between them. He offers his throne and all he has should they find him guilty, directly or indirectly, of Polonius' murder. Laertes agrees, but warns that he will examine all the evidence—the manner of death, the secret funeral, the lack of memorial or grave marker, the improper ceremony—all of which point to foul play. They leave together as Claudius vows that a great axe will fall on the man responsible for Polonius' death.

FLOWERS
The symbolism of flowers was well-known by Elizabethan audiences. A poem, "A Nosegay Always Sweet," first published in 1584, gives detailed meanings for many of the flowers handed out by Ophelia in this scene.

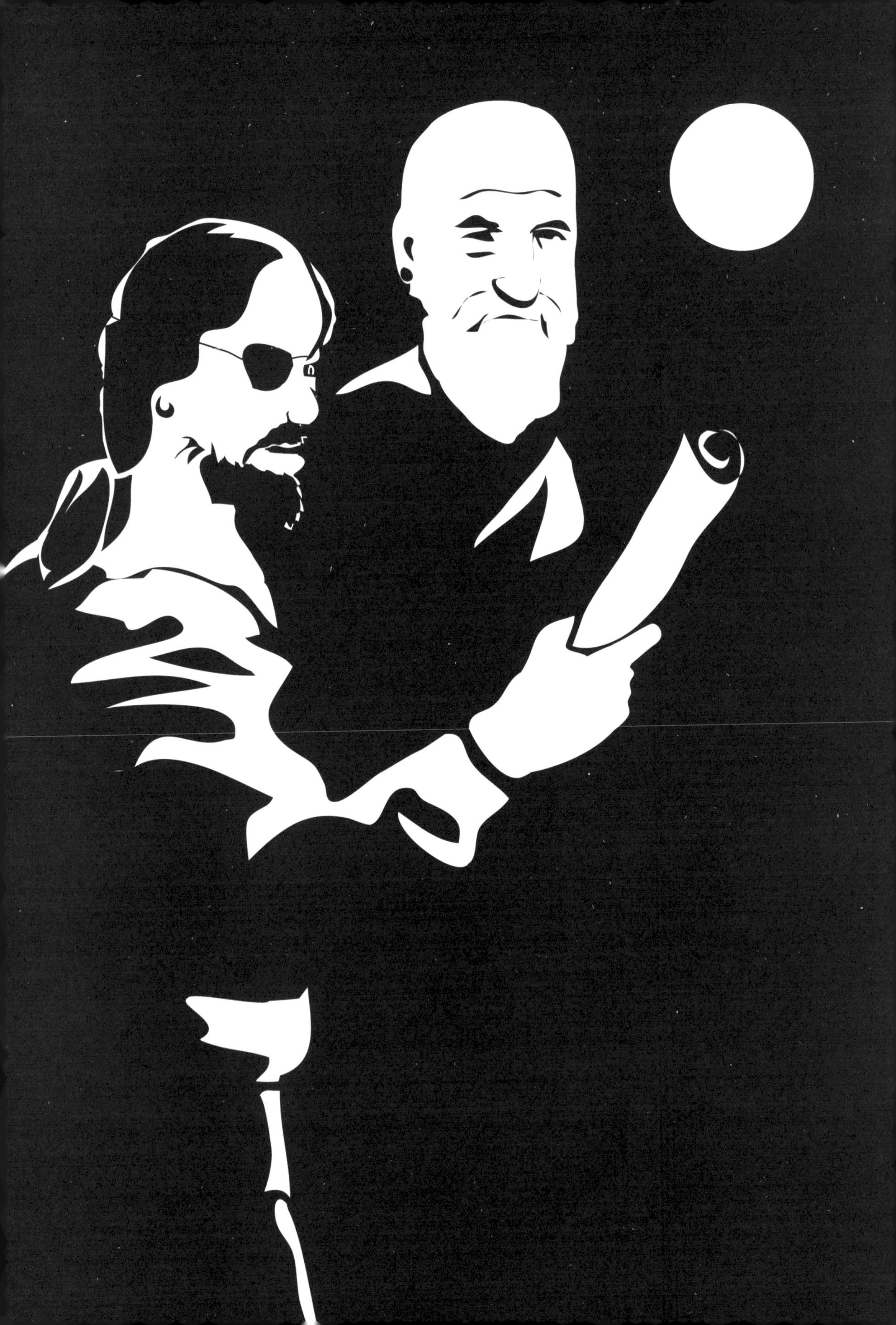

ACT 4, SCENE 6

The sailors bring a letter to Horatio with news of Hamlet's return.

HORATIO IS TALKING with a servant as the scene opens. He asks the servant to identify the people who are outside, waiting to speak to him. The servant answers that they are "seafaring men," which in the context of this scene can mean either pirates (who we will hear about shortly) or merchant sailors who have been paid by the pirates to act as middlemen in the transaction which follows. In any case, the servant says these men possess letters for Horatio.

Horatio tells the servant to bid the men come in. As the servant leaves Horatio conjectures that the letters must be from Prince Hamlet, by exclusion, since he knows no other person abroad who would write to him. At least two men enter, rustic and sea-weathered. The first sailor greets Horatio with a blessing and when Horatio returns the blessing, the sailor accepts it fatalistically, saying God *may* bless him, but only if it is in his will. The sailor then extends a letter to Horatio, saying it is from the Danish ambassador to England.

As Horatio guessed, the letter is from Hamlet and he quickly begins reading. It opens with a request: once you've read this, arrange for the men who brought it to you to meet with King Claudius; the men carry letters for the king from me. (The content of the letters to Claudius remains a mystery to the audience at this point in the play—we will see them presented to Claudius in 4.7.)

Then Hamlet tells a fantastic tale of adventure at sea. Before his ship to England had sailed for two days, a pirate ship, equipped with war armory, approached them and gave chase. The ship Hamlet was on proved too slow and was forced to engage the pirate ship, eventually running alongside it.

Finding the ships locked together for a moment, Hamlet boarded the pirate ship. The two ships unlocked and cleared one another, leaving Hamlet the sole prisoner of the combat. The letter goes on to say that the pirates treated him well, believing they would receive favor from the king upon his safe return (they believe Hamlet to be an ambassador). The letter then intimates that he has much more exciting news to communicate face-to-face. It closes, saying the sailors will bring Horatio to Hamlet after their meeting with the king and that Rosencrantz and Guildenstern are continuing to England.

Horatio leaves with the pirates, eager to take them to the king and then be taken himself to see Hamlet.

PIRACY
Piracy, or robbery at sea, was commonplace in Shakespeare's day and the English, possessors of the world's greatest navy at the time, were fascinated by it. In 1577, Queen Elizabeth I commissioned Francis Drake to plunder Spanish holdings and vessels in the Pacific. He was knighted four years later and made a national hero.

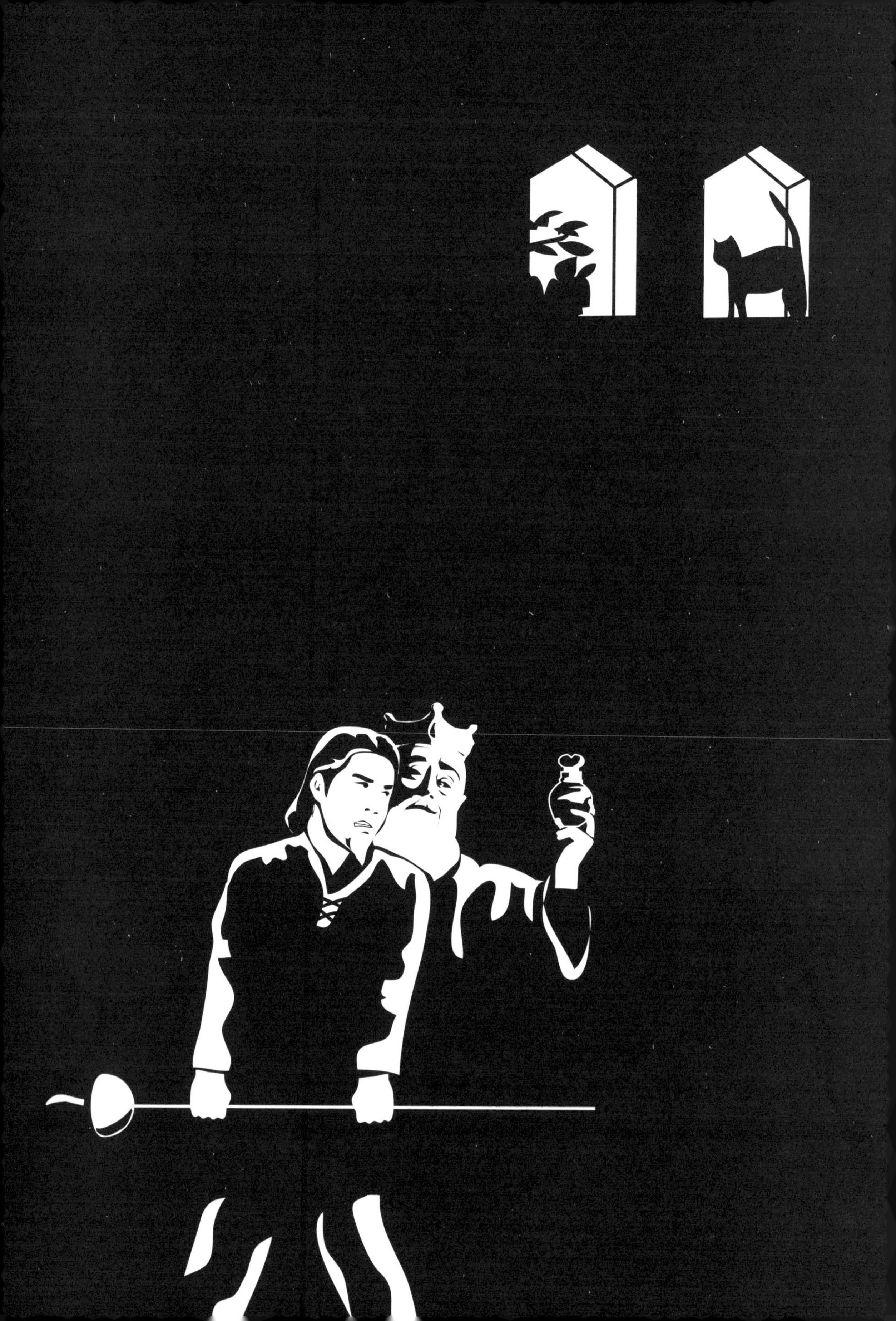

ACT 4, SCENE 7

Hamlet's letter; Claudius plots with Laertes; the drowning of Ophelia.

CLAUDIUS AND LAERTES enter discussing their reconciliation. The king says they have a common enemy in Hamlet, which solidifies their friendship. Laertes asks the natural question: Why haven't you, the king, taken legal action against Hamlet? Claudius answers, saying he hesitated because Gertrude cherishes her son, the people support him and the evidence against him was insubstantial. He reassures Laertes, however, that he has already taken care of the matter.

Before Claudius can expound upon his disposal of Hamlet, a messenger enters with the letter from the prince. Aghast, Claudius reads aloud: Hamlet has returned, stripped of all possessions, and will relate the details of his journey the following day. Claudius asks for Laertes' help in explaining this. Laertes is equally as confused as the king, but says he is glad Hamlet has returned, for now he can avenge his father's death. Claudius says if Hamlet will not continue his voyage, then he will prepare an accidental death for the prince that will fool even Gertrude.

Claudius sets up the details of his plot. Two months ago, he relates, a Norman horseman came to Denmark and amazed audiences with his riding expertise. After his performance, the horseman was speaking to the court and gave a first-rate appraisal of Laertes' swordsmanship, saying no one could rival his ability with a rapier. Hamlet, upon hearing this report, became green with envy and said he could think of nothing until Laertes returned home and could be engaged in a fencing contest.

The king then tells Laertes his idea: he intends to wager that Hamlet will win a fencing contest with Laertes. The prince will accept, not wishing to back down from the challenge. Laertes is to choose a sword with an unprotected tip and stab Hamlet during the contest. Laertes likes the idea, adding that he has procured a quick-acting poison which he will place on the tip, allowing him to merely scratch the prince for his revenge. Claudius, developing a back-up, says he will offer Hamlet a drink from a cup with this same poison, thereby ensuring his fate.

After this plotting, Gertrude runs in, frantic, saying Ophelia has drowned while placing flower garlands on the tree branches overhanging the brook. Laertes tries to hold back his tears, but is unable to and he leaves to grieve alone. Claudius asks Gertrude to follow Laertes with him, saying he has done everything to calm the young man's rage.

POISON
A favorite device of Shakespearean plot, poison appears in many well-known tragedies: *King Lear*, *Antony and Cleopatra*, *Romeo and Juliet*, and *Hamlet*. The playwright could assign qualities that were impossible in real life (such as Juliet's false death) and the theatrics of gagging and choking onstage were well received by audiences.

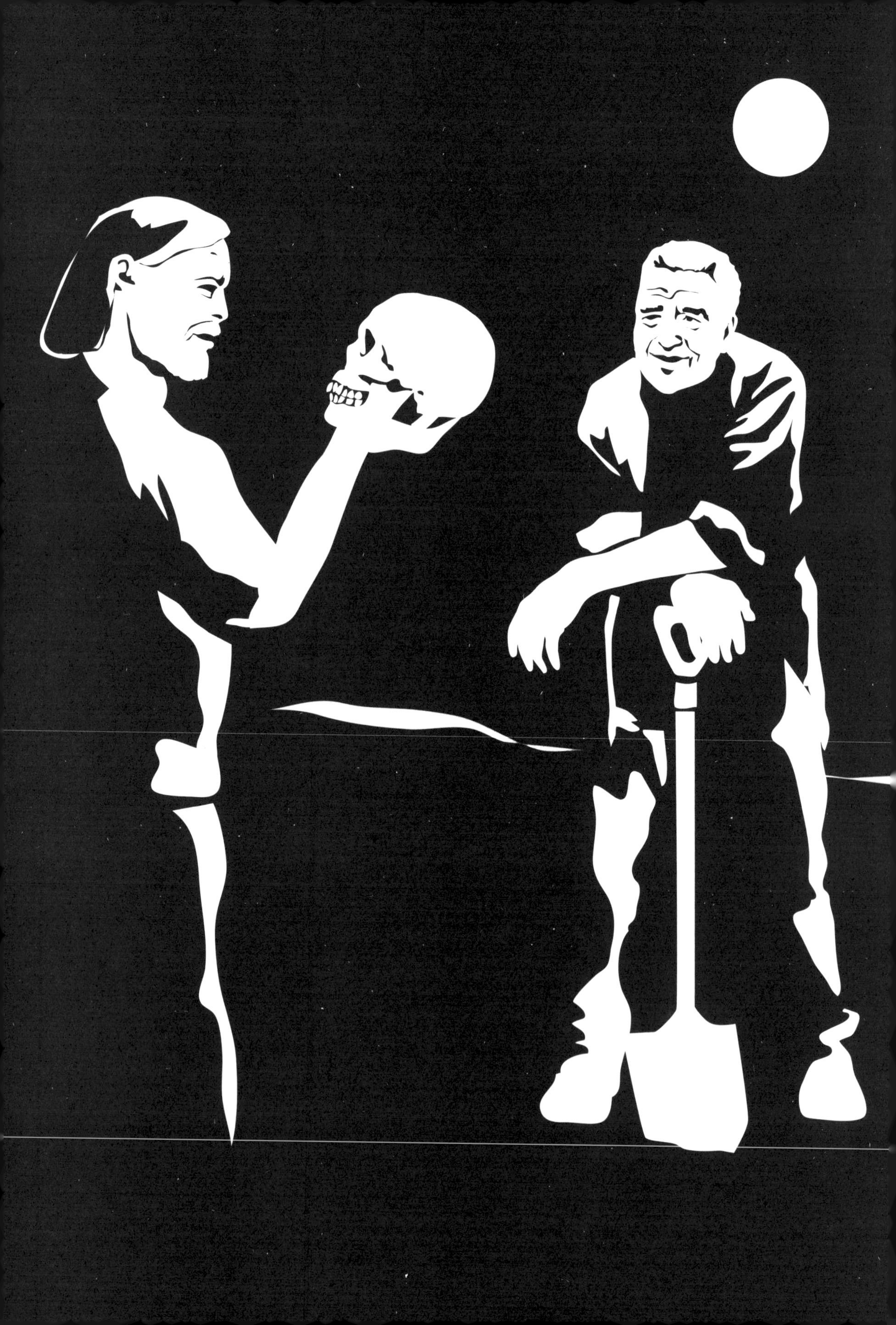

ACT 5, SCENE 1

Hamlet in the graveyard; his fight with Laertes at Ophelia's funeral.

ACT FIVE BEGINS the following day, with the Shakespearean clowns, gravediggers one and two, working in the graveyard. Using legalese they quibble in irreverent, low-comic fashion about death, including the spiritual loopholes of suicide. The second gravedigger is sent to the tavern for "a stoup of liquor" as Hamlet and Horatio approach. The first gravedigger, singing as he works, strikes a skull with his shovel and tosses it nonchalantly aside.

Hamlet muses over the fact that the skull might have belonged to a politician, a courtier or a lord—but now is only good for worms. Still singing, the gravedigger tosses aside another skull, which Hamlet speculates could have belonged to an attorney. Hamlet then jests with the man about who's grave he is now digging, without knowing that it is for Ophelia. The gravedigger says he has been working his trade since the day Old Hamlet slew King Fortinbras (the day of Hamlet's birth). He then picks up a third skull that once belonged to Old Hamlet's jester, Yorick.

Hamlet takes the skull, recognizing it as the friend of his childhood ("Alas, poor Yorick. I knew him Horatio...") and he speaks to the skull, requesting it to tell the queen she'll come to this same end.

A funeral procession approaches. The mourners include Gertrude, Claudius and Laertes, who is arguing with the priest for a more upstanding ceremony. The priest says that since the death may have been a suicide, the clergy can provide no higher memorial. Laertes replies that his sister will be a ministering angel in heaven while the priest howls in hell.

Hamlet can't believe his ears. The queen throws flowers in the grave and tells the dead Ophelia that she would have rather scattered flowers on her and Hamlet's bridal bed. Laertes curses Hamlet for depriving Ophelia of her reason and then leaps into her grave to deliver an emotional eulogy.

Hamlet rushes forward. He and Laertes struggle and must be forcibly separated. Hamlet maintains that he loved Ophelia greater than forty thousand brothers. He asks Laertes why he has besmirched him so.

The king and queen beg Laertes to restrain himself, saying Hamlet is mad and therefore not responsible for his actions. Hamlet leaves in disgust and Claudius whispers to Laertes to be patient, since his opportunity for vengeance will come soon.

CLOWNS
Shakespearean clowns, such as the two gravediggers, have a unique function in that they are allowed to expose some fundamental truths about their society through their low-comic humor. Other characters do not share in this privilege.

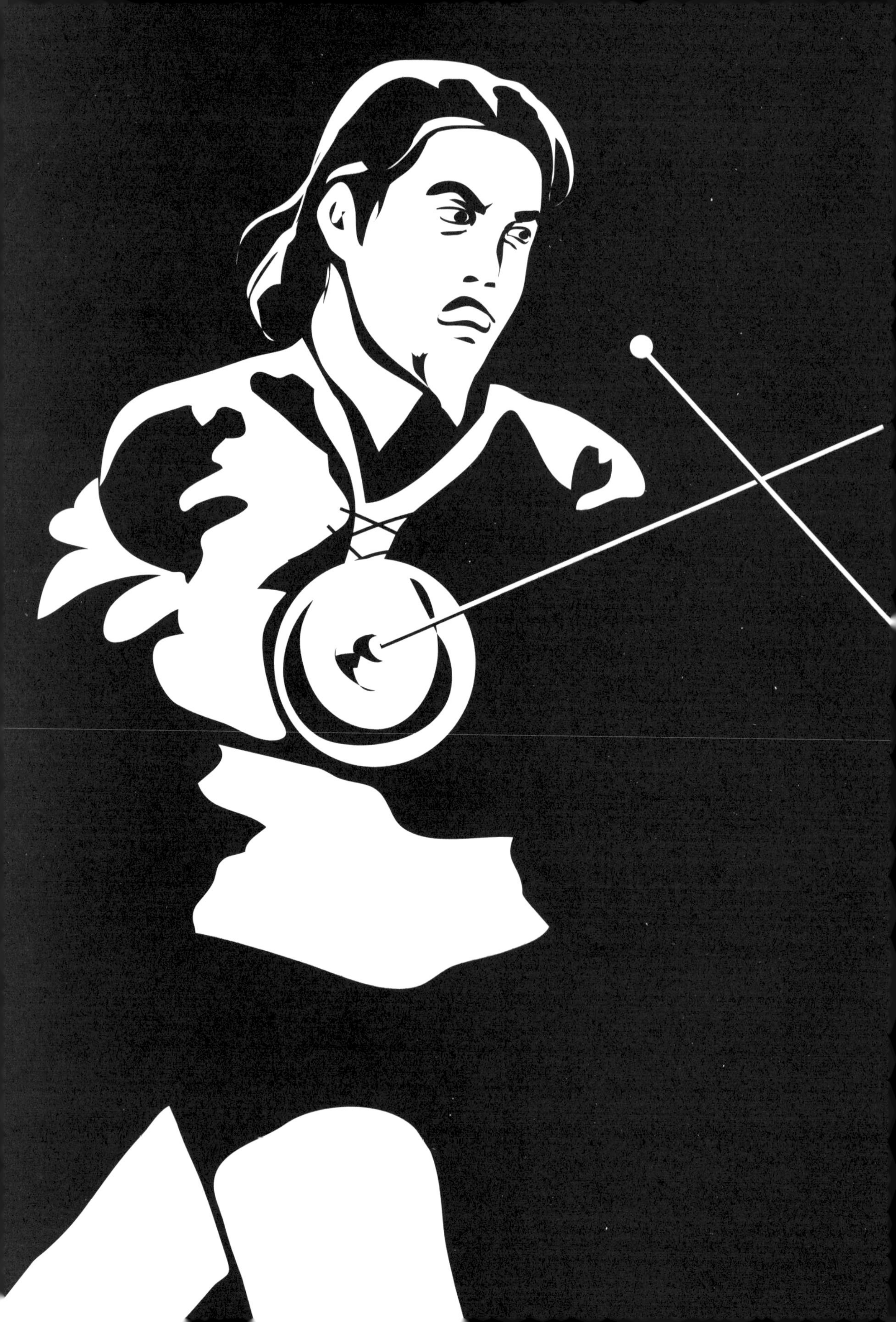

ACT 5, SCENE 2

Details of Hamlet's voyage; fencing match with Laertes; the deadly finale.

THE FINAL SCENE opens with Hamlet relating to Horatio the details of his voyage. The first night on the ship, Hamlet snuck into Rosencrantz and Guildenstern's cabin and stole the documents given them by King Claudius. After reading their request to execute him upon arrival, Hamlet forged new orders requesting the execution of the *bearers* of the documents—guaranteeing the deaths of his ex-friends. The capture by pirates was told previously in 4.6.

Hamlet and Horatio are then interrupted by Osric, a courtly sycophant whose high-flown fashion and speech are intended to impress those around him. The king, Osric communicates, has wagered six horses that Laertes will not score more than nine hits out of a twelve round fencing match with Hamlet. Hamlet—after having some fun at Osric's expense—accepts the challenge. Osric leaves and Hamlet confides that he has some misgivings about the match. Horatio encourages his friend to mind his instincts, but Hamlet waxes fatalistic and is escorted to the match hall.

Hamlet approaches Laertes and apologizes for his behavior at the funeral, assigning it to his recent madness. Laertes accepts it at face value, but does not unreservedly clear the offense. The contestants then take their rapiers (Laertes' is unprotected and poisoned) and ready themselves for the match.

The king drops a valuable pearl in a toasting cup—it's actually the poison—and says that he'll toast if Hamlet opens well in the match. The contest begins and Hamlet excels, scoring a hit. Claudius offers him the cup, but he refuses, wishing to continue. Again, Hamlet scores a hit and Gertrude offers him a handkerchief and drinks a toast from the poisoned cup before Claudius can stop her.

The third round is a draw, but as they are separated Laertes cuts Hamlet. In the ensuing scuffle, they accidentally exchange rapiers and resume. Hamlet cuts Laertes as the queen falls, stopping the match. The queen cries that she's been poisoned and Hamlet shouts, "Treason!" Laertes confesses the conspiracy and Hamlet, still holding the poisoned rapier, runs Claudius through and forces him to finish the poisoned drink. Hamlet and Laertes exchange pardons as Laertes dies. With his final breaths, Hamlet asks Horatio to tell his story. Prince Fortinbras enters on his return from Poland and Hamlet bequeaths him the kingdom. The curtain closes with Horatio's benediction and Fortinbras' request to give Hamlet a soldier's burial.

DEATHS
A typical question is, "How many deaths is Hamlet responsible for?" Perhaps a more interesting question is, "How many deaths is Claudius responsible for?" Surely Old Hamlet, Gertrude and Hamlet; but, indirectly, you can make an argument for Laertes, Rosencrantz and Guildenstern as well.

APPENDIX A: DRAMATIC MAPS

The Dramatic Maps which follow are schematic representations of *Hamlet*, by scene. In each case, the main ideas of the scene are highlighted on the timeline, alongside their initial corresponding line number. The brackets attempt larger groupings of the ideas to provide a sense of the overall movement of the scene. The line numbers of Shakespeare's *Hamlet* differ greatly between Quartos, Folios and consequently, publishers—each publishing is an interpretive work. Keep in mind they are guidelines for general assistance; your specific version may vary.

1.1

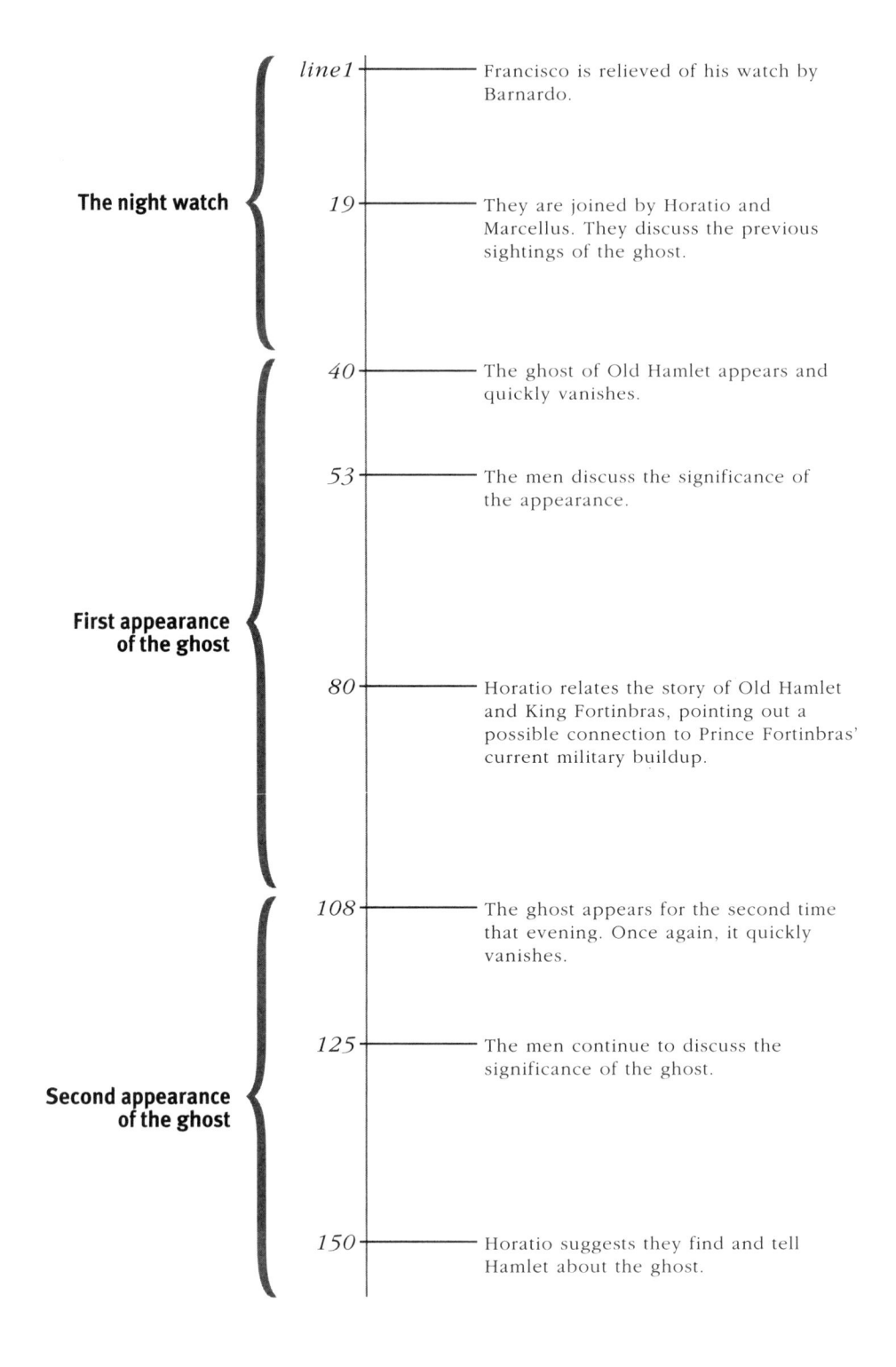

The night watch
- *line 1* — Francisco is relieved of his watch by Barnardo.
- *19* — They are joined by Horatio and Marcellus. They discuss the previous sightings of the ghost.

First appearance of the ghost
- *40* — The ghost of Old Hamlet appears and quickly vanishes.
- *53* — The men discuss the significance of the appearance.
- *80* — Horatio relates the story of Old Hamlet and King Fortinbras, pointing out a possible connection to Prince Fortinbras' current military buildup.

Second appearance of the ghost
- *108* — The ghost appears for the second time that evening. Once again, it quickly vanishes.
- *125* — The men continue to discuss the significance of the ghost.
- *150* — Horatio suggests they find and tell Hamlet about the ghost.

1.2

The king, queen and royal court enter. — *line 1*
Claudius addresses the court.

} **Affairs of state**

The ambassadors are sent to diffuse the — *33*
situation in Norway.

Laertes' petition to return to university in — *42*
France is discussed and settled.

The matter of Hamlet's gloom is addressed. — *64*

} **Personal affairs**

Hamlet is requested not to return to — *112*
university in Wittenberg.

Hamlet's soliloquy of despair. — *129*

} **Soliloquy**

Horatio and the soldiers enter and — *159*
describe the sightings of
Old Hamlet's ghost.

} **Hamlet is told of the ghost**

Hamlet decides to join the night — *244*
watch and swears Horatio and the
soldiers to secrecy.

DRAMATIC MAPS | 1.1 & 1.2 | 159

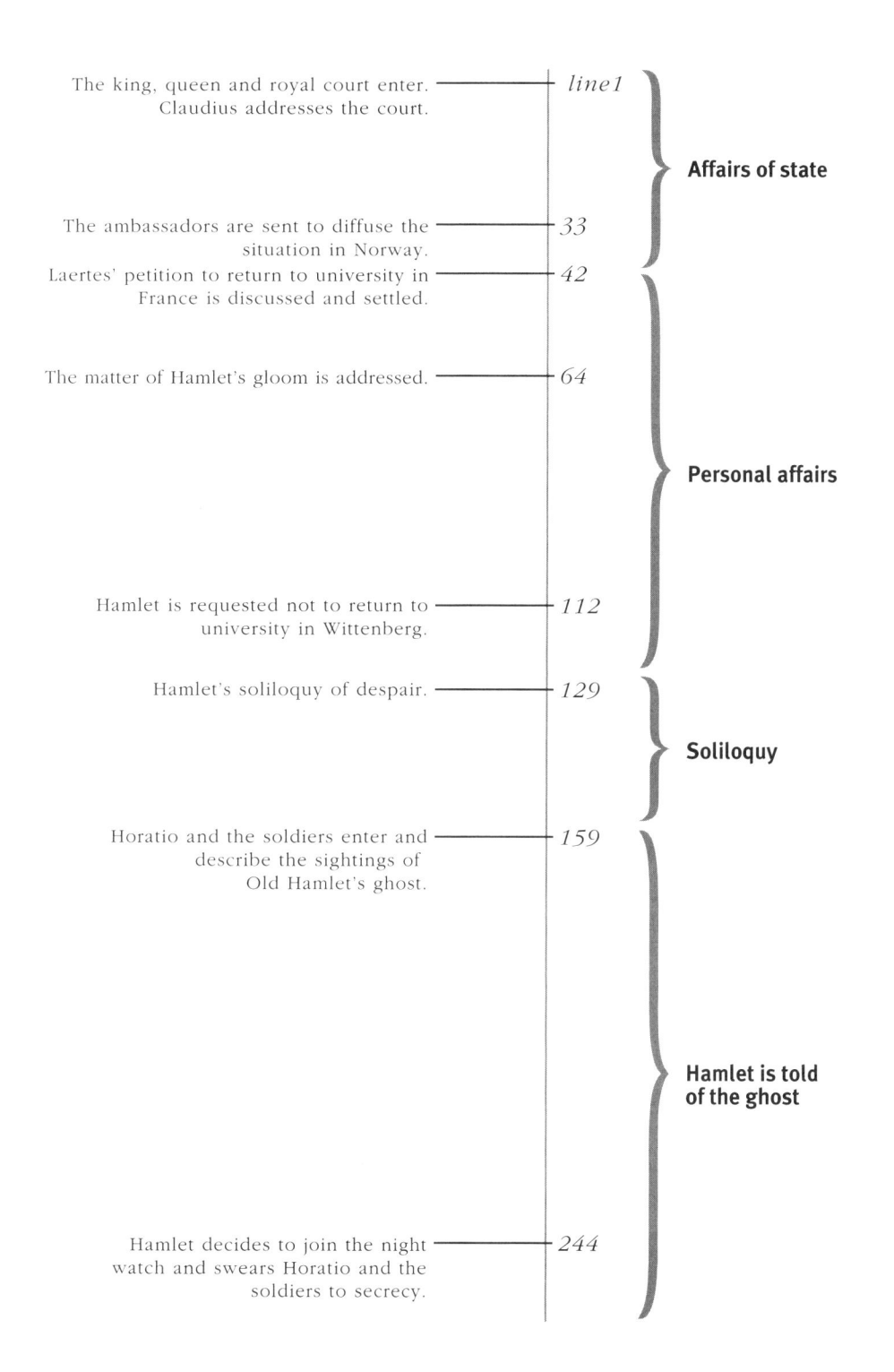

1.3

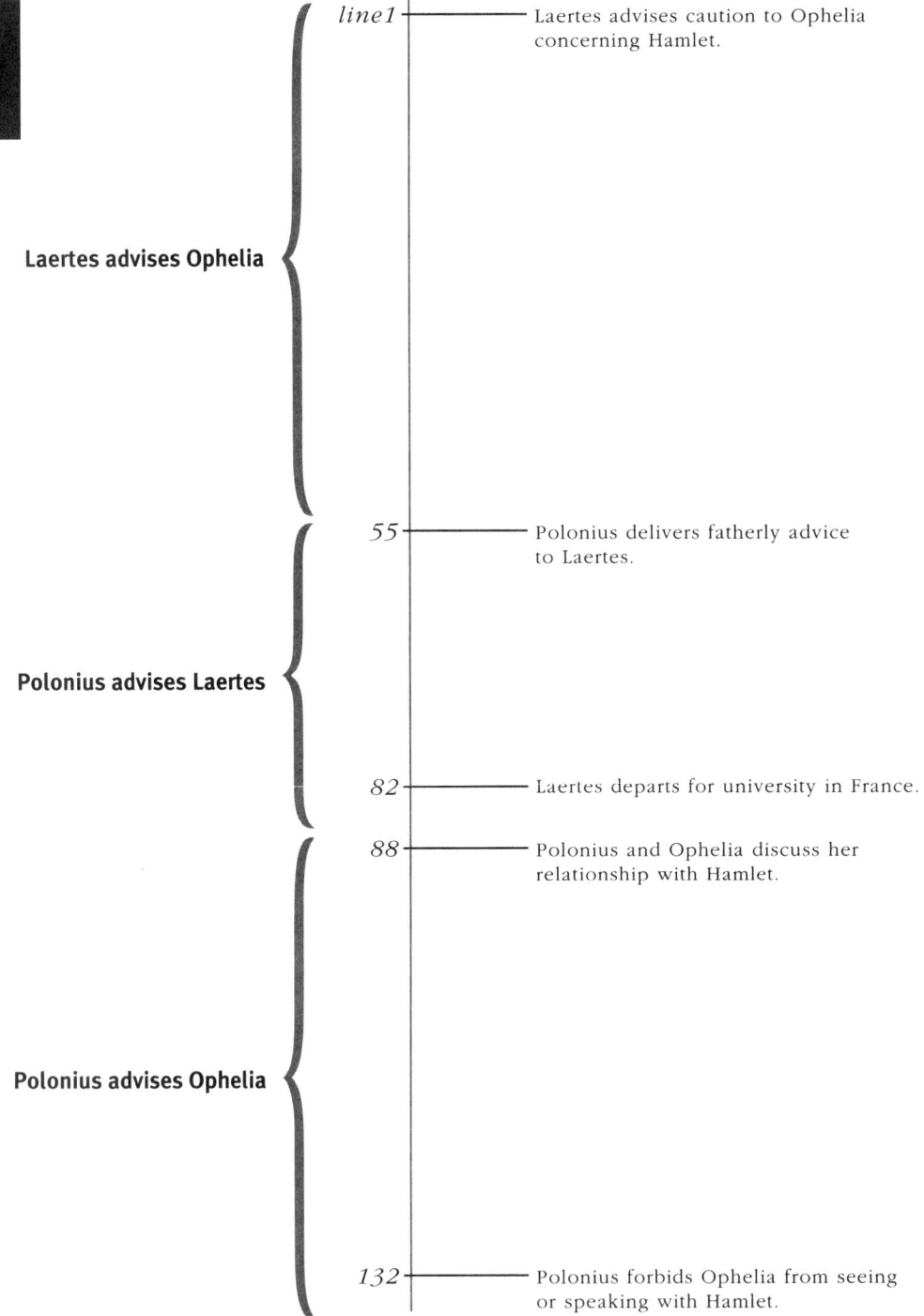

Laertes advises Ophelia
- line 1 — Laertes advises caution to Ophelia concerning Hamlet.

Polonius advises Laertes
- 55 — Polonius delivers fatherly advice to Laertes.
- 82 — Laertes departs for university in France.

Polonius advises Ophelia
- 88 — Polonius and Ophelia discuss her relationship with Hamlet.
- 132 — Polonius forbids Ophelia from seeing or speaking with Hamlet.

Hamlet joins the night watch.	*line 1*	
Hamlet and Horatio comment on the drunken revels of Claudius.	7	**The following night's watch**
The ghost appears and beckons to Hamlet.	17	**The ghost appears**
Horatio and Marcellus urge Hamlet not to follow the ghost.	41	**Hamlet's determination to follow the ghost**
Hamlet follows the ghost.	61	
Horatio and Marcellus follow after Hamlet.	63	

1.4

DRAMATIC MAPS | 1.3 & 1.4 | 161

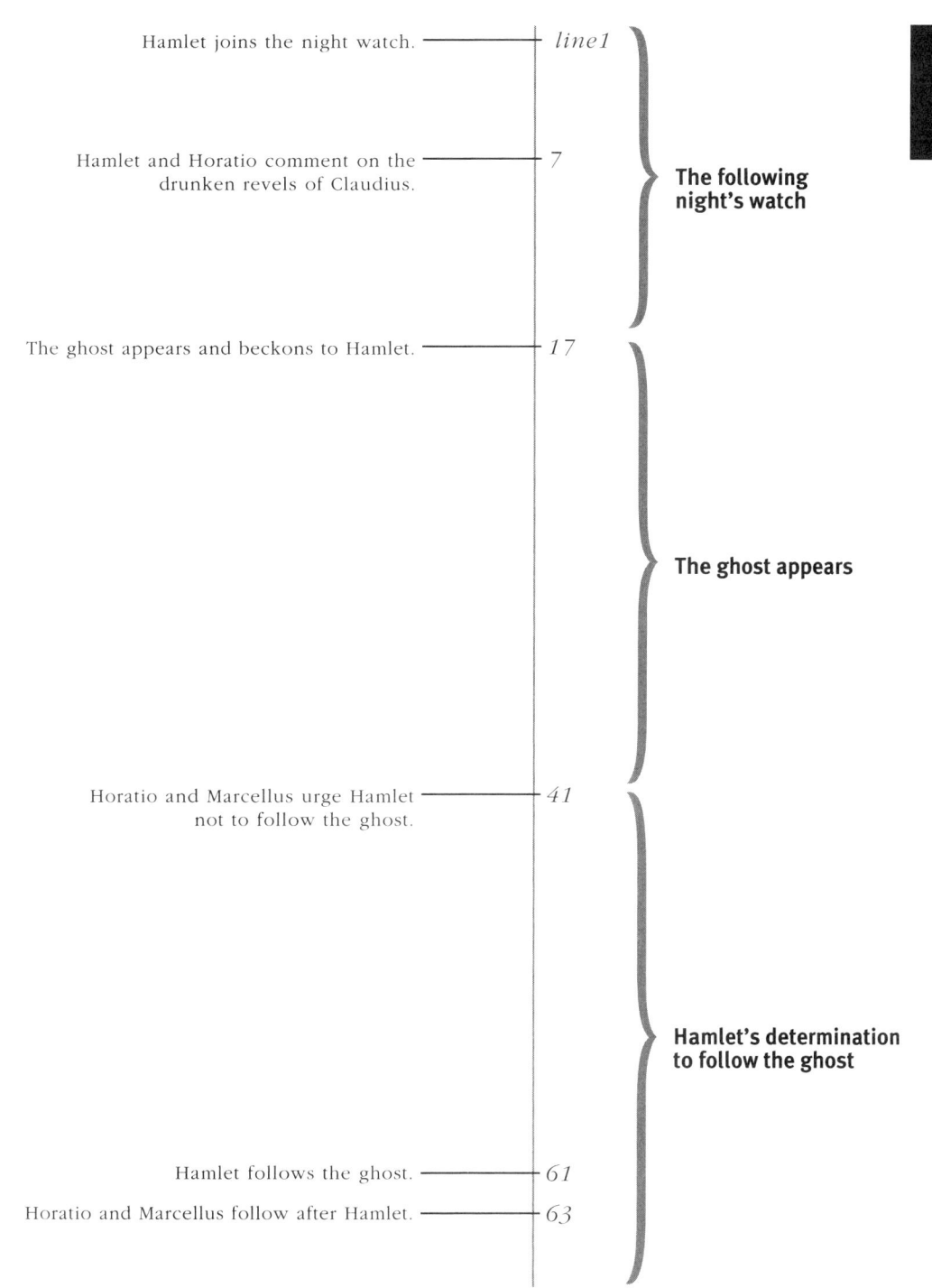

1.5

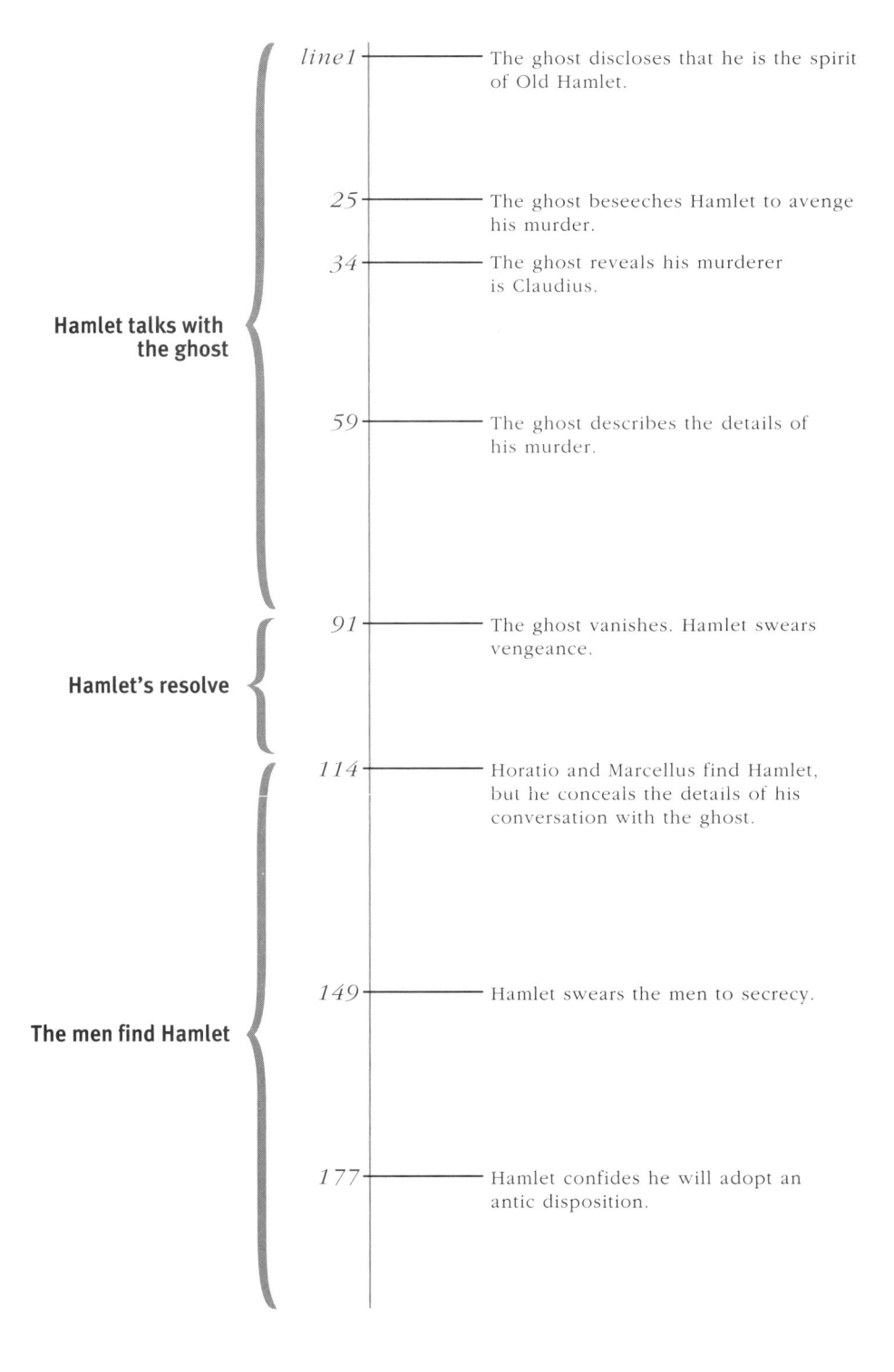

Hamlet talks with the ghost
- *line 1* — The ghost discloses that he is the spirit of Old Hamlet.
- *25* — The ghost beseeches Hamlet to avenge his murder.
- *34* — The ghost reveals his murderer is Claudius.
- *59* — The ghost describes the details of his murder.

Hamlet's resolve
- *91* — The ghost vanishes. Hamlet swears vengeance.

The men find Hamlet
- *114* — Horatio and Marcellus find Hamlet, but he conceals the details of his conversation with the ghost.
- *149* — Hamlet swears the men to secrecy.
- *177* — Hamlet confides he will adopt an antic disposition.

Polonius sends Reynaldo to spy on — *line 1*
Laertes in France.

2.1

} **Reynaldo sent to spy**

Ophelia bursts in, upset. She describes — *75*
her encounter with Hamlet.

} **The frightened Ophelia**

Polonius concludes that Hamlet's madness — *111*
has been caused by Ophelia's rejection.

Polonius and Ophelia go to the king. — *118*

2.2 part 1

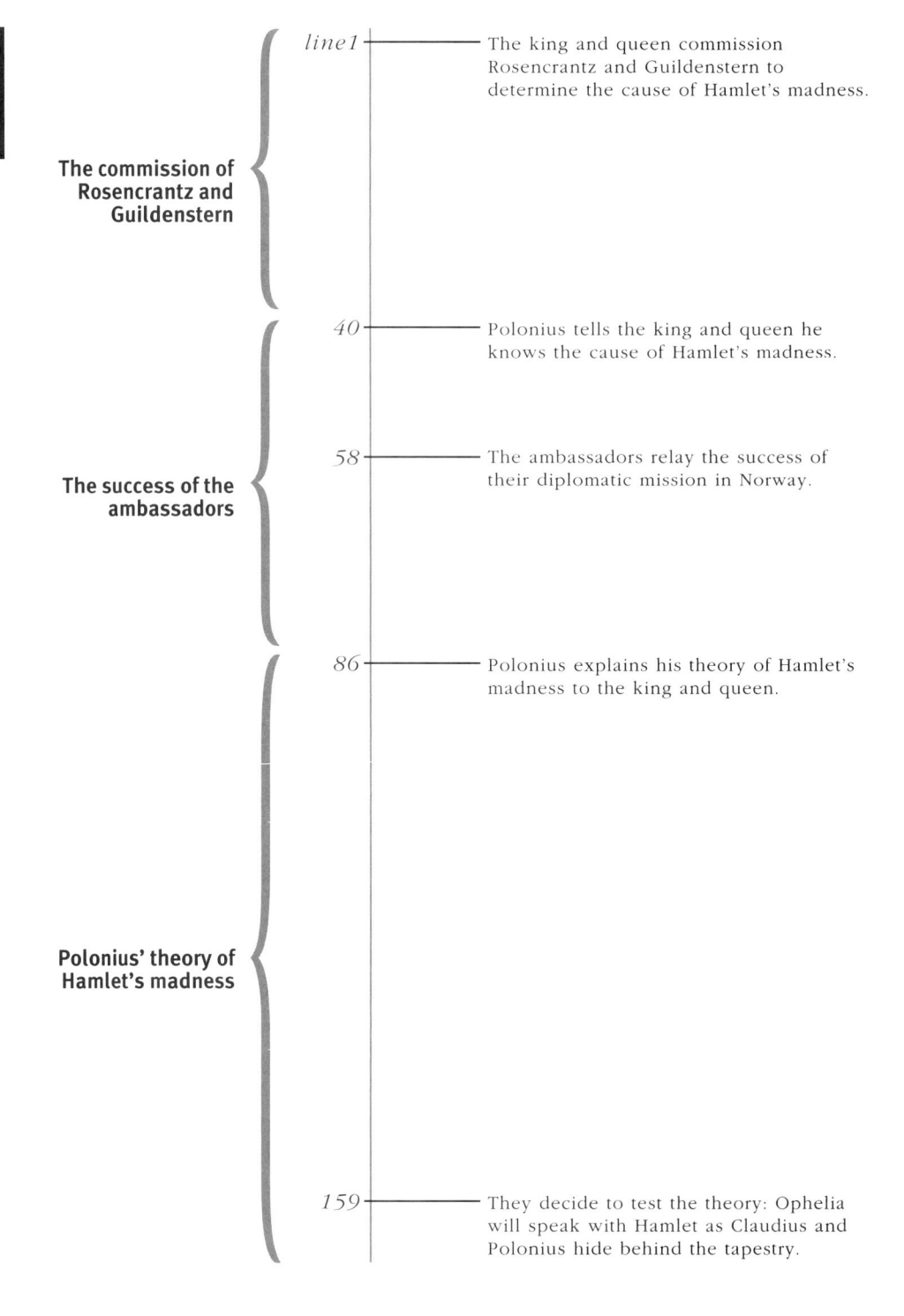

The commission of Rosencrantz and Guildenstern

line 1 — The king and queen commission Rosencrantz and Guildenstern to determine the cause of Hamlet's madness.

The success of the ambassadors

40 — Polonius tells the king and queen he knows the cause of Hamlet's madness.

58 — The ambassadors relay the success of their diplomatic mission in Norway.

Polonius' theory of Hamlet's madness

86 — Polonius explains his theory of Hamlet's madness to the king and queen.

159 — They decide to test the theory: Ophelia will speak with Hamlet as Claudius and Polonius hide behind the tapestry.

2.2 part 2

Hamlet speaks in antic fashion to Polonius. — *line 168*

} **Hamlet confounds Polonius**

As Polonius exits, Rosencrantz and Guildenstern enter. They speak with Hamlet, who uncovers their motivations. — *217*

Rosencrantz and Guildenstern tell Hamlet of the players. — *313*

} **Hamlet outmaneuvers Rosencrantz and Guildenstern**

Hamlet warns he is only feigning madness. — *371*
Polonius brings word the players have arrived in Elsinore. Hamlet jests with him. — *384*
The players arrive. — *414*
At Hamlet's request, the lead actor recites a speech about the fall of Troy. — *423*

} **The arrival of the players**

Hamlet commissions a performance of *The Death of Gonzago*. — *524*
Hamlet's soliloquy of self-admonishment. He decides to reveal Claudius' guilt with a play. — *537*

} **Hamlet's soliloquy of self-admonishment**

DRAMATIC MAPS | 2.2 | 165

3.1

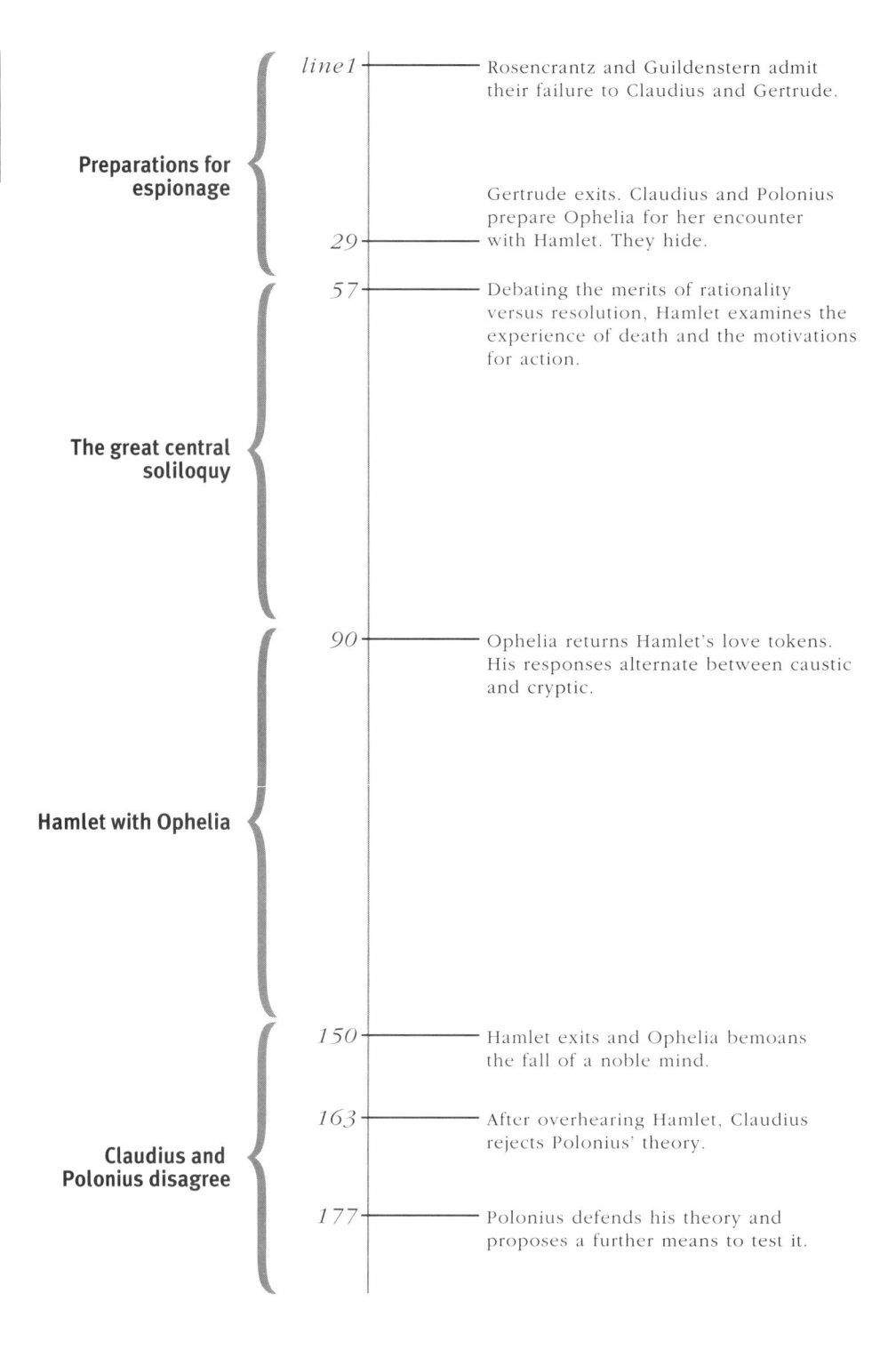

Preparations for espionage

- *line 1* — Rosencrantz and Guildenstern admit their failure to Claudius and Gertrude.
- *29* — Gertrude exits. Claudius and Polonius prepare Ophelia for her encounter with Hamlet. They hide.

The great central soliloquy

- *57* — Debating the merits of rationality versus resolution, Hamlet examines the experience of death and the motivations for action.

Hamlet with Ophelia

- *90* — Ophelia returns Hamlet's love tokens. His responses alternate between caustic and cryptic.

Claudius and Polonius disagree

- *150* — Hamlet exits and Ophelia bemoans the fall of a noble mind.
- *163* — After overhearing Hamlet, Claudius rejects Polonius' theory.
- *177* — Polonius defends his theory and proposes a further means to test it.

3.2

Line	Event	Section
line 1	Hamlet gives last-minute direction to the actors.	**Before the play**
47	Hamlet praises Horatio for his temperance. He assigns Horatio to watch Claudius' reaction to the play.	
85	The playgoers arrive. Hamlet jests at Polonius' expense, then makes innuendo-riddled wordplay with Ophelia.	
127	The pantomime begins.	**The Mousetrap**
139	The play begins. Hamlet interprets.	
249	Claudius runs out, stopping the show. Hamlet gloats over his victory.	**Gertrude sends for Hamlet**
279	Rosencrantz and Guildenstern inform Hamlet that the queen wishes to see him.	
317	Rosencrantz presses Hamlet for the cause of his distemper.	
356	Polonius tells Hamlet that the queen wishes to speak with him.	
370	Hamlet resolves to speak frankly with the queen.	

3.3

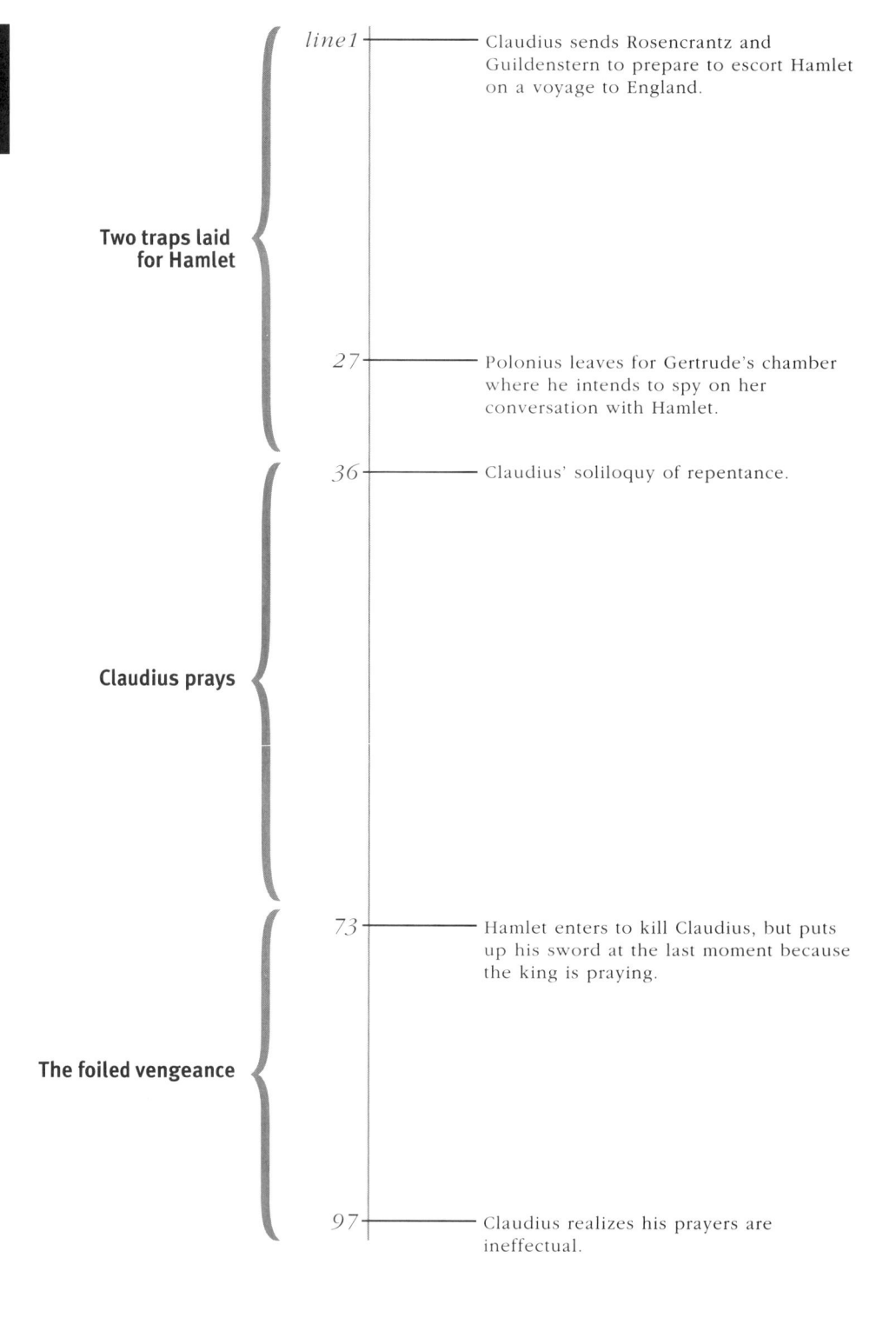

Two traps laid for Hamlet
- *line 1* — Claudius sends Rosencrantz and Guildenstern to prepare to escort Hamlet on a voyage to England.
- *27* — Polonius leaves for Gertrude's chamber where he intends to spy on her conversation with Hamlet.

Claudius prays
- *36* — Claudius' soliloquy of repentance.

The foiled vengeance
- *73* — Hamlet enters to kill Claudius, but puts up his sword at the last moment because the king is praying.
- *97* — Claudius realizes his prayers are ineffectual.

3.4

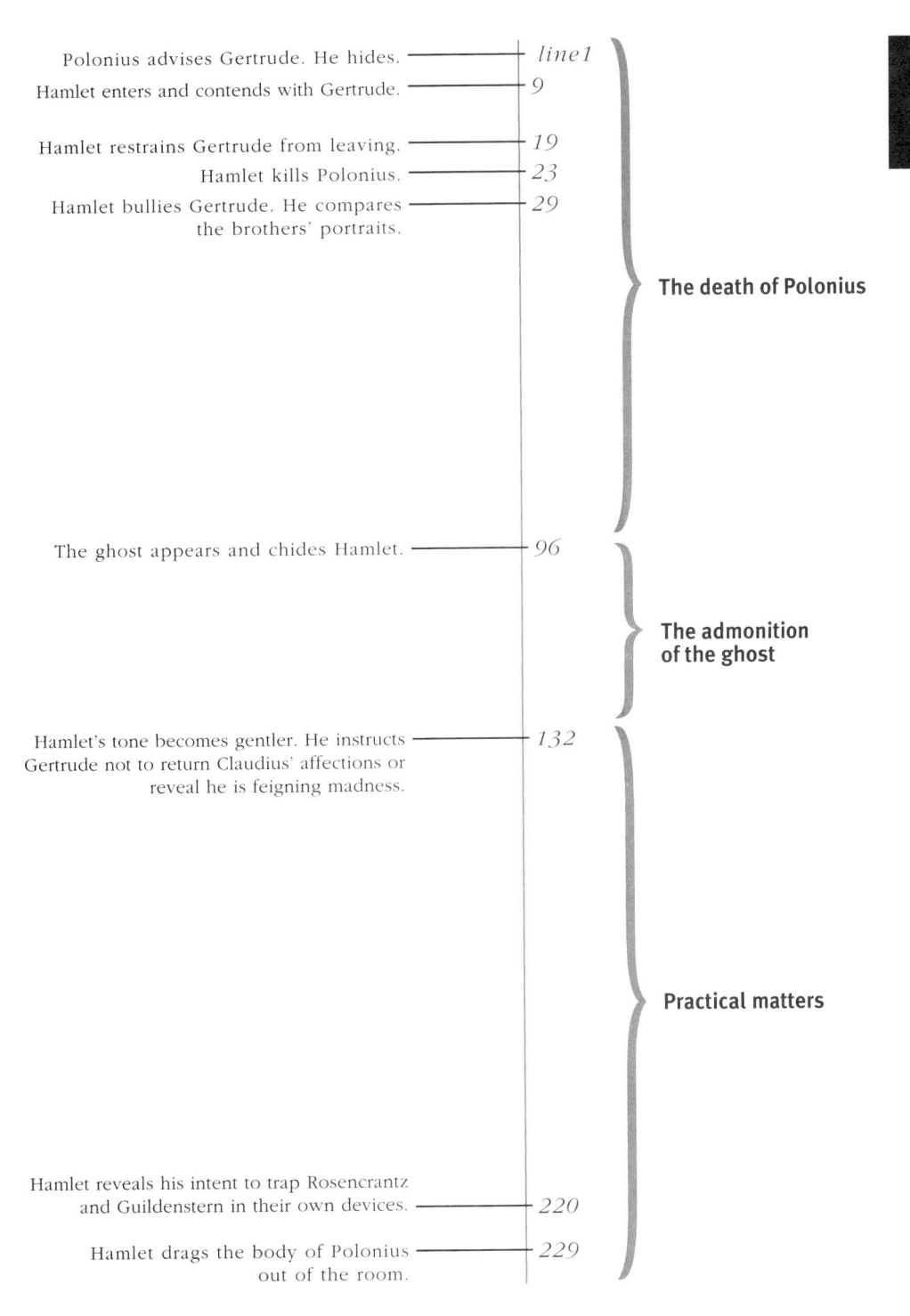

Polonius advises Gertrude. He hides. — *line 1*
Hamlet enters and contends with Gertrude. — *9*

Hamlet restrains Gertrude from leaving. — *19*
Hamlet kills Polonius. — *23*
Hamlet bullies Gertrude. He compares — *29*
the brothers' portraits.

The death of Polonius

The ghost appears and chides Hamlet. — *96*

The admonition of the ghost

Hamlet's tone becomes gentler. He instructs — *132*
Gertrude not to return Claudius' affections or
reveal he is feigning madness.

Practical matters

Hamlet reveals his intent to trap Rosencrantz
and Guildenstern in their own devices. — *220*
Hamlet drags the body of Polonius — *229*
out of the room.

4.1

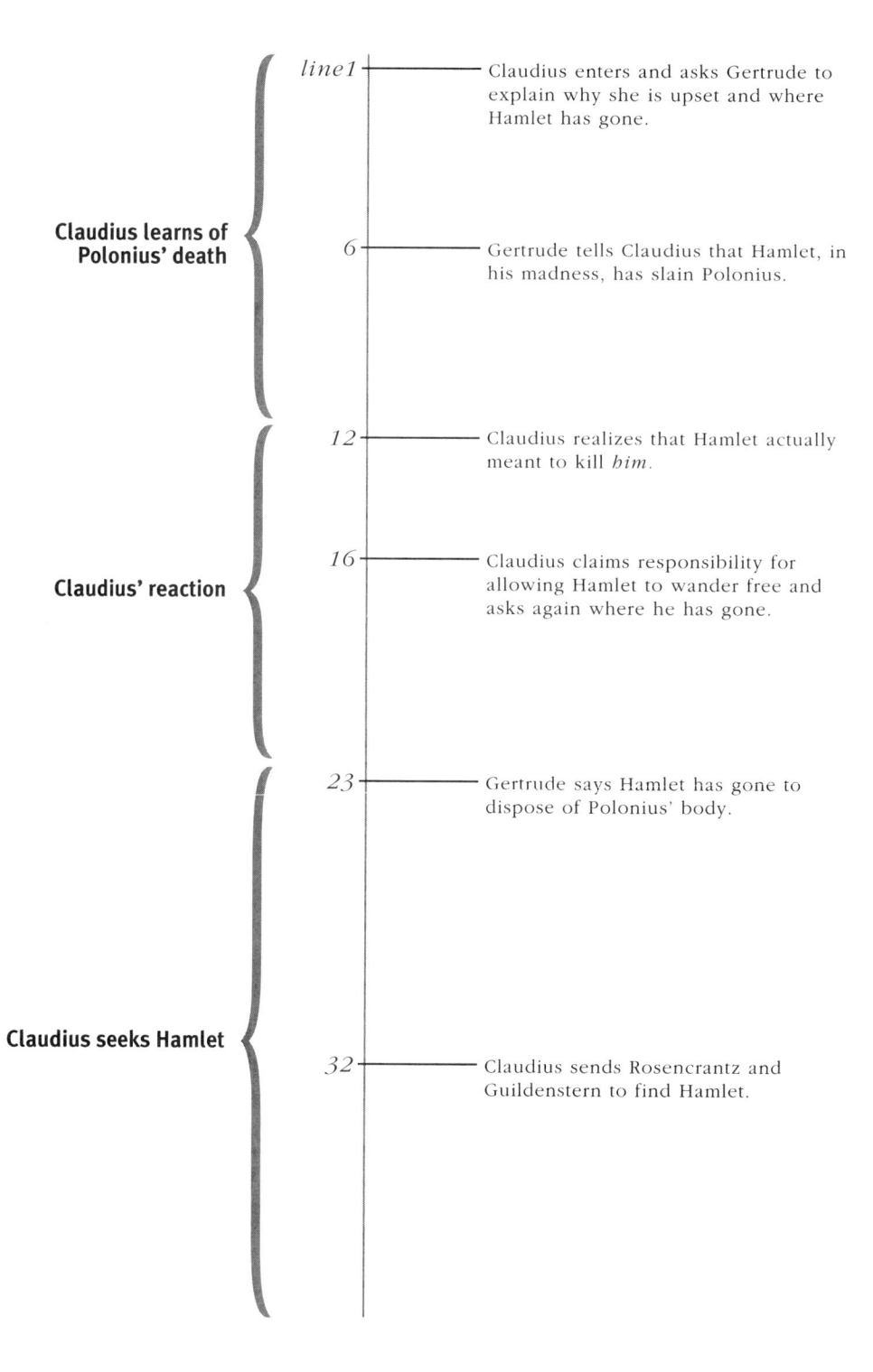

Claudius learns of Polonius' death

- *line 1* — Claudius enters and asks Gertrude to explain why she is upset and where Hamlet has gone.
- *6* — Gertrude tells Claudius that Hamlet, in his madness, has slain Polonius.

Claudius' reaction

- *12* — Claudius realizes that Hamlet actually meant to kill *him*.
- *16* — Claudius claims responsibility for allowing Hamlet to wander free and asks again where he has gone.

Claudius seeks Hamlet

- *23* — Gertrude says Hamlet has gone to dispose of Polonius' body.
- *32* — Claudius sends Rosencrantz and Guildenstern to find Hamlet.

4.2

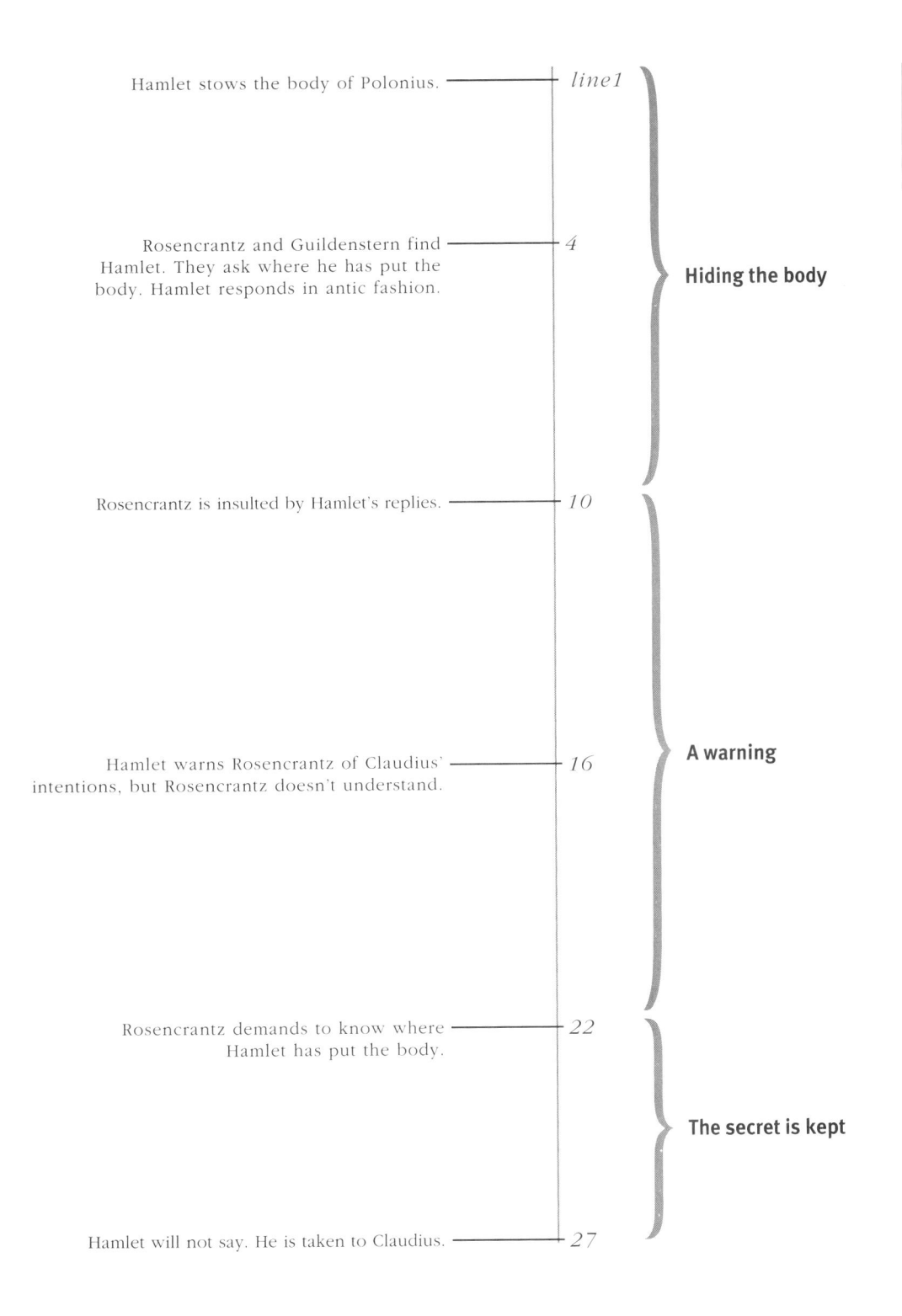

Hamlet stows the body of Polonius. — *line 1*

Rosencrantz and Guildenstern find Hamlet. They ask where he has put the body. Hamlet responds in antic fashion. — *4*

} **Hiding the body**

Rosencrantz is insulted by Hamlet's replies. — *10*

Hamlet warns Rosencrantz of Claudius' intentions, but Rosencrantz doesn't understand. — *16*

} **A warning**

Rosencrantz demands to know where Hamlet has put the body. — *22*

} **The secret is kept**

Hamlet will not say. He is taken to Claudius. — *27*

4.3

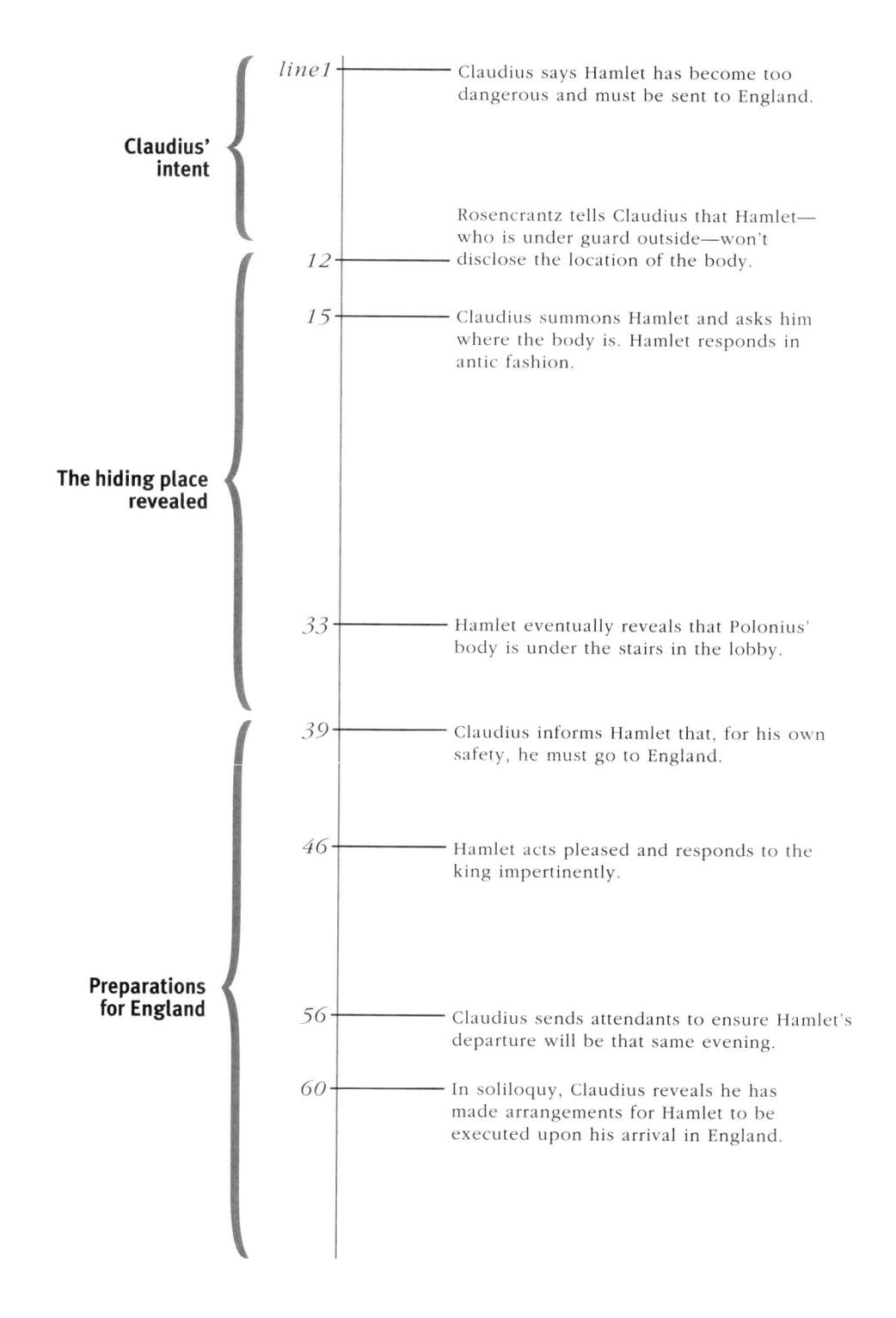

Claudius' intent

- *line 1* — Claudius says Hamlet has become too dangerous and must be sent to England.

The hiding place revealed

- 12 — Rosencrantz tells Claudius that Hamlet—who is under guard outside—won't disclose the location of the body.
- 15 — Claudius summons Hamlet and asks him where the body is. Hamlet responds in antic fashion.
- 33 — Hamlet eventually reveals that Polonius' body is under the stairs in the lobby.

Preparations for England

- 39 — Claudius informs Hamlet that, for his own safety, he must go to England.
- 46 — Hamlet acts pleased and responds to the king impertinently.
- 56 — Claudius sends attendants to ensure Hamlet's departure will be that same evening.
- 60 — In soliloquy, Claudius reveals he has made arrangements for Hamlet to be executed upon his arrival in England.

4.4

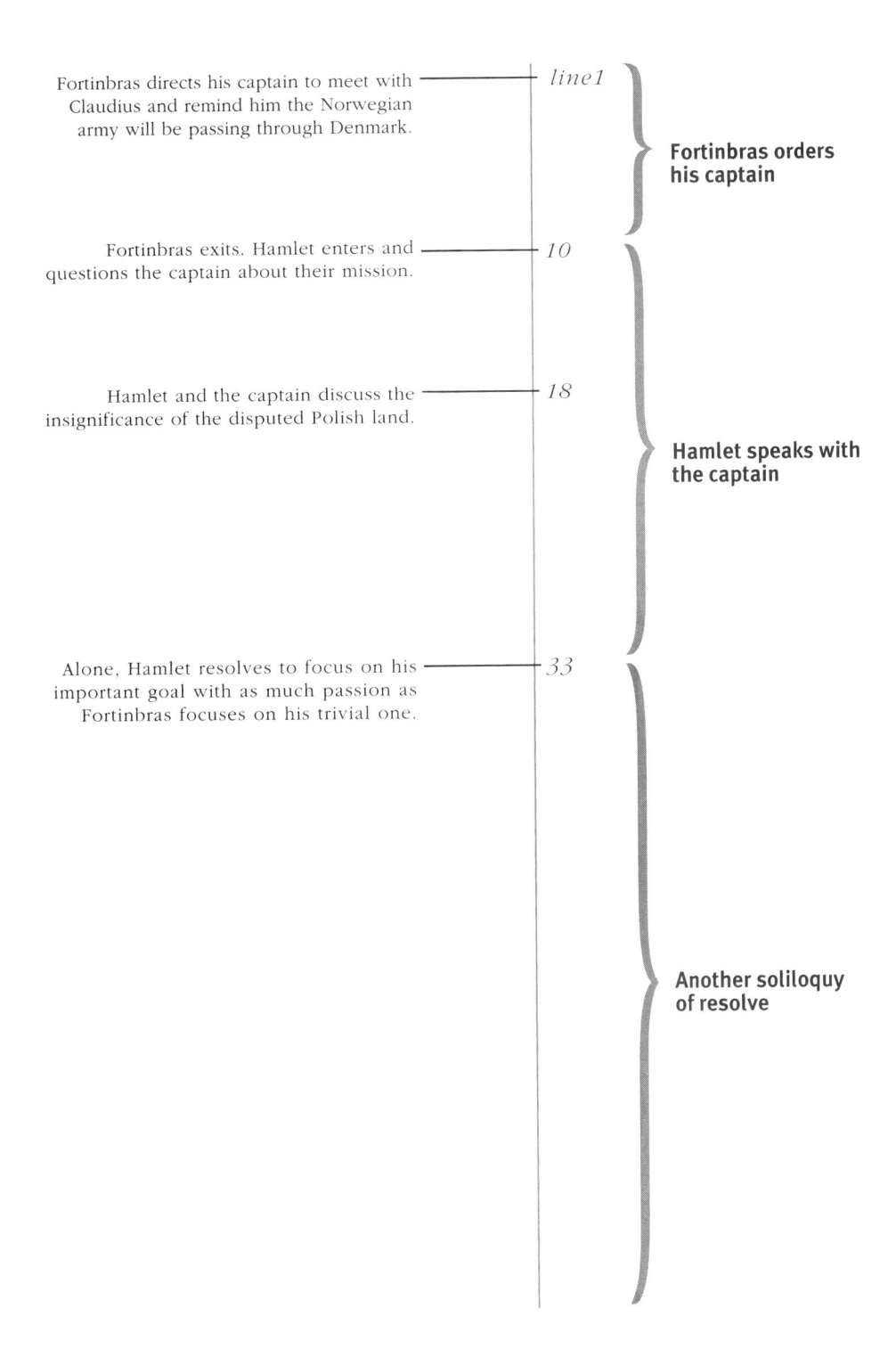

Fortinbras orders his captain

Fortinbras directs his captain to meet with Claudius and remind him the Norwegian army will be passing through Denmark. — *line 1*

Hamlet speaks with the captain

Fortinbras exits. Hamlet enters and questions the captain about their mission. — *10*

Hamlet and the captain discuss the insignificance of the disputed Polish land. — *18*

Another soliloquy of resolve

Alone, Hamlet resolves to focus on his important goal with as much passion as Fortinbras focuses on his trivial one. — *33*

DRAMATIC MAPS | 4.3 & 4.4 | 173

4.5

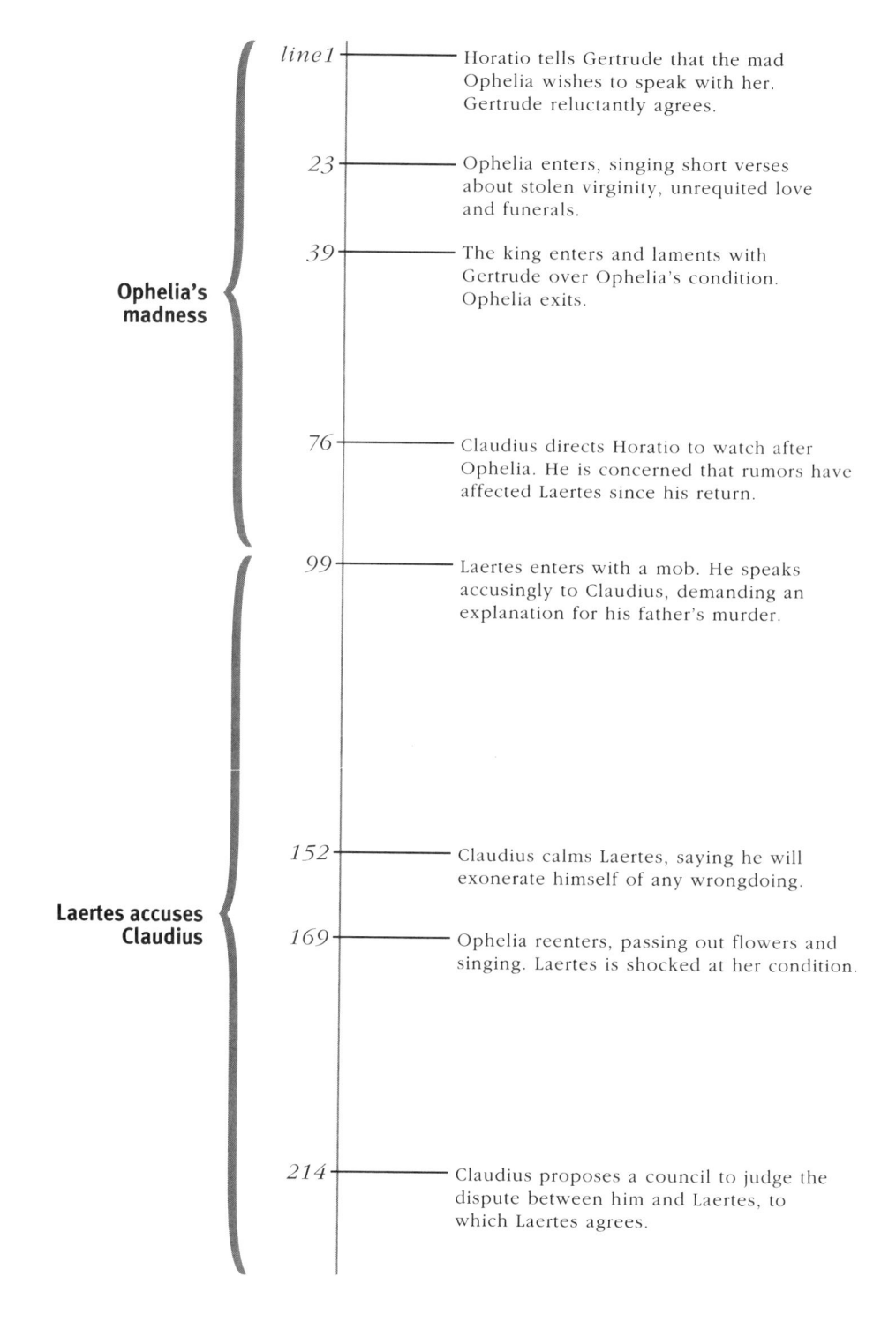

Ophelia's madness

- *line 1* — Horatio tells Gertrude that the mad Ophelia wishes to speak with her. Gertrude reluctantly agrees.
- *23* — Ophelia enters, singing short verses about stolen virginity, unrequited love and funerals.
- *39* — The king enters and laments with Gertrude over Ophelia's condition. Ophelia exits.
- *76* — Claudius directs Horatio to watch after Ophelia. He is concerned that rumors have affected Laertes since his return.

Laertes accuses Claudius

- *99* — Laertes enters with a mob. He speaks accusingly to Claudius, demanding an explanation for his father's murder.
- *152* — Claudius calms Laertes, saying he will exonerate himself of any wrongdoing.
- *169* — Ophelia reenters, passing out flowers and singing. Laertes is shocked at her condition.
- *214* — Claudius proposes a council to judge the dispute between him and Laertes, to which Laertes agrees.

4.6

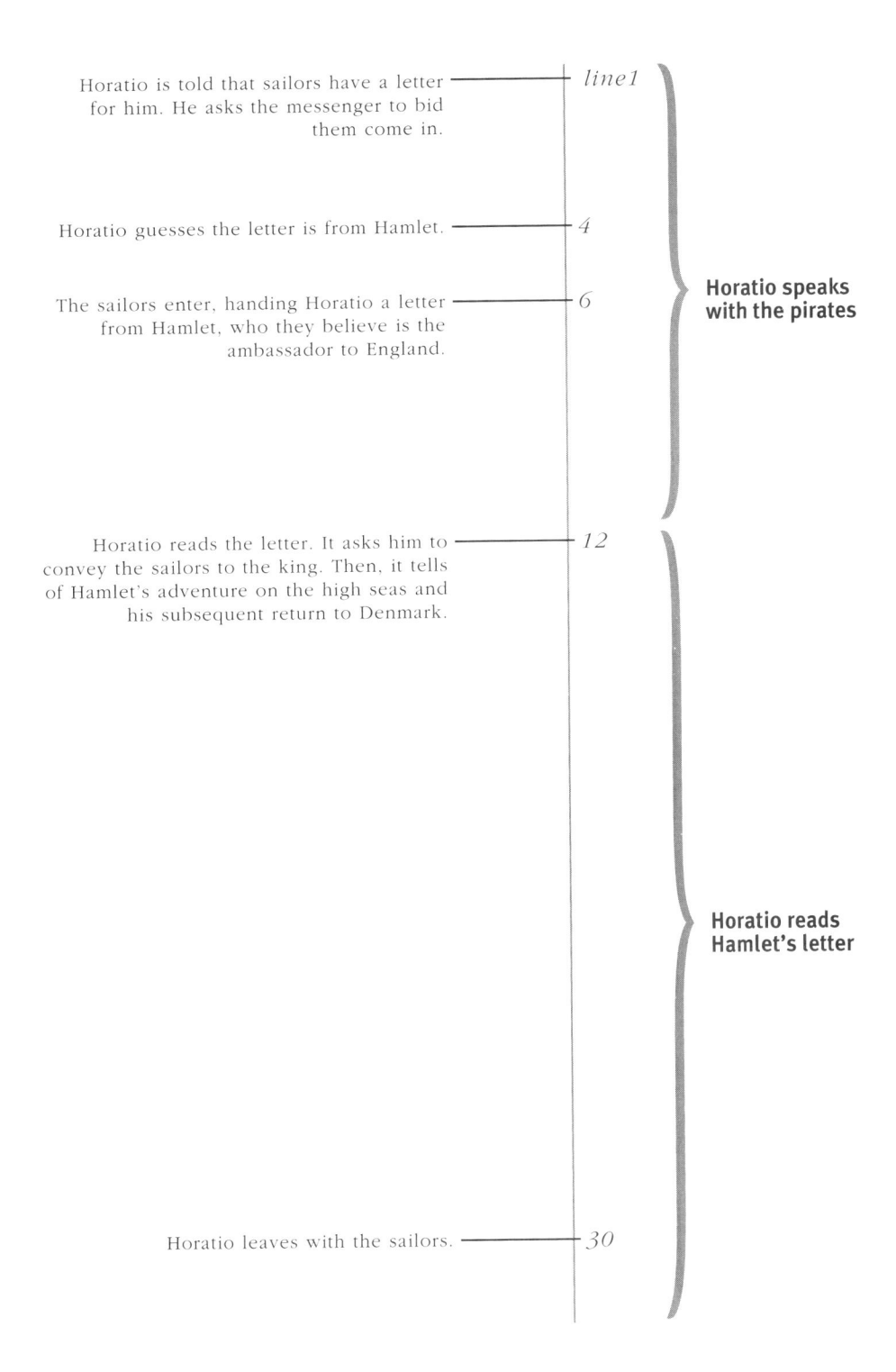

Horatio is told that sailors have a letter for him. He asks the messenger to bid them come in.	*line 1*	
Horatio guesses the letter is from Hamlet.	*4*	**Horatio speaks with the pirates**
The sailors enter, handing Horatio a letter from Hamlet, who they believe is the ambassador to England.	*6*	
Horatio reads the letter. It asks him to convey the sailors to the king. Then, it tells of Hamlet's adventure on the high seas and his subsequent return to Denmark.	*12*	**Horatio reads Hamlet's letter**
Horatio leaves with the sailors.	*30*	

4.7

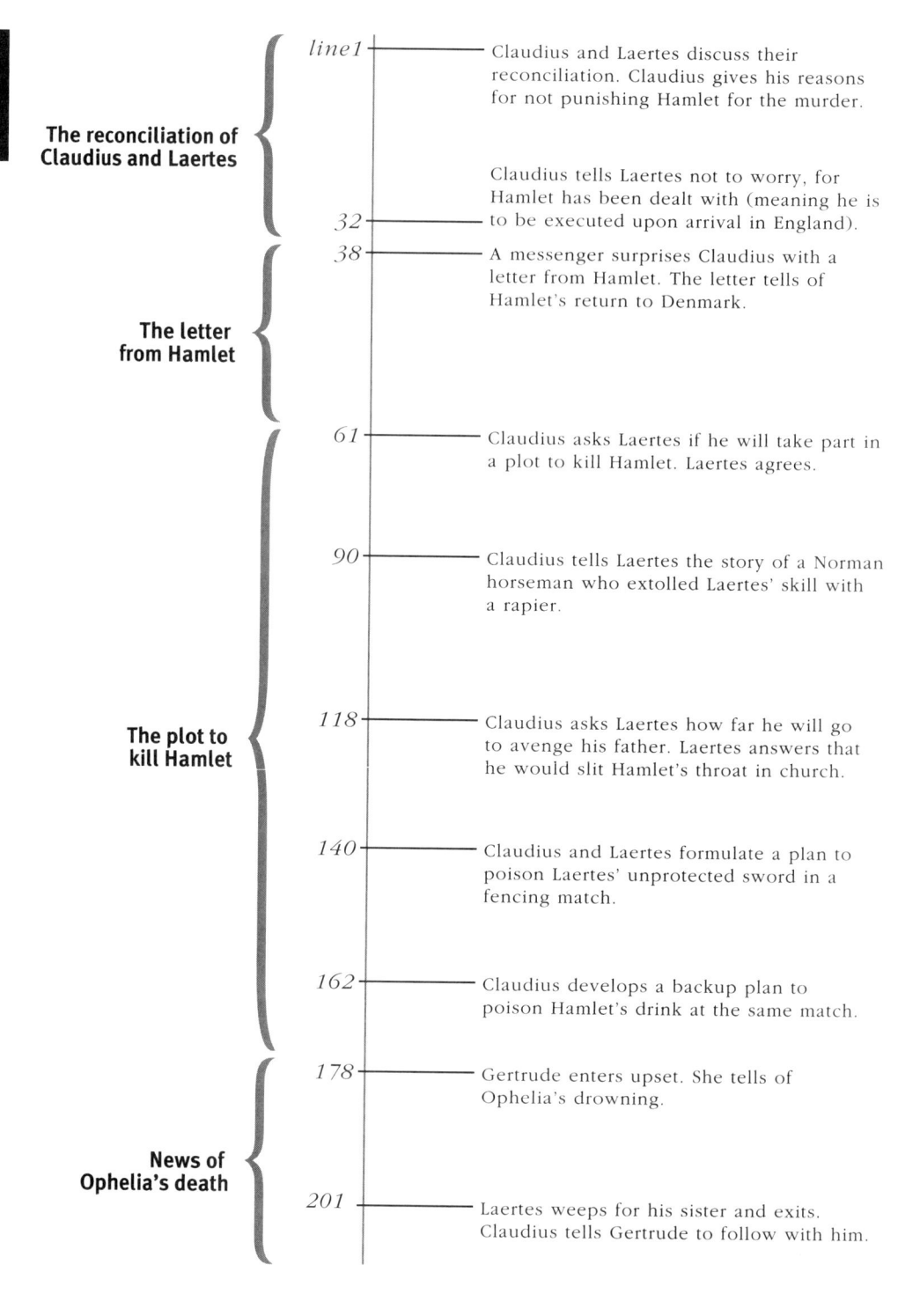

The reconciliation of Claudius and Laertes

- **line 1** — Claudius and Laertes discuss their reconciliation. Claudius gives his reasons for not punishing Hamlet for the murder.
- **32** — Claudius tells Laertes not to worry, for Hamlet has been dealt with (meaning he is to be executed upon arrival in England).

The letter from Hamlet

- **38** — A messenger surprises Claudius with a letter from Hamlet. The letter tells of Hamlet's return to Denmark.

The plot to kill Hamlet

- **61** — Claudius asks Laertes if he will take part in a plot to kill Hamlet. Laertes agrees.
- **90** — Claudius tells Laertes the story of a Norman horseman who extolled Laertes' skill with a rapier.
- **118** — Claudius asks Laertes how far he will go to avenge his father. Laertes answers that he would slit Hamlet's throat in church.
- **140** — Claudius and Laertes formulate a plan to poison Laertes' unprotected sword in a fencing match.
- **162** — Claudius develops a backup plan to poison Hamlet's drink at the same match.

News of Ophelia's death

- **178** — Gertrude enters upset. She tells of Ophelia's drowning.
- **201** — Laertes weeps for his sister and exits. Claudius tells Gertrude to follow with him.

5.1

Two gravediggers discuss the spiritual loopholes of suicide and the profession of gravedigging. — *line 1*

The second gravedigger is sent for a stoup of liquor while the first gravedigger continues working and singing. — *56*

} **The gravediggers jest**

Hamlet and Horatio enter. The gravedigger tosses up two skulls. Hamlet muses over their possible professions during life. — *63*

Hamlet and the gravedigger talk about the person whose grave he is digging (Hamlet doesn't yet know it's Ophelia's grave). — *110*

The gravedigger says he's been working his trade since the day of Hamlet's birth (He doesn't realize he's talking to the prince). — *138*

Seeing the skull of his childhood companion and father's jester, Yorick, Hamlet recalls fond memories. — *170*

} **Musings about life and death**

Ophelia's funeral procession enters. — *204*

Laertes jumps into Ophelia's grave and laments, cursing Hamlet. — *234*

Hamlet comes forward. He and Laertes fight. Gertrude says Hamlet is mad and therefore not responsible for his actions. — *244*

Hamlet leaves and Horatio follows. Claudius urges Laertes to be patient and tells Gertrude to tend to Hamlet. — *287*

} **Ophelia's funeral**

DRAMATIC MAPS | 4.7 & 5.1 | 177

5.2 *part 1*

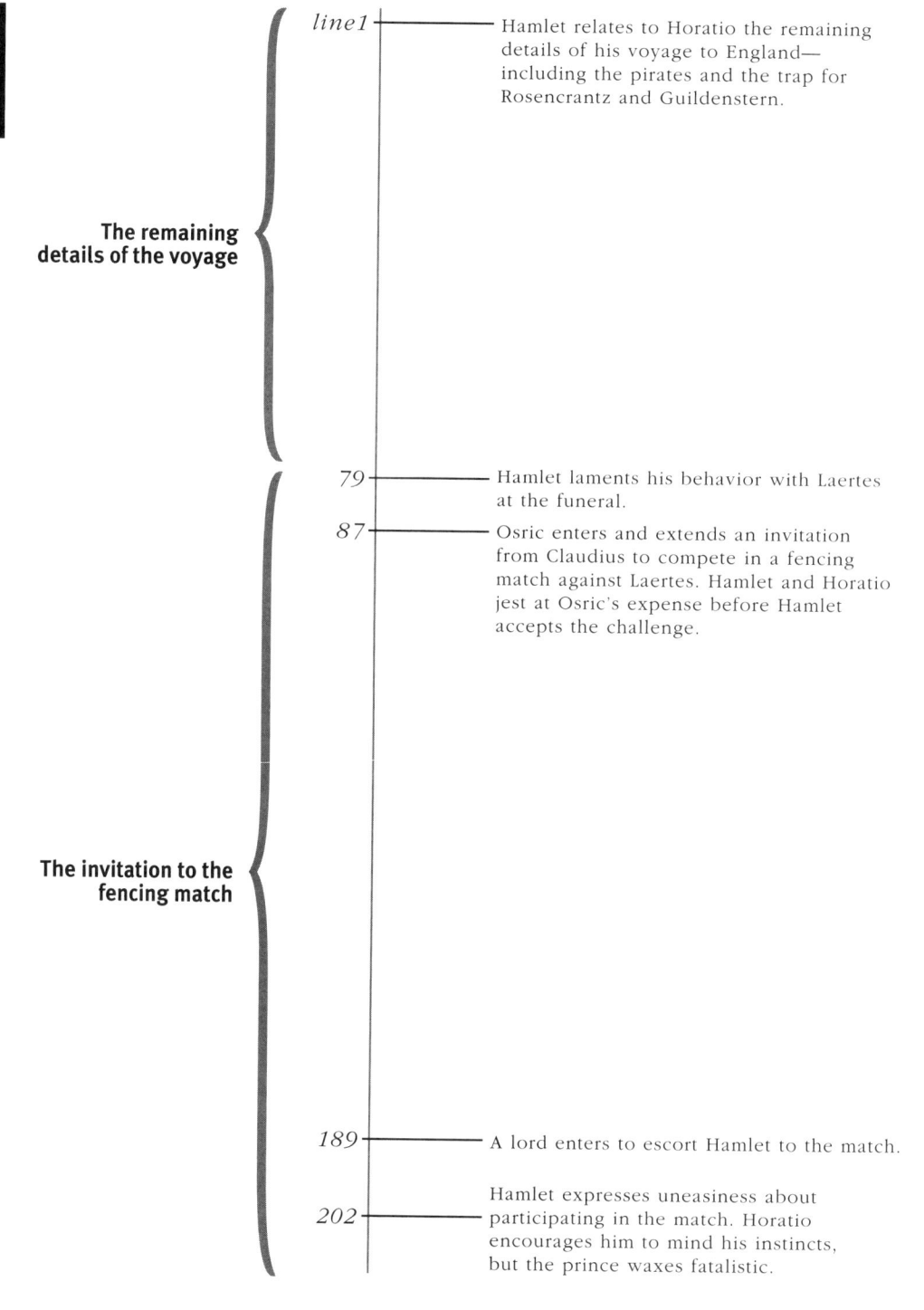

The remaining details of the voyage

line 1 — Hamlet relates to Horatio the remaining details of his voyage to England—including the pirates and the trap for Rosencrantz and Guildenstern.

The invitation to the fencing match

79 — Hamlet laments his behavior with Laertes at the funeral.

87 — Osric enters and extends an invitation from Claudius to compete in a fencing match against Laertes. Hamlet and Horatio jest at Osric's expense before Hamlet accepts the challenge.

189 — A lord enters to escort Hamlet to the match.

202 — Hamlet expresses uneasiness about participating in the match. Horatio encourages him to mind his instincts, but the prince waxes fatalistic.

Hamlet apologizes for his behavior at — 217
Ophelia's funeral. Laertes accepts it at
face value but does not unreservedly
clear the offense.

5.2 *part 2*

} **Hamlet's apology to Laertes**

Hamlet and Laertes choose their rapiers.
Laertes chooses the poisoned weapon.
Claudius proposes they toast if Hamlet
opens well in the match.
He poisons the cup. — 254

Hamlet scores the first hit. Claudius offers
the cup to Hamlet, who refuses it. — 276
Hamlet scores a second hit. Gertrude drinks — 286
from the cup ignoring Claudius' plea.
They play again to a draw. Laertes cuts — 306
Hamlet. In a scuffle, they exchange rapiers.
Hamlet cuts Laertes. Gertrude falls, poisoned.

Laertes confesses all, naming Claudius. — 323
Hamlet stabs Claudius and forces him to
drink the remaining poison. Claudius dies.
Laertes dies after an exchange of pardons. — 340
Horatio attempts suicide, but is stopped by — 350
Hamlet, who commissions him to tell his story.
Fortinbras is heard approaching. Hamlet — 362
bequeaths Denmark to the Norwegian
prince and then dies.

} **The deadly finale**

DRAMATIC MAPS | 5.2 | 179

APPENDIX B: BACKGROUND

We decided after careful thought to place the background material—generally the first information you see—at the end of the guidebook. The two most compelling reasons for doing so were, first, we did not want to lose the powerful beginning of the opening chapter ("This is Hamlet"); and, second, it has been our experience that the background material is usually passed over and then read last anyway. Having said this, we feel that the material in Appendix B is extremely useful to the reader wishing an expanded view of Shakespeare's life, sources, and personal investment in *Hamlet,* as well as the major versions of the play that exist today and a general discussion of the time setting.

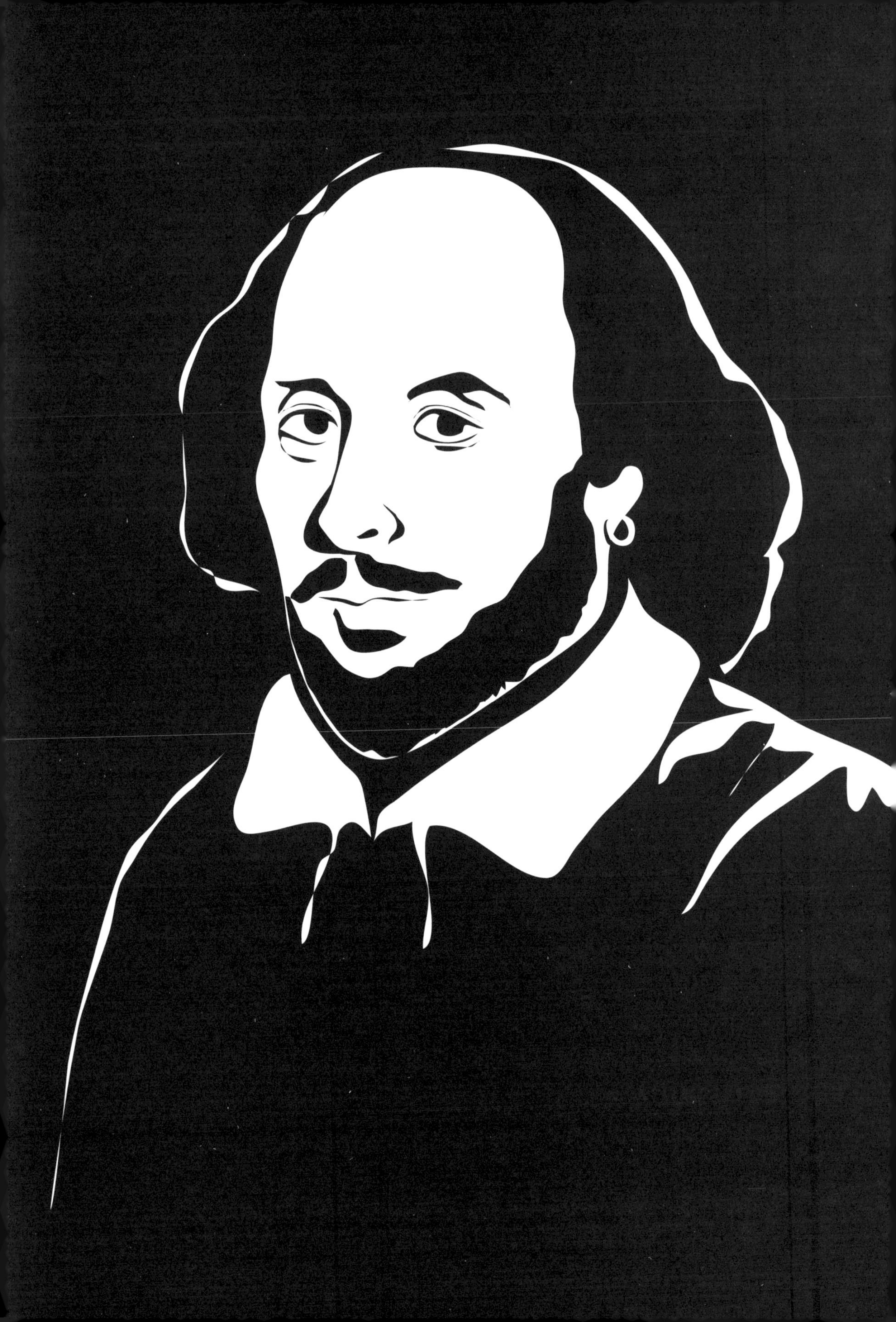

Shakespeare achieved success in his lifetime.

BUSINESSMAN. Born in 1564—the same year as Galileo—by the time William Shakespeare was 28, he had settled in London as an actor. At 30, he became a shareholder in the Lord Chamberlain's Men, a successful company who often staged plays at court for Queen Elizabeth I.

ACTOR. Shakespeare began as a player and part-time playwright, later focusing all of his energies on writing. He mostly acted character parts—not leading roles—although he is known to have played the character of Old Hamlet's ghost. He received far more income from his acting than from his writing royalties.

PLAYWRIGHT. He is widely regarded as the greatest dramatist of western literature and by some as the greatest thinker. Shakespeare's plays, replete with insights into human character, are performed more often than any other playwright's in history. He achieved success in his own lifetime and, by the time his wife died in 1623, a monument to Shakespeare had been erected in Holy Trinity Church in their hometown of Stratford.

1. Danish Oral Tradition

Most scholars believe *Amlódí* of oral tradition was the original Hamlet. He appears in a compilation of these traditions, known as the *Prose Edda*.

2. *History of Denmark* by Saxo Grammaticus

Saxo Grammaticus, c. 1200, wrote this nine volume work. One of the stories involves Amleth, son of Horwendil. In the story, Horwendil is murdered by his brother, Feng, to win the love of Gerutha. After he grows up, Amleth dedicates his life to avenge his father's murder. He feigns madness, but always speaks the truth, shrouded in riddle. A beautiful girl is sent to seduce Amleth to discover if he is bent on revenge, but his foster-brother warns him of the plot. Feng's counselor is murdered when Amleth is talking to his mother and discovers him hiding under the bed. Amleth feeds the body to the pigs. Feng sends Amleth to England with two escorts who possess a hidden order for Amleth's execution. Amleth switches the letter with one which calls for the execution of the escorts and calls for the King of England to marry his daughter to Amleth, which consequently happens. Amleth returns home to his own funeral, which he ordered his mother to observe before he left for England. His arrival creates a stir and eventually Amleth kills Feng with the king's own sword. He then tells his people what he has done and why. The people support Amleth enthusiastically, making him their next king.

3. *Tragic Histories* by Belleforest

In Belleforest's version of the story, which is largely identical to Saxo's, Fengon (the counterpart to *Feng*) is said to have desecrated his brother's marriage bed even before the murder. Geruthe strongly denies any complicity to the murder during an emotionally intense conversation with Amleth, after the discovery of the spying counselor. Belleforest describes Amleth as being overly melancholy and the author moralizes about the rightness of his passionate desire for vengeance.

4. The *Ur-Hamlet*

Ur is a German prefix meaning "proto, first or original." While only references to this play exist, we do have evidence that it included the introduction of the ghost of Hamlet's father, who calls for the vengeance of his murder. The play had average turnouts and apparently the phrase, "Hamlet, revenge!" became a popular jest. Whether Shakespeare or Thomas Kyd wrote this early version, no scholars believe it contained the depth of introspection that Shakespeare's subsequent version possesses.

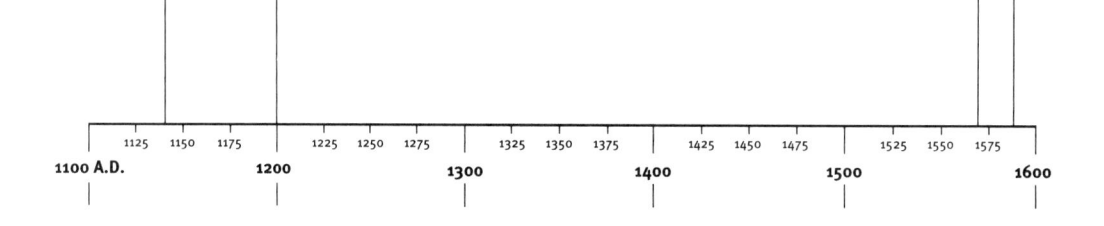

Shakespeare adapted the plot of *Hamlet*.

ORIGINAL STORY: *HISTORY OF DENMARK*, c.1200
Saxo Grammaticus, an early thirteenth-century historian, wrote the *History of Denmark*, including the first full account of the story of Amleth, son of a murdered king. The foundation of the modern story exists, but does not mention the ghost, the players, the play-within-the-play, Ophelia's madness and death, Laertes, the pirates, the gravediggers or Fortinbras.

SHAKESPEARE'S SOURCE: *TRAGIC HISTORIES*, 1570.
Saxo's story found its way into Francois de Belleforest's French translation, *Histoires Tragiques*. This is the source most likely used by Shakespeare. Belleforest's version shifts some possibility of blame for the king's murder to Gertrude's flirtations with her brother-in-law.

FIRST VERSION OF THE PLAY: *UR-HAMLET*, 1589.
An early version of *Hamlet*, called the *Ur-Hamlet*, is mentioned in a criticism of English literature, although no text of this play survives. Owing to a cryptic reference, many attribute this play to Thomas Kyd, author of the seminal revenge play, *The Spanish Tragedy*. Some believe it was instead Shakespeare's first version.

Hamnet Shakespeare born

Possibly named after his godfather, Hamnet was born in late January along with his twin sister Judith. Hamnet was Shakespeare's only son. Judith lived to be 77.

The *Ur-Hamlet* published

We know this proto-*Hamlet*, whose authorship can only be guessed at, included the innovation of a ghost to the storyline. It pulled average turnouts at the theater. No scholars believe that it contained the depth of character that the 1601 adaptation possesses.

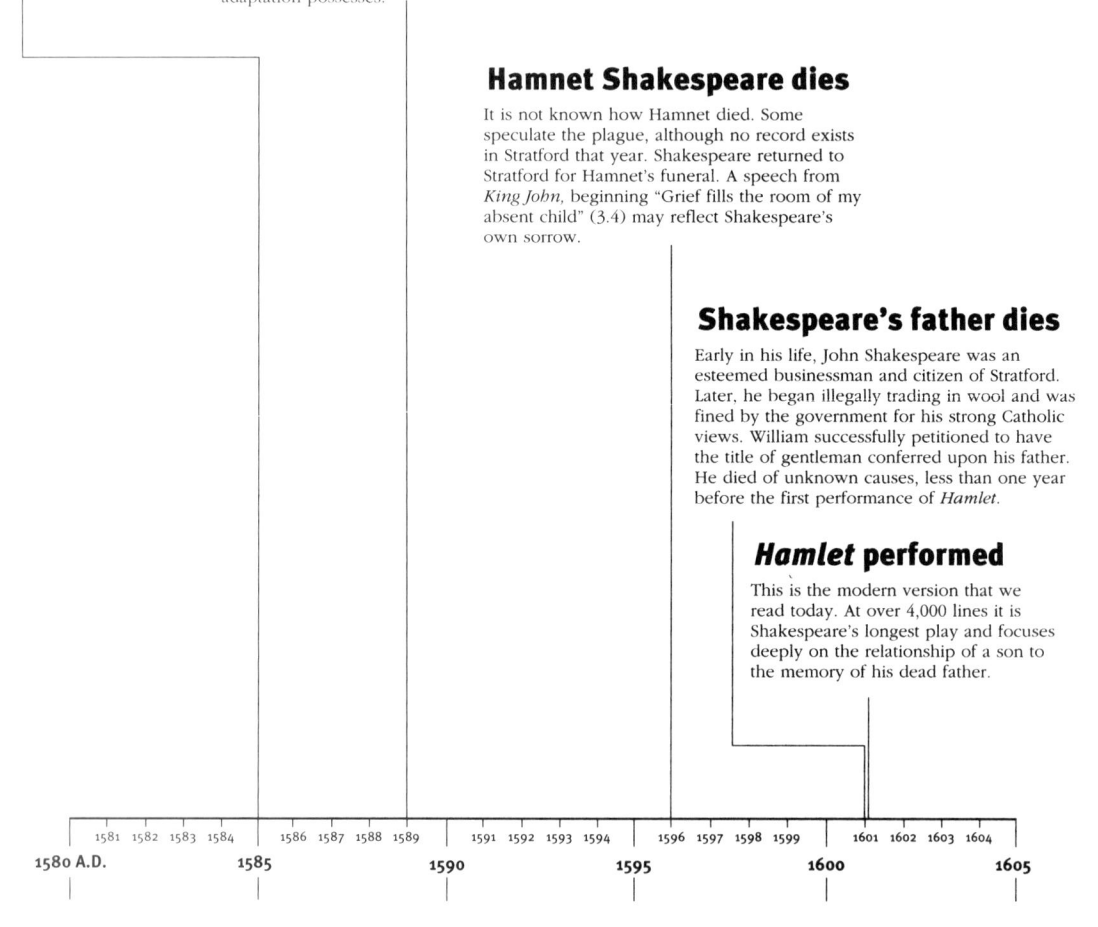

Hamnet Shakespeare dies

It is not known how Hamnet died. Some speculate the plague, although no record exists in Stratford that year. Shakespeare returned to Stratford for Hamnet's funeral. A speech from *King John*, beginning "Grief fills the room of my absent child" (3.4) may reflect Shakespeare's own sorrow.

Shakespeare's father dies

Early in his life, John Shakespeare was an esteemed businessman and citizen of Stratford. Later, he began illegally trading in wool and was fined by the government for his strong Catholic views. William successfully petitioned to have the title of gentleman conferred upon his father. He died of unknown causes, less than one year before the first performance of *Hamlet*.

Hamlet performed

This is the modern version that we read today. At over 4,000 lines it is Shakespeare's longest play and focuses deeply on the relationship of a son to the memory of his dead father.

1580 A.D. | 1581 1582 1583 1584 | 1585 | 1586 1587 1588 1589 | 1590 | 1591 1592 1593 1594 | 1595 | 1596 1597 1598 1599 | 1600 | 1601 1602 1603 1604 | 1605

Hamlet was a unique achievement.

INVENTIVENESS. Shakespeare's creative abilities were at a fevered pitch while writing *Hamlet*. Shakespeare not only used over 600 words unique to this play, he contributed more new words to the entire English language with the writing of *Hamlet* than any other playwright before or since.

SOLILOQUY. Nowhere in Shakespeare do we get such a marvelous insight into the depth of inner character than in *Hamlet*. Seven soliloquies, including the famous central soliloquy ("To be or not to be…"), stop the action so we may overhear a character's motivations, judgments and intent as they are developing.

FATHER-SON. Shakespeare's only son, Hamnet, died suddenly at age 11 in 1596, six years before *Hamlet* was first performed; Shakespeare's father died in 1601, less than one year before. The timeline on the opposite page describes this chronology. It is widely thought that the intense focus on the relationship between father and son in the play is a direct outgrowth of these two losses.

Hamlet performed

Most scholars date the first performance of Shakespeare's *Hamlet* around 1601, although more germinal versions were no doubt performed earlier.

First Quarto published

The First Quarto was published in 1603. It is called the bad Quarto and was probably written from memory by one or several of the actors. Here is an excerpt from its central soliloquy:
> To be, or not to be, aye there's the point,
> To Die, to sleepe, is that all? aye all:
> No, to sleepe, to dreame, aye mary there it goes…

Second Quarto published

We have two dates for the Second Quarto: 1604 and 1605. Q2 is considered the good Quarto—most of what we see in the modern printed versions comes from it. This quarto may have been compiled from Shakespeare's rough drafts.

First Folio published

The First Folio appeared in 1623. It is fairly consistent with Q2, but has some additions and deletions to the text. Some feel that Shakespeare may have had an editorial role in the development of this folio, resulting in his revising the original work while cleaning it up.

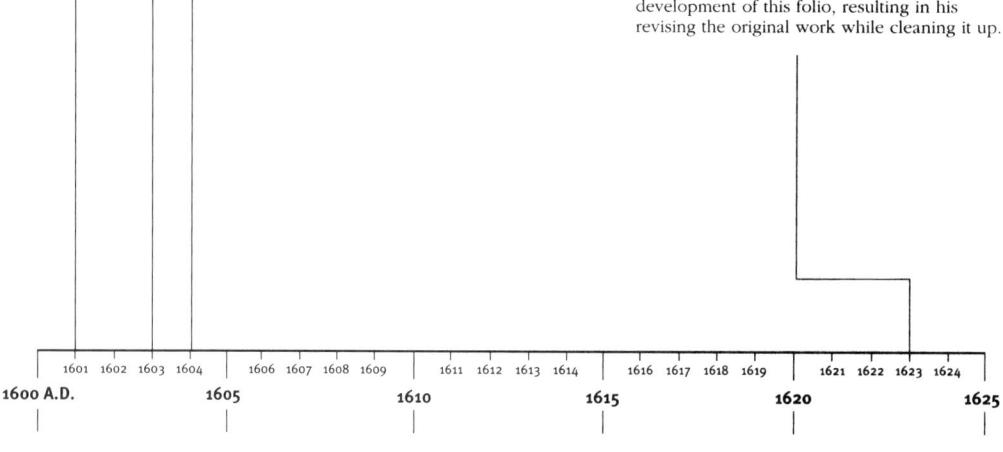

| 1600 A.D. | 1605 | 1610 | 1615 | 1620 | 1625 |

The *Hamlet* we read is a hybrid of versions.

QUARTOS AND FOLIOS. We date the first performance of *Hamlet* at 1601, about the midpoint in Shakespeare's career. There are three main printed versions of the play: two quartos and one folio. A quarto is a book made by folding a page twice, thereby quartering the original size of the sheet. A folio is a book made by folding a page once, thereby halving the width of the original sheet.

GOOD AND BAD QUARTOS. The First Quarto is referred to as the bad Quarto because of its unreliability, faulty grammar, poor usage and suspect dialogue. It is thought to have been written from memory by the actor playing Marcellus. The Second Quarto is about twice as long and is referred to as the good Quarto. It is much more reliable and is believed to have been written from Shakespeare's rough drafts.

FOLIO 1. The First Folio adds about 70 lines to Q2 after cutting more than 200. Along with Q1 and Q2, the First Folio is used to create a hybrid—a sort of "authorized" version—that we read today. It should be remembered that any modern version is an interpretive work.

Comitatus Society

The folktale of Amleth contains many of the elements of and Scandinavian warrior culture of the mid-eighth century:

- Howendil participates in the Viking tradition of roving (plundering neighboring lands).
- Howendil faces Koller in a single-champion dispute over land ownership.
- Howendil is given Gerutha as a peace bride.
- Amleth considers himself in the role of blood avenger. Later, the Danes confirm this by the unaminous affirmation of his revenge.
- The culpability of Gerutha is not even considered.

Saxo Grammaticus

Saxo's account commits the oral traditions to writing.

Francois de Belleforest

Belleforest's account introduces the *non-comitatus* notion of Geruthe's culpability. This is surely a transformation of societal mores, giving the female a more powerful responsibility with respect to influencing male behavior.

Renaissance World

Shakespeare's drama introduces late medieval and modern Renaissance ideas:

- Hamlet, Laertes and Horatio attend institutionalized higher education.
- Hamlet's thoughtful introspection slows his role as the avenger of blood.
- Court intrigues surround the centralized authority figure of Claudius.
- Hamlet espouses the belief that women have a negative influence on the actions of men.
- Hamlet's world is impregnated with doubt and the need for individual evaluation and responsibility.

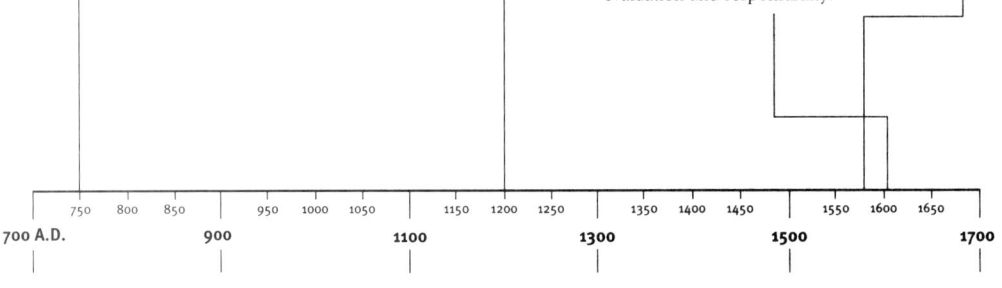

Hamlet is a collision of two time periods.

The question, "What is the time setting of *Hamlet?*" has in fact no simple response. There is evidence of a distinct juxtaposition between Old and New Worlds in the play.

MEDIEVAL SCANDINAVIA. The time setting of the first oral tradition's legendary trickster known as Amleth was probably contemporary with Beowulf, around 750 A.D. This is the early medieval world represented by Horwendil or Old Hamlet: Viking-like rovings, single champion combats, peace-weaver marriages and blood avengers. The oral folklore, undoubtedly edited for plausibility by each successive generation, was eventually recorded by Saxo in his *Danish History,* c.1200.

RENAISSANCE ANACHRONISMS. Shakespeare added many cultural anachronisms to his source, blending the *comitatus* society of Horwendil with the Renaissance world of court intrigue, central monarchies, diplomacy, university and social transition—in short, the world represented by Amleth, Claudius and Hamlet. Shakespeare's *Hamlet* then, becomes a collision of two time periods: eighth century and sixteenth century Europe.